The Labour of Laziness in Twentieth-Century American Literature

Modern American Literature and the New Twentieth Century
Series Editors: Martin Halliwell and Mark Whalan

The Labour of Laziness in Twentieth-Century American Literature

ZUZANNA LADYGA

EDINBURGH
University Press

Edinburgh University Press is one of the leading university presses in the UK. We publish academic books and journals in our selected subject areas across the humanities and social sciences, combining cutting-edge scholarship with high editorial and production values to produce academic works of lasting importance. For more information visit our website: edinburghuniversitypress.com

Edinburgh University Press Ltd
The Tun – Holyrood Road, 12(2f) Jackson's Entry, Edinburgh EH8 8PJ

Typeset in 10/13 ITC Giovanni Std Book by
Servis Filmsetting Ltd, Stockport, Cheshire,
and printed and bound in Great Britain.

A CIP record for this book is available from the British Library

ISBN 978 1 4744 4292 3 (hardback)
ISBN 978 1 4744 4294 7 (webready PDF)
ISBN 978 1 4744 4295 4 (epub)

CONTENTS

ACKNOWLEDGEMENTS

This book would not have been possible without the financial support of the Fulbright Senior Award, which provided me with time and resources to focus on my writing, and without the hospitality of the Humanities Department at the University of California Irvine, in whose intellectual atmosphere I had the privilege and pleasure to work during the initial stages of this project. I am especially indebted to James Kyung-Jin Lee for making my UCI experience possible, and Gabriele Schwab for her invaluable guidance, interest and care. I am grateful to Catherine Malabou, John Smith, Rajagopalan Radhakrishnan, Martin Harries and Virginia Jackson for sharing their wisdom with me. My special thanks go to Amanda Swain for giving me the best office space possible.

I would also like to thank my home university, the University of Warsaw, in particular Maria Dakowska, the dean of the Faculty of Modern Languages, Małgorzata Grzegorzewska, the head of the English Department, and Dominika Oramus, the deputy head, for supporting me in my scholarly effort.

I am especially grateful to my Americanist colleagues, who helped me a great deal at various stages of this project: Justyna Włodarczyk for countless discussions and feedback, Tomasz Basiuk for inspiration and comments on parts of the book, Marek Paryż and Aneta Dybska for precious editorial advice. Last but not least, I would like to thank Marek Wilczyński, Zofia Kolbuszewska and Martin Halliwell for their unwavering belief that what I am doing is worthwhile.

Nobody has been more important to the fruition of this project than the members of my family. I wish to thank my husband for his wide-ranging critique and editorial help on the book, and most of all, for years and months of filling in for me as parent when I was disappearing behind my desk. I also want to thank my parents and parents-in-law for their love and tremendous support. Most importantly, I wish to thank my children: Antosia for her great patience and for being my unending inspiration and Staś for giving me the deadline.

PREFACE

> Only in laziness can one achieve a state of contemplation which is a balancing of values, a weighing of oneself against the world, and the world against itself.
>
> John Steinbeck, *Log from the Sea of Cortez*

This book arose out of a passage in *Minima Moralia*, where Theodor Adorno speaks about the value of thought as measured by how free it is to wander and deviate from well-trodden paths:

> Every thought which is not idle, however, bears branded on it the impossibility of its full legitimation, as we know in dreams that there are mathematical lessons, missed for the sake of a blissful morning in bed, which can never be made up. Thought waits to be woken one day by the memory of what has been missed, and to be transformed into teaching.[1]

I often wondered about Adorno's choice of the metaphor of a lazy morning for the intimation that thoughts worth having and passing on to others are the ones that go against existing standards and the normative 'continuity of the familiar'.[2] Laziness, it seemed, was for Adorno the ultimate symbol of an unruly thought – the realm of thought being perhaps the only place where freedom is possible, or at least, as Marx also emphasised, where freedom begins. It took me a while to realise that Adorno's words resounded in my mind because they related to my own professional engagements. As a scholar working in the field of ethical criticism, I felt impatient with the solemnity of its discourse, the genteel humanitarianism of moralist verdicts upon art and literature as well as the universalist assertions of indifference to moralisation coming from the autonomist critics. In other words, I could neither fully relate to Martha Nussbaum's *Poetic Justice* nor to Lawrence Buell's *The Dream of the Great American Novel*. What Adorno helped me to understand about this impatience was that it had to do with an internal contradiction at the heart of ethical criticism – and perhaps, as Adorno suggested, of the academic industry in general – namely, the contradiction between a fundamental suspicion towards ethical regimes and a consensual compliance to the injunction to be productive, to propose meaningful 'solutions' to the world's problems. Indeed, by obeying the injunction, ethical criticism often conflates productivity with value, in the narrow axiological sense, as the value of value as such, and thus misses its point. As Adorno never tires of repeating, an ethical thought, a thought worthy of being transformed into teaching, is one that deviates from all normative valuation, the dictates of industriousness and the sabotage of universal communicability.[3] It is an idle thought on a lazy morning.

Adorno's metaphor from *Minima Moralia* was therefore what kindled my inquiry into the idea of laziness and its conceptual potential, particularly in relation to the notions of freedom and normativity. But, as I soon found out, the task of investigating this idea was harder than I expected, because as far as the notion of laziness was concerned, philosophers and artists – with few exceptions – had surprisingly little to say beyond standard stigmatisations or aphoristic glosses like the one by Steinbeck quoted in the epigraph.

My own initial reaction to Steinbeck's words was one of suspicion. Seriously, I thought, 'in *laziness*'? '*only*'? Steinbeck's certainty about the uniqueness of the lazy mood perplexed me, because no one ever thinks of laziness as something profound. In fact, if we ever give laziness a thought, we rather consider it a nuisance, and of a very shallow kind. In what the *Dictionary of Untranslatables* calls the class system of words,[4] laziness belongs among the lowest strata. Unlike languor or leisure, which have enjoyed some attention from artists and philosophers, it remains, very much like the sturdy beggar with whom it has been identified for centuries, untouchable and untranslatable into the language of philosophy or literary criticism. Aristotle, Cicero, Locke, Kant and Hegel singled out laziness as the exact opposite of contemplation. John Keats, whom the topic otherwise fascinated, complained that in contrast to languor, laziness was a rottenness of the senses with no 'teeth of pearl' nor 'the breath of lilies'.[5] All of which is to say that, in one way or another, the notion of laziness has continuously functioned as one of Western culture's more persistent stigmas, serving the disciplining registers of biopower that thwart individual claims to freedom of agency. Even today, curiously, laziness is policed no less vigilantly than in Antiquity or in early Christianity.

This oddity has been well captured by Roland Barthes, who once pointed out: 'Have you noticed that we always speak about the right to leisure, but never about a right to laziness? I wonder if here, in the modern Occident, *doing nothing* really exists.'[6] For Barthes, who as a French thinker was very familiar with the anti-work ethos born out of Paul Lafargue's 1883 manifesto *The Right to Be Lazy*, the question was not whether we can reclaim the notion of laziness in the service of some social cause – Barthes always distanced himself from such complacent political moralism – but whether Western thought is at all capable of thinking or performing 'doing nothing'. After all, Barthes observed, even those 'who have a completely different, tougher, more alienated and laborious life than my own don't do "nothing" when they're free. They always do something.'[7] Barthes's observation is casual but spot-on. It echoes Foucault on the normativisation of productive living, the social condemnation of idleness and the eventual internalisation of this sanction by individual subjects, but at the same time Barthes insists on exploring laziness beyond the level of its social function. Like Adorno, he links laziness with freedom of thought and imagination, bringing to mind Adrienne Rich's words from her 1972 essay 'When We Dead Awaken' about her desire for 'the one thing of which there was never enough: time to think, time to write'.[8] Precisely because the idea of doing nothing has always been so foreign to the modern Occident, Barthes argued, it deserves sustained philosophical reflection no less than it requires historicist scrutiny.

A long time has passed since Adorno's, Rich's and Barthes's remarks, yet in the present cultural climate they seem remarkably relevant. The twenty-first century is the epoch of hyper-activity and hyper-engagement, which renders the possibility of time for idle thinking as important and desirable as it is unwelcome and socially suspicious. We live in a culture where the imperative to do anything rather than nothing and to be productive has become the dominant value, if not the synonym of value as such. In everyday life, this manifests itself in the evaporation of the idea of free, private time, which becomes exchanged for complicated rituals of tech-assisted self-management. In the grip of a sentiment that Lauren Berlant has identified as 'cruel optimism', we enthusiastically trade our minimal spatio-temporal liberties for the sake of the biopolitical illusion of self-fulfilment.[9] Driven by the hope that new heartbeat tracking devices will take care of our health, we lose sleep over adjusting our profiles on social media. As documented in Jonathan Crary's *24/7: Late Capitalism and the Ends of Sleep*, the ethos of time-management has effectively erased the difference between free, private time and work time, with the former being redefined as nothing more than a reservoir of productive energies.[10] According to Crary, no aspect of *zoē* is now spared the incursion of global capitalist claims on individual privacy. The Debordian days when it was through the mechanism of the spectacle and entertainment that the masses were lulled into passive obedience towards economic systems are a thing of the past. Nowadays, entertainment and leisure have become strategic tools in the procedures of self-enhancement – 'mindfulness' techniques are supposed to *increase* one's creative skills; weight-lifting *fosters* one's stress endurance; having hobbies *enhances* one's performance at work. In short, self-development is not understood stoically, as self-care, an ethical goal in itself, but always as a means to the ultimate goal of productivity.

Of course, the injunction to stay productive and engaged controls not just the lives of those who happily indulge in the neoliberal rhythms of the self-management industry, but also of those who wish to oppose it and lead a slow, peaceful, eco-friendly existence, or those who want to analyse it critically. It transpires in the communitarian logic to promote citizens' active involvement in the problems of locality. It interpellates the *homo academicus* through the quantitative publish-or-perish doctrine. It calls on the free thinker to embrace the stance of a caring activist and participate in what Jacques Rancière calls the modern 'malaise of the ethical'.[11]

If this diagnosis seems violent or exaggerated, then consider some of the newest additions to the spectrum of approaches in literary studies. One example is the growing tendency in academic criticism to turn analytic attention away from literature itself towards circuits of readers' empathy and sympathy on internet forums and social networks.[12] Another is the trend for literary critics to write so-called biblio-memoirs, or autobiographical accounts of reading experiences and adventure stories of rescuing forgotten books from oblivion.[13] In both cases, the unusually strong emphasis on activity serves as a seal for what Solange Guènoun describes as the conflation of the 'global reign of economy' with 'the global reign of morality'.[14] In both cases the dominant sensibility is the fear of missing out, or FOMO as we nowadays call it, which is the dread of disconnecting from the networks of active engagement that is fuelled by a horrifying prospect of identity loss.

A case in point could be one of the recent FOMO-lit hits, Phyllis Rose's *The Shelf: From LEQ to LES. Adventures in Extreme Reading*, in which the author, who sacrificed her time to read forgotten novels, uses her own example to rekindle readers' awareness of the amount of still unconsumed literary produce stocked on library shelves. When unable to 'boost' a book herself, Rose starts fantasising that someone else will boost it instead: 'Does some future literary critic exist who can resurrect these books?'[15] In a similar tone, critical inquirers into empathic reader networks insist that analyses of reading communities are 'generative' of a 'genuine literary dialogue' between critics and ordinary consumers, as both groups 'do the "work"'.[16] Resurrecting books and generating critical work is evidently a goal in itself, which proves that the injunction to stay productive has infiltrated even the realm of literary criticism, which for a long time has claimed independence from the technologies of affect management that privilege active engagement over passive contemplation, the 'balancing of oneself against the world, and the world against itself'. It seems therefore that we have forgotten Nietzsche's warning that to equate value with productivity has profound ethical or epistemological consequences.

In the glorification of 'work', in the unwearied talk of the 'blessing of work', I see the same covert idea as in the praise of useful impersonal actions: the fear of everything individual. Fundamentally, one now feels at the sight of work – one always means by work that hard industriousness from early till late – that such work is the best policeman, that it keeps everyone within bounds and can mightily hinder the development of reason, covetousness, desire for independence. For it uses up extraordinary amounts of nervous energy, which is thus denied to reflection, brooding, dreaming, worrying, loving, hating; it sets a small goal always in sight and guarantees easy and regular satisfactions. Thus a society in which there is continual hard work will have more security: and security is now worshipped as the supreme divinity.[17]

Nietzsche, the great advocate of *otium* and *vita contemplativa*, was convinced that the general pressure to act, to move and to produce is the 'most odd mindlessness', which dresses up as moral concern, but is in fact a threat to individual differences and the diversity of cultural imagination. 'One is ashamed of keeping still ... one lives like someone who might always "miss out on something". "Rather do anything than nothing" – even this principle is a cord to strangle all culture', he wrote in *The Gay Science*, thus intimating that the fear of missing out is not a remedy for identity loss but an instrument of its extermination.[18]

If Nietzsche was right, I remember thinking at the start of my project, the ambition to explore the cultural and philosophical role of laziness is quite timely. The immediate circumstances of my exploration strengthened this conviction. I began writing this book in a busy, crowded university library by the Sea of Cortez. I remember thinking this place to be a perfectly ironic location for writing about laziness, because no one there seemed even slightly familiar with the idea of doing nothing. In the closed circuit of the university, designed deliberately as a community without a centre, with no area or square where people could engage in any form of idleness or unproductivity, everyone worked tirelessly from dawn to dusk, in perfect technological synchrony with the rest of the world. When tired or hungry, you could quickly feed on a protein drink my housemate recommended. For maintaining the work–leisure balance, she also suggested an activity tracker and a sleep monitor.

I remember observing it all and recalling Jean Baudrillard's impressions in *America*, where he lamented the predatorily entrepreneurial spirit of Silicon Valley and the cult of movement epitomised in the activity of jogging. Writing in the late 1980s, for Baudrillard both the Valley-like entrepreneurship and the view of runners impatiently skipping at traffic lights bespoke the same desperate denial of death, the inevitable, ultimate pause to all human action. Baudrillard was famous for poetic exaggerations of his American experience, but the geographical location of the Californian coast prompted a strong correspondence between his observations and Adorno's *Minima Moralia*, especially the argument about the bi-phasic character of free time in consumer culture. Indeed, as viewed through the windows of my office, free time seemed like a euphemism for productive activity outside of the workplace; free thought, an irresponsible folly.

One day, with Adorno's words in my head, I left the busy library and drove to the ocean to contemplate the autonomy of free time and idle thought. But getting back to the car after dark, I found a parking ticket for staying at the beach for too long, with my autonomy translated into a fine of ninety-six dollars. If I had any doubts about the project before, this unfortunate punishment convinced me that it was worthwhile. After all, I was in very good company, with Adorno, Barthes and Nietzsche, whose assured diagnosis of the Western privileging of work pointed towards the 'need for little deviant acts' of keeping still, doing nothing, dreaming and brooding – 'acting against one's better judgement when it comes to questions of custom'.[19] Writing *The Labour of Laziness* was my attempt to celebrate those philosophers and writers who have undertaken this preposterous, risky task.

Notes

1. Theodor Adorno, *Minima Moralia: Reflections from Damaged Life*, trans. E. F. N. Jephcott (New York: Verso, 2006), 81.
2. Ibid., 80.
3. Ibid.
4. Barbara Cassin, Steven Rendall and Emily S. Apter (eds), *Dictionary of Untranslatables: A Philosophical Lexicon, Translation, Transnation* (Princeton: Princeton University Press, 2014).
5. John Keats, *Poems and Selected Letters*, ed. Carlos Baker (New York: Scribner & Sons, 1962), 78.
6. Roland Barthes, 'Osons être paresseux', in *Oeuvres Complètes*, vol. 3 (Paris: Seuil, 2002), 760–6.

7. Ibid., 764.
8. Adrienne Rich, 'When We Dead Awaken. Writing as Re-Vision', in *On Lies, Secrets, and Silence: Selected Prose 1966–1978* (New York: W.W. Norton, 1979), 44.
9. Lauren Gail Berlant, *Cruel Optimism* (Durham, NC: Duke University Press, 2011).
10. Jonathan Crary, *24/7: Late Capitalism and the Ends of Sleep* (London: Verso, 2013).
11. Jacques Rancière, 'The Ethical Turn of Aesthetics and Politics', *Critical Horizons* 7.1 (2006), 1–20.
12. Dominick LaCapra, *History in Transit: Experience, Identity, Critical Theory* (Ithaca: Cornell University Press, 2004); Kathleen Fitzpatrick, *The Anxiety of Obsolescence: The American Novel in the Age of Television* (Nashville: Vanderbilt University Press, 2006).
13. Christine Smallwood, 'Ghosts in the Stacks', *The New Yorker*, 9 June 2014.
14. Solange M. Guènoun, 'Jacques Ranciere's Ethical Turn and the Thinking of Discontents', in *Jacques Rancière: History, Politics, Aesthetics*, ed. Gabriel Rockhill and Philip Watts (Durham, NC: Duke University Press, 2009), 179.
15. Phyllis Rose, *The Shelf: From LEQ to LES. Adventures in Extreme Reading* (New York: Farrar, Straus and Giroux, 2014), 17.
16. Ed Finn, 'Becoming Yourself: The Afterlife of Reception', in *The Legacy of David Foster Wallace* (Iowa City: University of Iowa Press, 2012), 171.
17. Friedrich Nietzsche, *Daybreak: Thoughts on the Prejudices of Morality*, trans. R. J. Hollingdale (Cambridge: Cambridge University Press, 1997), 173.
18. Friedrich Nietzsche, *The Gay Science: With a Prelude in German Rhymes and an Appendix of Songs* (Cambridge: Cambridge University Press, 2001), 183.
19. Nietzsche, *Daybreak*, 97.

Introduction: Doing Nothing in America

I wonder if here, in the modern Occident, *doing nothing* really exists.
Roland Barthes, 'Osons être paresseux'

To pre-empt the question that my oxymoronic title *The Labour of Laziness* suggests: this book is not an apology for doing nothing. I do not wish to rehabilitate the notion in the service of a specific political or aesthetic agenda, for that has already been done, and done with panache, by such eminent cultural figures as Paul Lafargue in *The Right to Be Lazy* (1883), Bertrand Russell in 'In Praise of Idleness' (1935), or Thomas Pynchon in 'Nearer, My Couch, to Thee' (1993). What I intend to do, however, is to argue the pertinence of laziness as a concept-metaphor and map the metaphorological field of how the term generates meanings in philosophical and literary discourse. 'Metaphorological field' is to be understood here in Hans Blumenberg's terms as referring to the epistemologically fluid paradigm of images, figurative characterisations and symbols that determine the way a particular notion functions in discourse and stabilise its ideological role and sociopolitical capacity. In the case of laziness, this discursive function emerges in the crowded network of relations among signs such as sloth, inertia, impotence, indolence, nausea, fatigue, *acedia*, aboulia, melancholia, unproductivity, passive resistance, *daemon meridianus*, the loafer, the idler, the delinquent, the vagabond and many others.

In *Paradigms for a Metaphorology*, Blumenberg posits that to recognise a metaphorical structure of a notion is to critically reflect upon, unmask and counteract its potential inauthenticity and in this way designate its true philosophical potential.[1] It is to separate where a concept 'lies' from where it tells us something important. Laziness is a promising candidate for such metaphorological analysis due to its unique history as one of Western culture's most notorious stigmas, a mysterious disease of the mind and of the body, to use the language of the early Church Fathers. Its enigmatic status is confirmed by modern neuroscience, which admits that laziness is still too complex an experiential phenomenon to be explained scientifically.

Nothing generates more metaphorological potential, Susan Sontag once observed, than an aura of mystery. The moment a phenomenon is considered mysterious, it becomes acutely feared, considered 'morally, if not literally contagious', a 'shameful' perversity that one ought to hide.[2] From there, a straight path leads towards trivialisation or total neglect. Such at least has been the story of laziness, a seemingly transparent term that philosophy has found unworthy of its attention. The basic premise of my metaphorological approach is therefore that the notion of laziness deserves to be examined because of how it attests to the limits of Western thought, in the sense Blanchot gives to the idea of the limit as one of those 'obscure' gestures 'by which a culture rejects something that, for it, would be the Exterior'.[3] It is a limit-term at the horizon of Western sensibility which, if given a chance, might tell us something about American and European culture with its privileging of activity and productivity that we do not necessarily like to hear or are not ready to admit.

As a limit-term, laziness benefits most from being approached syncretically, in the spirit of what Jacques Rancière has called 'thinking between disciplines' of literature, art and philosophy. In *The Labour of Laziness*, I therefore start from building a metaphorological framework for laziness as a concept by mapping the yet-uncultivated philosophical field that the notion circumscribes, to later move to explorations of the motif of laziness in modern American literature, where I argue that it performs important counter-normative protest work by generating meanings and subject positions that destabilise and redistribute the *partage du sensible* of a given epoch. That my literary examples are works by twentieth-century American authors follows from the fact that they emerged in a culture emphatically founded upon what Max Weber in *The Protestant Work Ethic* (1905) famously called the ethos of toil, that is to say, a culture where the imperative of productivity and the proscription of laziness have been cultivated more consistently than anywhere else. Therefore, it is in the aesthetic responses to the American cultural milieu that the counter-normative potential of laziness features in its fullness in this book. But before outlining the American literary coordinates of this book, it is important to understand the semantic and cultural genealogy of laziness, which takes us as far back as Antiquity.

A Brief Genealogy of Laziness

'Whereof one cannot speak, thereof one must be silent' is Wittgenstein's famous maxim from *Tractatus*, which may well be a good summary of the history of the word 'laziness' in the English language. The modalities of *cannot* and *must* are very relevant here because laziness is one of those entrenched nuisances whose semantic scope is as annoying as is its unclear etymological origin. Although dictionaries agree that the adjective 'laysy' appeared in the English language for the first time in 1549 as a back-formation from *layserly* or leisurely, the accounts of the origin of the word are more contradictory. Some etymological dictionaries derive 'lazy' from the Middle Low German *lasich* meaning 'languid', 'idle', 'weak, feeble, tired';[4] others associate it with the Swedish *loski*, *lase* and German *leisa* and *lata*: 'to loose, relax, be slow, late';[5] but laziness is also linked with German *erleswen* (to grow weak), Old Icelandic *lasinn* (weak, slack, limp), Bulgarian *loš* (bad, wicked) and Tocharian *ljask* (softness). Yet what dictionaries classify as obscurity of origin is also an indication of metaphorological potential. Even a basic sample of the cognates of 'laysy' suggests quite significantly that the word may refer to animate as well as inanimate entities, moral gestures, affective states and bodily dispositions. Its capaciousness denotes somatic sensations, such as in 'lax, loosened, derailed', but also the psychological sensibilities of 'passivity, inertia, apathy', and attitudes such as 'unwilling to work', 'unproductive', 'slackening' or 'resisting effort'.

The one thing that all dictionaries agree upon is that the first recorded usage of the word 'lazy' with a 'z' appears towards the end of the sixteenth century in Shakespeare's *Midsummer Night's Dream* when Theseus says:

> Say, what abridgement have you for this evening?
> What masque? what music? How shall we beguile
> The lazy time, if not with some delight?

Historians would emphasise the ingenious radicalness of how Shakespeare's enunciation of an uncourtly word 'lazy' challenges and makes more pluralistic the Renaissance perception of the stylised lifestyle that the French called *oisiveté* as the exclusion marker and symbolic capital of privileged social groups.[6] Indeed, Shakespeare's 'lazy' makes leisure thinkable outside of the leisure class, and, even more importantly, breaks the connotation with the poor and vagrancy laws that located 'laysy' in the registers of the medieval penal code.[7] Yet, as far as a metaphorological framework is concerned, the Shakespearean context also imposes a limitation to consider the term primarily *vis-à-vis* pastoral aesthetics and its ethico-political background. This criterion is particularly fitting for American letters, the history and development of which overlap with the consolidation of the pastoral paradigm in and beyond the mid-nineteenth century. I will argue in this book that whatever archaic or futuristic existential or political connotations the trope of laziness mobilises in the works of American authors, its metaphorological capacity is, to a significant degree, restricted by the horizon of the pastoral. This, however, in no way implies that laziness as an idea has no history beyond this horizon.

As Roland Barthes notes in 'Osons être paresseux' (1979), the Greek understanding of laziness is devoid of any moral undertones. The word for laziness is *argos*, the contraction of *a-ergos*, which means simply 'he who does not work', that is to say, he who has free time on his hands.[8] But this original reference to power over one's time is lost in other terms for 'not-working' such as the idea of leisure, or *skhole*. The Latin *scholar* and English 'school' derive from this word precisely because the Greeks' understanding of leisure did not involve absence of activity but indicated a structured effort at intellectual self-development. It is in this transition from *argos* to *skhole* that the first proscriptive gesture is effected. There were good and bad ways of spending free time in Antiquity – free time is not entirely free and it is spent well only if it is spent productively. What goes with this first proscription is also the cultural perception of leisure as, on the one hand, the ultimate object of pursuit of an aspiring intellectual, and on the other hand, a marker of status distinguishing free aristocracy from slaves and other labouring groups.

Thus, Aristotle states in his *Politics* that 'the first principle of all action is leisure'. Both leisure and work are necessary, 'but leisure is better than occupation and is its end', a view that does not speak in favour of idleness. Occupation is understood here as the daily routine of tending to one's business or as political action, whereas leisure is simply a different sort of work. Aristotle offers clear advice for going about these leisurely activities: 'we ought not to be amusing ourselves, for then amusement would be the end of life'. Amusement is unacceptable because it brings 'the emotion of relaxation', and relaxation prevents one from properly engaging in leisure, with 'exertion and effort', and thus reaching true 'enjoyment'. The idea formulated in *Politics* that there should be no unstructured idleness or relaxed pleasure in free time sets the parameters for the Western ethos of productivity, which would dominate its culture long after Aristotle. His argument documents the formation of the paradigm of perceiving human life in terms of productive rhythms and the symbolic intervention into the realm of the bodily. According to its logic, one's free time is not the time to loosen up and enjoy the sensation, since the goal of life is effort and exercise, which keep the body in rigid control. In other words, Aristotle's ethics of leisure is that of abstention from relaxation and laziness, with the latter becoming devalorised as the evil face of free time associated with time spent unproductively.

The repercussions of this idea were felt in modern ethical systems. Around the middle of the fourth century in Alexandria, Evagrius Ponticus, the father of Christian mysticism, developed the idea of *acedia*, laziness born out of boredom, which was to be the basis for the Christian definition of the sin of sloth. Escaping the tumult of the city of Constantinople to live among the hermits of Mount

Nitria, Evagrius hoped to find peace of thought in the desert, but once there, he discovered an obstacle to meditative life greater than the bustle of city life, which he identified as *daemon meridianus*:

> The demon of *acedia*, the 'noonday demon' is the most oppressive of all demons. He attacks the monk about the fourth hour and besieges his soul until the eighth hour. First he makes the sun appear sluggish and immobile, as if the day had fifty hours. Then he causes the monk continually to look at the windows and forces him to step out of his cell and to gaze at the sun to see how far it still is from the ninth hour, and to look around, here and there, whether any of his brethren is near. Moreover, the demon sends him hatred against the place, against life itself, and the work of his hands, and has him think he has lost the love among his brethren and that there is none to comfort him. He stirs the monk also to long for different places in which he can find easily what is necessary for his life and can carry on a much less toilsome and more expedient profession.[9]

Daemon meridianus thus imparts slowness and boredom, which infect the soul but also make the monk long for an existence outside of the hermitage.

What might explain the links built here between boredom, slowness and ease is the origin of the very term *acedia*. Evagrius did not invent the term himself, given that *acedeia*, which literally meant 'lack of care, *incuria*',[10] was borrowed from the writings of Hippocrates and Cicero, where it enjoyed a more ambivalent status. Although 'lack of care' denoted an impedimental state of weariness, exhaustion and apathy that needs to be cured, it also carried a more positive sense of carelessness or freedom from life's sorrows.[11] In Ancient Rome, the state of *acedia* was one of the possible consequences of having too much free time or too monotonous a life. These went under the category of *otium*, a term approximating the Greek *skhole* in the sense of 'leisurely time', being, however, of a much wider semantic range. The term was first used in the context of Roman military life, during the periods of seasonal unemployment and boredom among the army. There was thus *otium otiosum*, which denoted idleness caused by too much free time at hand, doing nothing, and its opposites *otium negotiosum* and *otium privatum*, which corresponded to Aristotle's idea of busy leisure. *Otium otiosum* was a dangerous type of time expenditure because it could lead to boredom, which in turn could bring about all sorts of transgressions against the norms of social life. In short, the Romans recognised the dissensus potential of *acedia* as connected to having too much free time. Evagrian anthropomorphisation of the idea was therefore yet another step in the creation of the ideological apparatus of sanctioning this freedom and the temporalities of private existence. Ironically, however, the connection established between *otium otiosum* and acediac boredom, through the emphasis on bodily stasis and immobility, also laid the first foundations for the modern concept of passive resistance, so often employed in political apologies for laziness as a mode of anti-work protest. Finally, it was none other than the notion of *acedia* that opened the door to idleness as a psychological disposition belonging to what today we call the depressive spectrum.[12]

The figure credited with extending the meaning of idleness into the domain of the *sacrum* was the fourth-century theologian John Cassian, who both compiled the list of sins and established the conceptual link between the Evagrian *acedia*, sloth, and the mood of melancholy.[13] In Cassian's definition, *acedia* gave rise to somnolence, rudeness, restlessness, wandering about, instability of mind and body, verbosity and curiosity.[14] What strikes one as particularly revealing about Cassian's list is that, by concatenating *acedia* with vagrancy, mental instability and rudeness, it supplied a religious rationale and a moral legitimacy to legal restrictions on otherwise quite unrelated sentiments and forms of behaviour.[15] It might therefore be argued that, already in the fourth century, sloth began to function as a code word for a variety of mental and physiological conditions that were undesirable from the perspective of state power. Thus, in the late Middle Ages sloth became one of the main concepts underlying the construction of poor and vagrancy laws, which criminalised idle behaviour and translated it into the language of both moral and economic failure. At the same time, however, the associations of sloth with acts of restlessness, curiosity and talkativeness illuminate the question of the term's relation to civil disobedience. The idea that slothfulness would imply verbosity and inquisitiveness suggests that in early Christian thought there already functioned some degree of association between lazy behaviour and the dissentient, an unruly attitude of saying 'too much' or asking too many questions.

At the time when Thomas Aquinas produced his *Summa Theologica*, which pronounced sloth to be synonymous with pure evil – *tristitia de spirituali bono*[16] – it was thus altogether difficult to pin down the essence of its evilness. Was it to be understood in temporal terms as freedom of time, or in terms of bodily weariness and loss of vitality? As dejection or as inquisitiveness, sorrow of lack thereof? These questions were never answered, probably because their stakes were different than the spiritual scenario implied, and had to do with the down-to-earth, corrective work that the term 'sloth' was to perform in the social arena. Such at least seems to be the prompt given by the medieval penitence tariffs, whose framing of sloth seems to have served as a cover story for state-ordained control of the population. It is quite possible, in other words, that when Cassianic or Gregorian penitentials chastised in particular three aspects of sloth – idleness, somnolence and instability – they did so because these vices were, at that time, most threatening to the sociopolitical order.[17] There is almost no difference between the language of early medieval penitentials and the formulations of poor and vagrancy laws, introduced in the fourteenth century after the Black Plague, and later applied in Europe and the United States in times of crisis such as epidemics, war and climate-related migrations to regulate the distribution of cheap workforces, control population mobility and stabilise state power. The standard lexicon of corrective jurisprudence contained phrases such as 'to set to work', 'sturdy beggar and vagabond' or 'idle and desolate persons', where 'setting to work' was a euphemism for compulsory labour, often preceded by public flogging or imprisonment without the possibility of an appeal, and where 'sturdy' was an overstatement of an idler's physical capacity for prolonged activity.[18] The harshness of vagrancy laws was disproportionate to the severity of the crime, and religious sermons mobilised the logic of inurement into productivity:

> a sturdy beggar who for laziness, and avoyde the toyle of manuall travel, loyter in idleness, should be constrained to desist their villainies, by the infliction of condigne penalties; they should, I say, be moved up

in Bridewels,[19] or houses of correction, forced to learn the mysteries of mechanical Artes.[20]

American colonies, albeit opposing the Old Continent in religious spirit, adhered nevertheless to the uncharitable British poor and vagrancy laws, which were later renamed as 'tramp acts'.[21] In 1619 the Virginia Assembly legalized compulsory labour for the 'slothful', whereas under the rule of the Act of 1672, workhouses and 'houses of correction' were erected throughout the American colonies to punish lazy and 'recalcitrant' servants and sturdy beggars and vagabonds deemed capable of working though unwilling to do so.[22] Ironically, many towns spent more on keeping out the vagrant and the idle than they would have spent on providing them with assistance.[23]

All in all, for the majority of the population in sixteenth- and seventeenth-century Europe and its colonies, sloth served as a category of social repression. To use Michel Foucault's famous formulation, it was a time when the demarcation line between labour and idleness virtually 'replaced the exclusion of leprosy'.[24]

> The asylum was substituted for the lazar house, in the geography of haunted places as in the landscape of the moral universe. The old rites of excommunication were revived, but in the world of production and commerce. It was in these places of doomed and despised idleness, in this space invented by a society which had derived an ethical transcendence from the law of work, that madness would appear and soon expand until it had annexed them . . . It was in this other world, encircled by the sacred powers of labor, that madness would assume the status we now attribute to it.[25]

Thus, in the discourse of the sixteenth and seventeenth centuries, idleness was no longer recognised as an irrational disposition received from elsewhere, as in Evagrius's conception of *daemon meridianus*, but became associated with an internal, 'degenerative malady' and a social stigma.[26] This segregationist ethos persisted until the eighteenth century, when proscription extended to all forms of unproductivity and social uselessness, now automatically subsumed under the category of criminal acts. The eighteenth-century Enlightened penitentials listed 'passivity' and 'shame on honor, through cowardice, that is to say, laziness'[27] among the most incorrigible and therefore most dangerous pathologies, while an elaborate canon of didactic literature aided the institution of 'communal correction'[28] disseminated across the so-called 'networks of good will'.[29] Finally, as far as the nineteenth century is concerned, criminalisation of all forms of inactivity ran concurrently with and was closely linked to the Industrial Revolution, the evolution of new production technologies and fluctuant labour demographics.[30]

Theorising Laziness

This historical and genealogical context enables us to see the importance of laziness in the formation of the disciplining regime of productivity as the governing logic of what Foucault calls biopower. If any one period in its modern history deserves emphasis, it is the sixteenth and seventeenth centuries, when laziness became secularised and its religious parameters replaced by socio-economic ones. As Foucault explains in the first volume of *History of Sexuality* (1984), biopolitical technologies of control over individuals' private lives originated at the time when the idea of freedom to live as one likes, including the freedom to take life away, gave way to notions of 'fostering' or 'disallowing' its temporal rhythms, as 'methods of power and knowledge assumed responsibility for the life processes and undertook to control and modify them'.[31] In short, at the time when life became thinkable only as a productive endeavour involving the mind as well as the body:

> all this was ensured by the procedures of power that characterized the disciplines: an anatomo-politics of the human body. The second, formed somewhat later, focused on the species body, the body imbued with the mechanics of life and serving as the basis of the biological processes: propagation, births and mortality, the level of health, life expectancy and longevity, with all the conditions that can cause these to vary. Their supervision was effected through an entire series of interventions and regulatory controls: a bio-politics of the population. The disciplines of the body and the regulations of the population constituted the two poles around which the organization of power over life was deployed.[32]

The intersection of the discipline of the body and control of the population is where Foucault locates his famous concept of the 'norm' as a tactic of governance that serves biopower by disseminating state control among multiple networks and sites of micro-power, such as the family or community, to render the disciplining process natural and transparent. The norm serves the role of a biopolitical mask for the conflation of biological life and political life, a mask which conceals the disciplining work of macro-power apparatuses. In the case of the regime of productivity, this discipline is maintained by the regulation of free time, control of geographical mobility and investment in the subjected bodies' vitality resources, all of which are possible through the mobilisation of discourse that stigmatises rest, idleness and lack of vigour.

Like all stigmas, which, sociologists of deviance agree, are always arbitrarily normatised,[33] the stigma of laziness is situated at 'the realm of the seams' of power and morality, where 'boundaries of different symbolic-moral universes meet and touch', where they 'use and abuse' each other,[34] even though, as Howard Becker observes, laziness is 'not a quality of the act a person commits, but rather a consequence of the application by others of rules and sanctions to an "offender"'.[35] This view dates back to Max Weber, who was the first to identify its logic in the Protestant ethos of industriousness. As he argued in *The Protestant Ethic* (1905), not only did this ethos provide a basis for the capitalist equalisation of moral virtue with economic value, but more importantly, it went hand in hand with the regulation of individual freedom and privacy. The emergence of the ethos of productivity, Weber observed, was not unrelated to 'the quiet disappearance of the private confession',[36] and the substitution of this intimate ritual with the institution of home visits. Three-quarters of a century later Foucault agrees. The biopolitical dynamics of communal control over private space, bodily intimacy and free time 'was, without question, an indispensable element in the development of capitalism; the latter would not have been possible without the controlled insertion of bodies into the machinery of production'.[37]

Inasmuch as such diagnoses are always products of arbitrary historical emplotments, the idea that post-sixteenth-century moral regimes stigmatised laziness in order to normalise productivity finds strong confirmation in the early American literature. From Puritan texts, through the writings of Benjamin Franklin and Jonathan Edwards, to the literary output of the New Republic, idleness evolves from a stigmatising marker of deviance into a powerful trope of dissent and self-preservation *vis-à-vis* the norm of productivity and its oppressive *dressage*.

Without doubt, laziness is not the only trope of defiance in American letters. But as I argue in the chapters of this book, it is unique in how it connects the material sphere of the body with the non-material sphere of the mind. As a signifier for corporeal laxation, recalibration of the senses, intellectual drifting and withdrawal from the world, the motif of laziness maps the same cognitive field that is targeted by the norm of productivity. It is therefore a perfect candidate for a concept-metaphor by means of which philosophers and writers pinpoint a particular stage of this norm's formation, as well as inventing models of its evasion. It is this convergence of literary and philosophical concepts in this book that enables me to analyse the trope of laziness on a spectrum of connotations.

But what does it mean to say that the semantic scope of laziness overlaps with that of the norm? In 'The King's Two (Biopolitical) Bodies', the philosopher Catherine Malabou examines Foucault's definition of the norm as a mask for the conflation of biological life and political life in order to argue that, despite claims to the contrary, Foucault's project of critique of biopower and normativity fails as a result of his inattention to the modalities of biological materiality. In other words, Malabou claims that Foucault's understanding of 'biological' and 'bodily' are not as physiological and 'bare-life'-centred as we like to think. 'The problem', she writes, is that for Foucault, 'biology is always presented as intimately linked with sovereignty in its traditional figure ... as a power of normalization' and never as something real, something which could also serve as the basis of dissentient power-as-*puissance*.[38] It is as if, in Foucault's project of the critique of biopower, 'there can't be any biological resistance to biopower', because *bio* is continuously de-somaestheticised by the symbolic language of philosophy.[39]

Taking a prompt from Malabou to enter a conversation with philosophers who are perhaps more open to the materiality of the body than is the author of *Discipline and Punish*, I use the first chapter of this book to argue that it is precisely in the blind spot of Foucault's argument, captured by the phrase 'there can't be any biological resistance to biopower', that the question of laziness can be inserted. Indeed, as the rare instances of philosophical inquiry into unproductive idling that I discuss in Chapter 1 suggest, laziness marks the horizon of biological dissent to a biopolitical norm, and the horizon of thinking about the sense of agency, self-affirmation and self-preservation. As I will indicate in turn, this is the case with Martin Heidegger's notion of *Lässigkeit* as the basic existential sensibility, Emmanuel Levinas's *paresse* as a position of refusal towards life, and Giorgio Agamben's *inoperativity*. But it is also the case when Roland Barthes and Theodor Adorno define idleness in terms of insubordination to pedagogical rituals or as a position of ethical neutrality, when Georges Bataille forges the concept of energy expenditure, when Sandor Ferenczi discovers the principle of neocatharsis in relaxation, or when Donald Winnicott dwells on the benefits of laziness as a psychosomatic symptom. When those ideas are juxtaposed against the political models of passive dissent, such as the *parrhēsia* model of Diogenes the Cynic or the socialist strike model proposed by Paul Lafargue, laziness emerges as a valuable signifier for the complex haptic-affective mechanism of counter-normativity. As I argue, the type of discourse that laziness mobilises across disciplines proves that this scandalous notion lays bare and unmasks the hidden conflation – within this norm – of the biological, the symbolic and the political. Or, as one might also put it more positively, the conceptual field demarcated by the meanings of laziness allows philosophy to (re)construct the language of docility and therefore reduce its biological bias. In this way, Chapter 1 develops the theoretical framework for the subsequent chapters, which focus on literary experiments with the figure of laziness undertaken by twentieth-century American writers.

The literary dimension of *The Labour of Laziness* demonstrates the cultural significance of those experimentations. For my American writers, laziness is more than just a theme; they use it as a unique metonym that connects *zoē* and *bios*, a figure that contains an archaeology of subjectivity, thus offering insight into the essential questions about the limits of subjective freedom. Although American literature features many works where the topos of being lazy plays a role, I limit my focus to authors who go beyond its purely aesthetic or strategically political use and recognise its tremendous philosophical and ethical counter-normative potential. That this potential is at its strongest, as I argue, in the works of such twentieth-century writers as Gertrude Stein, Ernest Hemingway, Donald Barthelme and David Foster Wallace does not mean that counter-normative uses of the laziness trope have no precedent in American literature before 1900. Accordingly, I devote my second chapter to a genealogy of the trope in pre-twentieth-century American literary history. In this way, Chapter 2 plays the role of an intermedium between the first philosophical chapter and the literary interpretations of twentieth-century literary works that are the main focus of *The Labour of Laziness*.

Chapter 2 serves as a historico-philosophical introduction to this twentieth-century focus, by giving an overview of how the motif of laziness functioned in the early Puritan literature, how this function was broadened in eighteenth-century secular and religious didactic literature, and how it eventually developed into an aesthetic device at the time of the Early Republic and American Renaissance. I will argue that Washington Irving's 'Rip Van Winkle' (1819) enriched the American cultural imaginary with a new trope, which combines the high Romantic aesthetics of the pastoral with unrefined motifs of vagabondage and delinquency, and in this way addresses the cultural desire for freedom from the norm of collective labour and from patterns of inclusion and exclusion within the consensual networks of social participation. Similarly, the engagement with the topos of laziness of such American Romantics as Ralph Waldo Emerson, Walt Whitman and Herman Melville in the 1840s and 1850s stands in sharp contrast to the ideologically and ethically prescriptive pastoral aesthetics of idle repose that dominates American literature of the first half of the century. Analysing their work, I draw a map of interrelations between several aspects of the Romantic sensibility, such as the pastoral idea of leisure and the democratic ideas of freedom and communitarianism, in order to indicate how the theme of laziness interrupts their ideological congruity and, in a counter-normative way, undermines their pedagogical efficiency. In Emerson's elaborations of passive contemplation I find the approximation of what, in the twentieth century,

Roland Barthes will call the position of the neutral that consists in withdrawal from social engagement and the obligation to judge. My reading of Whitman locates his famous trope of loafing less within the democratic framework than that of the Cynical tradition of performative indomitability as *parrhēsia*, or speaking truth to power. Finally in this chapter, I turn to Melville and his elaborate exploration of the theme of laziness in *Typee*, which, by employing the tactics of exaggeration and extravagant haptic poetics, stages a critique of Romantic moralism. I argue that Melville's debut novel is an experiment in the poetics of tactility, whose camp exaggerations enable him to criticise both the ideology of colonialism and the hypocrisy of compassionate Orientalism. Above all, however, the haptic aesthetics (that is, an aesthetics based on references to the sense of touch) allows Melville to stage a protest against an emerging ethico-aesthetic norm of his time for literature to be productively instructive.

One of the inevitable disadvantages of being a literary theorist rather than a historian of literature is that one's literary examples are always necessarily selective and exclusive. My 'historico-philosophical' approach in Chapter 2 does not explore in detail such key writers of the American Renaissance as Henry David Thoreau and his idea of passive resistance, or Frederick Douglass, whose writing documents the counter-systemic potency of laziness as a form of passive resistance to the antebellum slaveocracy. This omission on my part is, however, entirely deliberate: not only did I not want to intrude into the territories of the political history of resistance and protest, and the history of the South and the ways in which laziness, as a moral category and as a form of passive resistance, is intertwined with the history of American slavery (both are scholarly fields of their own), but I also decided to focus primarily on the philosophical dimension of the laziness metaphor and its less ostensibly ethical implications.

The Labour of Laziness in Twentieth-Century American Literature

In the remaining five chapters of this book, I combine close readings of some important twentieth-century literary works and philosophical analysis that amplifies the various tropes of laziness that these authors deploy. The reason for this is that I wish to demonstrate how an approach to literary texts via the concept-metaphor of laziness opens the possibility of what I call 'non-normative ethical criticism'. By this I mean a kind of reading that registers a text's ethical intervention, without classifying it as morally good and productive or immoral and culturally useless. These five chapters are divided into two parts, each being devoted to a particular moment in American literary history – 'The Modernist Moment of Laziness' and 'The Postmodern Moment of Laziness' – where 'moment' is understood here not as a point in time but in Lyotard's terms as an 'event' when the idea of laziness intervenes in the process of aesthetic normatisation with unusual directness and power. As section headers, 'The Modernist Moment' and 'The Postmodern Moment' are thus not simply chronological markers, but events of shift within what Raymond Williams called value systems and structures of feeling. In both parts, I argue that literary engagements with the figure of doing nothing for Gertrude Stein, Ernest Hemingway, Donald Barthelme and David Foster Wallace are unique in that they challenge modernist and postmodern ethical regimes, which situate literary creativity among other forms of community-serving productivity.

Chapter 3, 'Cessation and *inaction externe*: Gertrude Stein and Marcel Duchamp', focuses on the first instance of counternormative work that the trope of laziness performs with respect to the twentieth-century distribution of the sensible. I discuss the modernist fascination with vitality and movement, exemplified by the modernist manifestos of avant-garde artists and poets, to show how this 'vitalocentric' tendency is matched by a cultural counter-current of the aesthetics of cessation. Using Raymond Williams's concept of emergent cultural value, I argue that in the art theories of Gertrude Stein and Marcel Duchamp one finds the embryonic form of the sensibility of exhaustion, traditionally associated with modernism's successor, postmodernism. Unlike the discussion of Romantic writers, Chapter 3 is counter-Rancièrean, in the sense that, contrary to the philosopher's view of modernism as naively unaware of art's usurpation by the market, I insist on its recognition of art's co-optation by the capitalist norm of productivity, and highlight the concepts and aesthetic modes by means of which this awareness – an awareness underpinned by dissent – is communicated.

While Chapter 3 focuses primarily on theories of art, Chapter 4 illustrates how the modernist mode of cessation enters literature. I discuss Ernest Hemingway's late 1940s novel *The Garden of Eden* (published posthumously in 1986), which stands at the threshold of modern and postmodern aesthetic regimes, and therefore offers a useful point to start an investigation of how modernist inoperativity is wrested from its embryonic state and given a literary form. Hemingway's novel captures the tension between creative potency and impotency by dramatising it as a conflict between two characters, Catherine and David Bourne, each haunted by their individual, internal conflict between creative vigour and creative resistance. The tension sustains *The Garden*'s narrative and dictates its pace. Occasionally, however, there occur in the story languorous moments of slowing down and the drawing off of vigour, when the interpersonal and internal conflicts cease, while the text itself approximates a self-reflexive commentary on its own power dynamics. Self-referential as those fragments are, however, they are also exercises in haptic aesthetics in that their insight into the essence of creativity incorporates, via the theme of laziness, the bodily, sensuous dimension of all creative endeavours. I argue that Hemingway's manipulation of the theme is a radical attempt at articulating by literary means the sensibility of exhaustion that underlies the modernist love of action. In *The Garden of Eden*, the poetics of laziness serves a double function. First, it expresses the idea of a privative origin of creative power, via Hemingway's engagement with the poetics of touch; and second, it critiques the capitalist emphasis on productivity and the economic dimension of writing. As a story centred upon the question of what it means to create, a story that the author rewrote many times and could not bring himself to finish, *The Garden of Eden* provides a unique sample of a modernist text struggling to give shape to an inexpressible, pre-emergent sensibility of exhaustion, cessation and impotency. Read metafictionally, the novel is a story about what stylistic measures it takes to spell out by literary means of vitalocentric norm that element of impotency/inoperativity that defines the poetic act, and therefore inevitably counters that norm.

Chapters 5, 6 and 7 represent 'The Postmodern Moment' in the evolution of twentieth-century value systems and structures of feeling. In the first of this group of chapters, 'Exhaustion of Possibilities: Harold Rosenberg, John Barth and Susan Sontag', I turn to postmodern manifestos to analyse their embrace of inaction, exhaustion and cessation, and show that despite their claims, these manifestos contain an internal contradiction. If postmodernists' declared assent to the mode of exhaustion of aesthetic possibilities, articulated in its theorists' and writers' penchant for self-referentiality, intertextuality and metafiction, gives an impression of a full-fledged embracing of doing nothing, this insight might actually be misleading. A careful look at postmodern manifestos, such as those by Harold Rosenberg, John Barth and Susan Sontag, suggests that the appropriation of the limit-trope of doing nothing as postmodernism's very own is in fact quite artificial. Rather than realising the counter-normative potential of the trope, the dominant postmodern rhetoric nullifies it by rephrasing productivity in terms of hyper-productivity and hyper-engagement. For example, in Rosenberg's theory of Action Painting and John Barth's notion of ultra-productive weariness with tradition, certain modes of inactivity such as passivity or uninterest are revitalised as states of heightened cognition. Thus, rather than inaugurating a 'new' representational and ethical regime, postmodern manifestos are quite reactionary in that they reiterate the ideologically troublesome Romantic notion of the artist's active role in the process of artistic production.

Yet this is not the whole story. Just as individual modernists saw through the vitalocentric norm and looked for ways of evading it, some postmodern artists radically opposed the dominant post-Romantic intellectual current of the 1960s and 1970s. Resistance is one of the themes of Thomas Pynchon, but the one postmodern writer who seems to have made Romantic mystification and its twentieth-century versions the central theme of his fiction is Donald Barthelme. Therefore, Chapter 6 looks at his work through the prism of variants of sloth and laziness such as inertia and indolence – themes that Barthelme used to dramatise Anton Ehrenzweig's concept of unconscious scanning – in order to map his position *vis-à-vis* productivity. From Barthelme's early renditions of the figure of the artist such as the Pollockian Paul in *Snow White* (1967), who spends his life on long baths and inert contemplation of empty canvases, to the half-dead-half-alive carcass of D.F. in *The Dead Father* (1975), who personifies the idea of writer's block, or finally to the lassitude-driven architect in *Paradise*, Barthelme's characters and plots seem to stand in contrast to dominant ideas of the 1960s. I argue that Barthelme's views on action/inaction in art were fundamentally different from those voiced by Harold Rosenberg in *The Tradition of the New* (1959). In fact, no author of American postmodernism has done more to counteract the Rosenbergian post-Romantic idea of the heightened sensibility of passive repose than did Barthelme. The purpose of this chapter is to bring the themes of inertia and *sterēsis* to the foreground via a detailed reading of Barthelme's most famous stories and novels to argue that his insight into creative processes exceeds the postmodern ethical and aesthetic regime. In essence, it challenges, via the themes of inertia, the ideological underpinnings of literary creation.

The argument in Chapter 7, devoted to David Foster Wallace, is an elaboration of these conclusions. If writers such as Hemingway and Barthelme use the trope of doing nothing to announce protest against the absorption by the regime of productivity of the individual (writer's or reader's) privacy and freedom, then writers of the second half of the twentieth century such as Wallace face a very different problem. In other words, in the late 1980s and 1990s the counter-normative potential of the trope of doing nothing is appropriated as one of the marketing strategies of the art market. By the turn of the century, I argue, it becomes *the* promotional tactic. Requiring writers to engage in book tours or publicising the themes of personal distress, insecurity and weakness, as seems to be suggested by the steady upsurge in popularity of failure novels, the publishing industry consolidates the biopolitical normativisation of productivity. If we view this trend on the continuum of American literature, we might recall Marx's famous line about history happening first as tragedy and second as farce, in the context of which one cannot but view the modern trend for productive self-fashioning as a farcical caricature of the Protestant work ethic and its biopolitical reach for the lives of the seventeenth-century American settlers as outlined in Weber's *The Protestant Ethic or The Spirit of Capitalism*. Indeed, the authors of the important *addendum* to the Weberian legacy entitled *The New Spirit of Capitalism*, Luc Boltanski and Eve Chiapello, characterise the recent mutations within capitalism along those very lines:

> It becomes difficult to make a distinction between the time of private life and the time of professional life, between dinners with friends and professional lunches, between affective bonds and useful relationships ... At the same time, the whole work ethic or, as Weber put it, the ethic of toil, which had permeated the spirit of capitalism in various forms, was affected. Associated in the first state of capitalism with rational asceticism ... it tends to make way for a premium on *activity*, without any clear distinction between personal or even leisure activity and professional activity. To be doing something, to move, to change – this is what enjoys prestige.[40]

While it seems impossible to invent aesthetic modes that would evade this new logic and reach for a position at its limit, a case can be made for David Foster Wallace's novel *The Pale King* (2011), which employs *acedia* as the mode of its subjectivity and its main theme, thus creating the effect of a recursive loop, or as the author himself calls it elsewhere, a 'feedback glare'. The result of recursive dynamics, the novel creates a series of micro-events of what Lauren Berlant calls 'self-interruption', which guard the heterotopic territory of the subject's (as well as the author's) agency against interpellative calls from the book industry for self-exploitation and productivity. Thus, I end the book with a discussion of a literary text that is also fundamentally a philosophical one in its foregrounding of the theoretical connotations of laziness that are embedded in its genealogy and development.

Notes

1. Hans Blumenberg, *Paradigms for a Metaphorology*, trans. Robert Savage (Ithaca: Cornell University Press, 2010), 3.
2. Susan Sontag, *Illness as Metaphor* (New York: Picador, 2013), 6–8.
3. Maurice Blanchot, *The Infinite Conversation* (Minneapolis: University of Minnesota Press, 1993), 196.
4. Robert K. Barnhart and Sol Steinmetz (eds), *The Barnhart Dictionary of Etymology* (New York: H. W. Wilson Co., 1988); John Thomson, *Etymons of English Words* (Edinburgh: Oliver & Boyd, 1826).

5. Walter W. Skeat, *An Etymological Dictionary of the English Language* (Oxford: Clarendon Press, 1958).

6. Virginia Krause, *Idle Pursuits: Literature and Oisiveté in the French Renaissance* (Newark, DE: University of Delaware Press, 2003), 16.

7. Jeffrey S. Adler, 'A Historical Analysis of the Law of Vagrancy', *Criminology* 27.2 (1989), 209–29; Stephen Pimpare, 'Vagrancy and the Homeless', in *Crime and Criminal Behavior*, ed. William J. Chambliss (Thousand Oaks, CA: SAGE Publications, 2011), 254–68.

8. Roland Barthes, 'Osons être paresseux', in *Oeuvres Complètes*, vol. 3 (Paris: Seuil, 2002), 760.

9. Siegfried Wenzel, *The Sin of Sloth: Acedia in Medieval Thought and Literature* (Chapel Hill, NC: University of North Carolina Press, 1967), 5.

10. Stanford M. Lyman, *The Seven Deadly Sins: Society and Evil* (Lanham, MD: Rowman and Littlefield, 1989).

11. Wenzel, *The Sin of Sloth*, 6.

12. In *The Seven Deadly Sins*, Morton Bloomfield also traces the psychological sense to the Septuagint which connects *acedia* to 'faintness, weariness, anguish', as in Psalm 128, verse 28: 'My soul has slumbered because of acedia.' Emphasising the pre-Christian roots of *acedia*, Bloomfield sees its origin in the Babylonian myth of the Soul Journey, where a man's soul after death has to pass a series of demons who are connected with specific sins and who judge the soul with regard to a particular sin. These demons are sometimes connected to the seven planets. See Morton Bloomfield, *The Seven Deadly Sins: An Introduction to the History of a Religious Concept, with Special Reference to Medieval English Literature* (East Lansing: Michigan State University Press, 1967), 7, 15.

13. William F. May, *A Catalogue of Sins: A Contemporary Examination of Christian Conscience* (New York: Holt, Rinehart and Winston, 1967), 195.

14. Qtd. in Bloomfield, *The Seven Deadly Sins*, 17.

15. The Cassianic list should also be appended by the observations of Pope Gregory the Great, who explicitly merged *acedia* with sorrow (*tristitia*), as well as by the ideas of Peter Damiani, a Benedictine monk serving under Pope Leo IX, who detected it in the physiological symptoms of drowsiness and weariness. Similarly, in the writings of a twelfth-century monk, Aelred of Rievaulx, *acedia* is defined as exhaustion with religious activity and decrease of life energies. As Wenzel notes, the physical 'lack of fervor' was understood in the Middle Ages as the antecedent of death, the final state of atrophy of the soul that has grown bored not just with God but also with the world. In short, it is a crime against life, against vitality.

16. 'sorrow in the Divine Good'.

17. Wenzel, *The Sin of Sloth*, 70.

18. Pimpare, 'Vagrancy and the Homeless', 257.

19. From the mid-sixteenth century, 'bridewell' was a synonym for a petty offender prison, named after London's St Bride's Well.

20. Luke Rochfort, *An Antidot for Lazinesse, or A Sermun against the Capitall vice of Sloth and Sundrie Evill Effects Thereof by L.R.* (Dublin: Printed by the Society of Stationers, 1624), 8–9.

21. Dorothy Moses Schultz, 'Vagrancy', in *Encyclopedia of Homelessness*, ed. David Levinson (Thousand Oaks, CA: Sage Publications, 2004), 587.

22. C. J. Ribton-Turner, *A History of Vagrants and Vagrancy, and Beggars and Begging* (London: Chapman and Hall, 1887), 357.

23. Michael B. Katz, *The Undeserving Poor: America's Enduring Confrontation with Poverty*, 2nd edn (Oxford: Oxford University Press, 2013).

24. Michel Foucault, *Madness and Civilization: A History of Insanity in the Age of Reason* (New York: Vintage, 1988), 135.

25. Ibid.

26. Rochfort, *An Antidot for Lazinesse*, 9.

27. Michel Foucault, *Discipline and Punish: The Birth of the Prison*, trans. Alan Sheridan (New York: Vintage, 1995), 221.

28. Michel Foucault, *The Birth of Biopolitics: Lectures at the Collège de France, 1978–79* (New York: Palgrave Macmillan, 2008), 259.

29. Deborah Weiss, 'Maria Edgeworth's Infant Economics: Capitalist Culture, Good-Will Networks and "Lazy Lawrence"', *Journal for Eighteenth-Century Studies* 37.3 (2014), 396.

30. John Hatcher, 'Labour, Leisure and Economic Thought before the Nineteenth Century', *Past and Present* 160.1 (1998), 64–115.

31. Michel Foucault, *The Foucault Reader*, ed. Paul Rabinow (New York: Pantheon Books, 1984), 261, 264.

32. Ibid., 261–2.

33. Erving Goffman, *Stigma; Notes on the Management of Spoiled Identity* (Englewood Cliffs, NJ: Prentice-Hall, 1963); Norbert Elias, *Quest for Excitement: Sport and Leisure in the Civilizing Process* (Oxford: Blackwell, 1986); Norbert Elias, *Involvement and Detachment* (New York: Blackwell, 1987); Howard S. Becker, *Outsiders: Studies in the Sociology of Deviance* (New York: The Free Press of Glencoe, 1963); Steven M. Elias (ed.), *Deviant and Criminal Behavior in the Workplace* (New York: New York University Press, 2013).

34. Nachman Ben-Yehuda, *The Politics and Morality of Deviance: Moral Panics, Drug Abuse, Deviant Science, and Reversed Stigmatization* (Albany: State University of New York Press, 1990), 3.

35. Becker, *Outsiders*, 9.

36. Max Weber, *The Protestant Ethic and the Spirit of Capitalism* (London: Routledge, 2001), 62.

37. Foucault, *The Foucault Reader*, 263.

38. Catherine Malabou, 'The King's Two (Biopolitical) Bodies', *Representations* 127.1 (2014), 100–1.

39. Ibid., 101.

40. Luc Boltanski and Eve Chiapello, *The New Spirit of Capitalism*, trans. Gregory Elliott (London: Verso, 2007), 155.

PART I

The Philosophical and Literary
Contexts of Laziness

CHAPTER 1

Laziness as Concept-Metaphor

Some concepts must be indicated by an extraordinary and sometimes
even barbarous or shocking word.

Gilles Deleuze, *What is Philosophy?*

Western thought has always been extremely attached to the idea of
activity, says Giorgio Agamben in his essay 'The Power of Thought'.
The belief that the power of human faculty lies in its potency to act,
in its dynamic capacity to actualise itself, has 'grown and developed'
in history 'to a point of imposing its force over the entire planet'.[1] As
a result, we have lost the more fundamental understanding of our
relation to power. Agamben attempts to recover this lost meaning
from *De Anima*, where Aristotle says that the essence of power is not
to be sought in the dynamic potency of human faculty (*dunamis*),
but in the capacity to withhold potency and action, in privative
power or *sterēsis*. The possibility of thinking power as privation
has been almost entirely repressed by the Western philosophical
tradition, to the point that it is now an incredibly difficult idea
to promote. The fact that Agamben's argument, which originally
appeared in the 1999 collection of essays *Potentialities*, was repub-
lished in *Critical Inquiry* in 2014 suggests that the demand to recon-
sider the repressed concept of *sterēsis* is germane to contemporary
discussions of power.

Here is how Agamben justifies the pertinence of *sterēsis* for our
understanding of power. In Aristotle's theory there is, he says, a
specific ambivalence

of every human power that in its original structure maintains itself in relation to its own privation; it is always – and with respect to the same thing – power to be and not to be, to do and not to do. It is this relation that constitutes . . . the essence of power. The living being that exists in the mode of its power is capable of its own powerlessness and only in this way possesses its own proper power . . . In power, sensation is constitutively anesthesia, thought non-thought, work worklessness . . . The greatness of [man's] power is measured against the abyss of his powerlessness.[2]

The capacity to *not do* things, powerlessness (*impotenza*) – this is where power finds its apotheosis. What lies at the core of the concept of power is the condition of having a faculty but refraining from using it, a situation of 'availability/inactivity' of the faculty and its simultaneous 'exertion and nonexertion'.[3]

The reason why Agamben thinks it crucial to revive the notion of *sterēsis* today is because it bears a direct relation to the idea of freedom. It is possible, Agamben writes, 'to glimpse in this doctrine, in the amphibolic nature of every power, the place in which the modern problem of freedom may be discovered at its foundation'.[4] For the very idea of freedom 'as a problem' is born precisely with the emergence of the possibility of being capable to act or not to act. Such a definition of freedom is more elemental than the idea of freedom as the right to choose; freedom is not so much 'a right or a property' one has or performs, but rather 'an experience that puts the entire being of the subject in play' and a way of being in relation to a *sterēsis*.[5] Just as power is essentially based on the modality of availability/inactivity, the idea of freedom it gives rise to accommodates simultaneously the potential for exerting and for not exerting power. In short, *sterēsis* is the proper site of freedom. It comprises within itself the active position of actualising potency as well as the passive position of abstaining from actualisation.

Having searched Western thought for approximations of *sterēsis*, Agamben concludes that it is almost entirely extinct, lost somewhere on the margins of philosophy. Philosophical tradition has no formula for a truly privative position of 'hovering between affirmation and negation, acceptance and rejection, giving and taking, except, perhaps, for the Skeptics' notion of "suspension" (*ou mallon*)'.[6] Agamben's diagnosis holds true as long as one looks exclusively at the history of what are considered to be legitimate philosophical concepts. Yet some concepts, as Gilles Deleuze points out in *What is Philosophy?*, are indicated by most bizarre, 'barbarous and shocking' words, or by words that are so plain and ordinary that they remain 'imperceptible to a nonphilosophical ear'.[7] One potential candidate for a concept of this kind, which would allow us to retrieve the formula for suspension, is the word laziness. Though rarely invoked due to unequivocally negative cultural connotations, when laziness does appear in philosophical writing, it punctuates precisely those blank spots on the horizon of Western thought where the ancient notions of *sterēsis* or *ou mallon* could be reinserted. This is so precisely because of its stigmatic attributes such as unproductivity, inaction, indolence, boredom, absence of *élan vital*, passivity, inertia, stasis, lifelessness and death. With those negatives in its spectrum, laziness signals a forbidden attitude of being poised between assent and dissent.

This chapter is devoted to a reflection on laziness as a concept. I look at the ways in which philosophers employ the notion of laziness in the service of their arguments, the ideas with which it is clustered and to what ends. I specifically examine Emmanuel Levinas's notion of *paresse* in relation to Martin Heidegger's fundamental boredom (*Lässigkeit*), as well as Barthes's notion of the *neutral* and Adorno's concept of *gaps*, in order to argue that laziness emerges from these accounts as a concept denoting an attitude of withdrawal – or, more specifically, a position of suspension motivated by a desire for freedom, where freedom is understood as ethico-political neutrality.

The theoretical framework derived from this philosophical analysis will serve as an interpretative reference point for the discussion of literary texts where the trope of laziness mediates the elusive problems of subjective freedom and literary productivity. Considering laziness as a lay term for the position of *sterēsis*, which 'contains an archeology of subjectivity', I use my philosophical examples to demonstrate that the figure of laziness affords access to those subtle moments of privative power that define literature's relation to freedom.[8] Not all literature centred around the topos of freedom engages with this archaeological dimension of what it means to be free. Indeed, as I argue in the following chapters of

The Labour of Laziness, few writers in the history of literature have accepted the risk of failure and rejection to explore the relation between subjective freedom and the norm of productivity. The ones chosen for this book have all done so by discovering the power of *sterēsis* in the trope of laziness.

The Existential Perspective

In *Existence and Existents* (1978), Emmanuel Levinas addresses the notion of *paresse* – the French term for laziness – very directly. One of his opening claims is that *paresse*, although never 'examined by pure philosophical analysis outside of moral preoccupations', is relevant to philosophy, since 'in its very occurrence' it denotes 'a position taken with regard to existence', a position of dissent to the fact that one has to participate in being.[9]

Levinas's opening claim thus situates laziness at the very heart of the problematics of being. While Levinas considers it necessary to reconfigure laziness in philosophical terms, he is aware that to conceptualise such a banal and apparently transparent notion is to oppose the entire Western philosophical tradition, especially that of the Enlightenment, which boldly excluded laziness from the sphere of philosophical interest. In Locke's *Of the Conduct of the Understanding*, for example, laziness features as that which prevents the mind from thinking rationally, allowing it to wander in all directions, merely scratching the surface of things, obstructing the force of reason.[10] In *Lectures on Anthropology*, Kant not only subsumes laziness under the category of 'natural predisposition' and 'savage' inclinations that we have a moral duty to eradicate, but identifies laziness in '*Was ist Aufklarung?*'as the main obstacle to Enlightenment, equal in its destructiveness only to cowardice.[11]

Of course, to a reader brought up on the principles of Deleuzian hermeneutics of nomadic thinking, Kant's and Locke's denials of the rhizomatic dynamics of thought processes can be perhaps dismissed as historical trivia. Levinas, however, takes such dismissals as his starting point for restoring the relevance of laziness to philosophical inquiry. The uncanny presence of laziness at the 'margins of normalization'[12] is precisely what he finds intriguing. In his view, the experience of laziness attests to what Blanchot has called 'the limits of thought'.[13] Following Blanchot, Levinas finds in the not-doing-anything of *paresse* the most fundamental existential moment of a refusal to be, a refusal which is empirically impossible – we can only experience it after we've been plunged into being – but whose impossibility gestures towards the limits of thought. In this way, he reasons, laziness opens up the question of exteriority, which is to say, the fundamental metaphysical question about the beyond or the transcendental. If Levinas is right, then there is definitely a reason to consider *paresse* philosophically, to think of it as a gesture of ontological attentiveness to oneself, a certain position.

Levinas's desire to reignite philosophy's interest in experiences that have always occupied its margins resonates with Heidegger, who in his 1929–30 lectures *The Fundamental Concepts of Metaphysics* opens his analysis of attunement (*Stimmung*) by arguing for a philosophical relevance of prosaic dispositions in the following way:

> Attunements are the fundamental manner in which we find ourselves disposed in such and such a way . . . And precisely *those* attunements to which we pay no heed at all, the attunements we least observe, those attunements which attune us in such a way that we feel as though there is no attunement at all, as though we were not attuned in any way at all – these attunements are the most powerful.[14]

Heidegger's suggestion that we should look for answers to fundamental philosophical and, indeed, metaphysical questions in the phenomena where nothing seems to be happening, and which we scarcely ever consider important at all, paves the way for Levinas's claim about laziness. Not only because laziness shares the etymological paradigm with Heidegger's boredom (the German *Langeweile* literally means 'long while' and signifies 'long, and/ or easy time'), on the grounds of which Heidegger develops his concept of *Stimmung*, but also because laziness is a mood, or a sentiment, whose meaning consists, primarily and exclusively, in a feeling that there is no attunement – in doing and feeling nothing.

Crucially, this doing and feeling nothing in laziness is just as much an (in)activity of the mind that wanders around in, to use Locke's words, 'lazy recumbency and satisfaction on the surface of things', as it is also an act of the body.[15] As medieval theologians observed when tracing the influence of *daemon meridianus* in the slow movements of monks, laziness articulates itself primarily in the loose pose of the body, in the relaxation of its outer shell. To do its existential work, laziness must engage the bodily dimension; for as Catherine Malabou points out in her reading of Heidegger's *Stimmung*, without consideration of the 'ontico-ontological membrane' of the flesh, the entire mechanism of tuning in and out with the world and oneself makes little sense.[16] The issue of the bodily threshold is thus crucial to philosophical inquiry into moods, while it is also that which the discipline finds most problematic. Because laziness seems for Levinas to be the mood whose entire meaning is indivisible from the body's materiality, it is one that puts the traditional mind/body dialectic into question in the most radical way. This is, therefore, how he announces his attempt at challenging philosophical tradition in *Existence and Existents*:

> To see the truth of the operation [of how the existent relates to existence], let us ignore all attitudes towards existence which arise from reflection, attitudes by which an already constituted existence turns back over itself. The attitudes involved in the meditation on the 'meaning of life,' pessimism or optimism, suicide or love of life, however deeply they may be bound up with the operation by which a being is born into existence, take place over and beyond that birth.
>
> We must try to grasp that event of birth in phenomena which are prior to reflection. Fatigue and laziness, which have never been examined by pure philosophical analysis outside of moral preoccupations, are in their very occurrence, positions taken with regard to existence.[17]

To be fair, some philosophical attention has already been given to laziness in relation to fatigue. John Locke discussed the two together in *The Conduct of the Understanding*, in his argument about the necessity of intellectual exercise, where he defined laziness as a reaction of aversion to effort developed in situations when a mind takes upon itself a task that exceeds its capacities. Locke found this aversive response analogous to the reaction of a body which, exhausted by lifting a weight too heavy for its strength, grows fatigued and unable to move. But what for Locke was only an analogy, for Levinas becomes a pretext for a metaphysical inquiry.

However, Levinas's primary interlocutor for *Existence and Existents* is neither John Locke nor Edmund Husserl with his theory of passive synthesis, but Martin Heidegger. The point many readers of Levinas often raise as to whether the quoted words announce a break from or a continuity with Heidegger is for now of secondary importance.[18] What is more pertinent is how Levinas conducts his dialogue with Heidegger and how he articulates his reinsertion into philosophy of ordinary experiences such as *paresse*.

Levinas says that the only way to grasp the instant of one's coming into existence is to turn to experiences that precede conscious thought, reflection and attitude: that is to say, to modes of perception that are more basic than phenomenal sensibility. He also intimates that the precedence of those modes is not simply temporal, in the sense that pre-reflective phenomena come *before*, but also ontological, in the sense that they are *prior* to reflection. Notably, the quality that makes a phenomenon *prior* in both senses of the term is apparently not present in all pre-conscious phenomena, but is uniquely specific to fatigue and laziness, which entail 'the refusal to exist'.[19] Fatigue and laziness are 'made up of that refusal', because 'refusal is *in*' laziness and fatigue; it is their very structure: the two sentiments not only lend themselves to 'pure' philosophical analysis, but indeed 'must' become its object.[20] In other words, not only is laziness relevant to philosophical inquiry into existence, but it is absolutely essential to it, as in its occurrence it articulates the limits of our understanding of what existence is. Clearly then, apart from undermining Kant's relegation of laziness to the sphere of moral predispositions, Levinas also works against the formula of transcendental deduction which places the conditions of possibility outside empirical experience. Not only does he reinstate the cause 'prior' to reflection into the sphere of perceptual experience of doing nothing, but, as we shall see, he identifies in this experience a specific mode of pre-conscious perceptivity.

Paresse, Stimmung and Proprioception

Levinas's line of attack on the Kantian *a priori* via emphasis on perception makes most sense when read in the context of Heidegger's

Being and Time (1927), which defines attunement in terms of self-localisation among the phenomena of the world, or *Befindlichkeit*. It is precisely in *Befindlichkeit*, the sensation of corporeal orientation in space and time, that Heidegger situates the precondition of all attunements. Moreover, Heidegger identifies the character of this sensation in explicitly Kantian terms, as 'the condition of possibility', thus indicating that perception of our body's abjectness may indeed mark a blank spot in the concept of the transcendental.[21]

At first glance, Levinas's claims about laziness and fatigue in *Existence and Existents* seem to differ from *Befindlichkeit* only in the degree of concretisation: the former marks orientation *vis-à-vis* the world, whereas *paresse/fatigue* denotes the sense of being burdened by its presence. But it is precisely this degree of concretisation that makes all the difference. The sense of orientation that Heidegger's German term captures linguistically is amplified by Levinas through the insertion of laziness-as-withdrawal, and thus highlights the idea that the essential component of one's sense of existence should be sought in the act of *refusal to be attuned* rather than in the act of attunement as such. Simply put, Levinas thinks there is something about the way one attends to the spatial burdensomeness of one's body in laziness that very literally actualises the impossible refusal of being. In ontological terms, the experience of inactivity expressed in laziness compels us to a unique kind of attention to the fact of our existence as material objects.[22]

When Levinas develops the idea, it becomes clear that the attention to one's objectness takes place on a specific level of perception. The impossible dissent, which is built into the structure of existence, is most purely revealed not in the *content* of the experience of laziness, but in its *form* on a bodily level. Levinas's phrase 'position with regard to existence' should thus be understood in a very literal sense, as a bodily pose. For when 'we take fatigue and laziness as contents', Levinas argues, 'we do not see what is *effected* in them', namely, 'the event of refusal to act' and to engage with existence – a hopelessly 'impossible' event of 'an impotent nonacceptance'.[23] The lazy pose enunciates an objection towards activity on the somatic level, in a fleeting event of corporeal self-mapping, before any faculty to act upon and transform this objection into reflection or awareness becomes activated. Consequently, what Heidegger's

Befindlichkeit denoted semantically, Levinas's *paresse* captures somatically, as *paresse* situates the event of existence on the surface of the ontico-ontological membrane of the human skin.

In Levinas's preliminary remarks about laziness, fundamental questions about the essence of existence are interspersed with empirical observations of ordinary, somatic states of perception. The extent of this 'somaticization'[24] of philosophical jargon is gradually revealed as Levinas develops his argument to explain that the event of laziness is expressed through 'inhibition': 'laziness concerns beginning, as though existence were not there right off, but preexisted the beginning in an inhibition. There is more here than a span of duration, flowing imperceptibly between two moments.'[25] The position of refusal is now concretised even further. It is not simply a pose, but a pose of *inhibition*: that is to say, a *poise*. The withholding of action and movement occasioned in laziness does not have the temporal structure of retrospective withdrawal or seizure of perceptive faculties; rather, it functions as a threshold phenomenon from the vantage point of which all future sensory experience can be derived. What we colloquially call laziness emerges from Levinas's analysis as a preparatory instance of attention-scaling, whose purpose is to calibrate channels of more complex interactions with the world on the level of sensibility and reflection. In other words, if we normally associate laziness with the opposite of poise – that is with looseness and rest – it is because we fail to observe that laxity, when considered on the level of heed, is a manifestation of specifically understood, deeper tension within our perceptive apparatus.

The emphasis on inhibition adds to the empirical sense that Levinas gives to *position*, for as remarked earlier, he does not use the term 'position' in a strictly philosophical sense, as an assertion of an assumption performed by reason, but in the sense of position*ing* one's limbs, head and body, which in the case of a lazy pose is lax, almost lifelessly limp, as if entirely made up of a refusal to move. Inhibition is thus a crucial term in Levinas's somatic semantics (or should we say 'semantics') of the prior position, because the arresting of senses that inhibition presupposes is for Levinas a distinct kind of sense itself. This at least seems to be the meaning of Levinas's assertion that the phenomenon of refusal to act *effects* *itself*, as if it belonged to a different order of faculty arrangement. It effects itself, 'just as in the order of experience, vision alone is the apprehension of light and hearing alone the perception of sound'.[26] The special properties of the power of refusal suggest that Levinas understands inhibition occasioned in laziness in terms of *sterēsis*, as the ability to suspend faculty that is prior to and more fundamental than the power to activate the senses. Just as the power of vision finds its essence when the eyes are closed, being finds its essence in the suspension of activity.

If inhibition is a kind of sense, how does it work and on what level of perception? While the concept of *sterēsis* concerns any privation of faculty, Levinas focuses on one specific case of its suspension, the inhibition of action and movement. He argues that this sense or mode of perception, which characterises *paresse*-as-prior-position, coincides with 'an impulse' at the beginning of action, which 'conserves itself' the moment it occurs.[27] The position of *paresse* 'lies between the clear duty of getting up and the putting of the foot down off the bed'.[28] Thus, just as physical gestures precede and shape their affective content, the prior position enunciates the refusal in the pose of inhibition, which only later may become the content of a reflection. In short, *paresse* is Levinas's term for an experience of self-conserved reflex suspension that has to do with the distribution of oneself 'in relationship with a place', with the world.[29]

This experience is entirely prior to any conscious reflection. Consciousness, Levinas says, 'comes out of rest, out of a position, out of this unique relationship with a place . . . out of an immobility'.[30] The position of rest is 'a commitment which consists in maintaining itself in uncommittedness' and which is 'a condition'.[31] Everything that follows from this state – such as sensory 'contact with the earth' and conscious emotions – is already secondary and obstructive to the sense of 'gathering oneself up' that is effected in inertia.[32] One might conclude, therefore, that Levinas not only associates the prior position with the body at rest, given that 'the body [is] the very advent of consciousness', but is also careful to disambiguate the level of bodily perception he prioritises.[33] What he has in mind is 'the *irruption* in anonymous being of *localization* itself': namely, the impulse of self-mapping.[34]

Translated into the language of biology, the impulse of self-mapping that Levinas isolates in the experience of laziness is referred to as *proprioception*. Proprioception is the knowledge of the body's location in space, made possible by sensory receptors called 'proprioceptors' located in the skin, muscles and joints, whose combined input helps maintain a sense of bodily integrity. According to the neurophysiologist Charles Sherrington who coined the term proprioception in 1906, proprioceptors are to be distinguished from 'interoceptors', which provide the brain with information about internal organs, and 'exteroceptors', which provide information about the external world.[35] As inferred from the Latin prefix *proprio-* ('one's own'), proprioception has to do with the ability to sense that our bodies are ours, as it yields knowledge of the body's coherence and orientation in space, the positioning and movement of our limbs and torso, the sense of effort, force and heaviness. In short, the 'direct, immediate and spontaneous knowledge of the body' contributes to our sense of body ownership and the knowledge that our body belongs to us and not someone else.[36] All conscious awareness of being in the world as well as all reflection about separateness, sovereignty and freedom – all 'meditation on the "meaning of life", pessimism or optimism, suicide or love of life' – starts with this elementary perceptivity.

That proprioceptive awareness of one's body might be relevant to the analysis of existential matters seems to be the underlying assumption of Levinas's concept of 'position with regard to existence'. His extreme empiricism in this respect can be interpreted as an attempt to describe the sense of dissent to being as neither an act of volition nor an act of protest against necessity. *Paresse* construed as an exercise of the will, a decision to escape it, or a heroic protest against its undeniable presence would no longer be an elemental suspension of engagement in being. Thus, Levinas develops a radical vision of a poised body, a body whose entire life function is suspended (if only for a brief moment), in order to draw attention to his insight on the nature of freedom that this position captures: that freedom is never fully available unless in suspension.

In Levinas's radical vision, the position and the body are one and the same thing. As he puts it, the body 'as a means of localization' of the sense of self-weight 'is not an instrument, symbol, or symptom of a position, but *is position itself* [my emphasis]'.[37] Therefore, against the conventional understanding of lazy languor, the philosopher says that there is more to laziness than relaxation. In Levinas, laziness is 'neither peace nor softness'; it only 'weighs us down'.[38] The phrase *weighs us down* brings together empirical observation and philosophical reflection, framing laziness as a mode of sensory awareness of one's body, a sense of suspension, a state prior to unconscious muscle tension, and thus prerequisite to all activity.

In Levinas's model of prior position, the sense of suspension is communicated at the semantic level by the word *paresse*, derived in French from *parare*, to prepare, which emphasises the sense of priority that Levinas insists on in his argument. According to John Llewelyn, 'the essential laziness and lethargy with which Levinas is concerned here is a prevaricatory preparation that constitutes and accomplishes the effortfulness of the beginning of an instant'.[39] As a pre-arrangement, laziness is a rudimentary phenomenon of self-location, a state of heightened proprioception that makes us, so to speak, alert to the fact that our existence is inscribed within the material object of the body.

Levinas's point that there is more to *paresse* than a span of duration is further developed in his discussion of the expression *weighs us down*. The emphasis on corporeality brought forth in the assertion of contingency between *paresse* and fatigue remains to be explained. If the entire philosophical impact of the idea of laziness depends on that contingency, we have to ask how the spatial logic of weight relates to the temporal logic of inhibition.

From *Stimmung* to *Lässigkeit*

The question of fatigue once again takes us back to Heidegger, since the expression *weighs us down* happens to be the key expression in his discussion of the experience of time in fundamental attunement. As we shall see, Levinas's appeal to the materiality of self-weight in *Existence and Existents* might be read as gesture of reinserting the problematics of the body into Heidegger's theory of how we tune into contact with being. If one turns to Heidegger's *Fundamental Concepts of Metaphysics*, one initially notes a striking similarity between his and Levinas's analyses of this process, a resemblance which, nevertheless, soon betrays a fundamental difference. First, let us focus on the similarity.

Heidegger opens the discussion of attunement by investigating the concept of inhibition. He starts by saying that the understanding of attunements is essential for addressing metaphysical questions about the world, finitude and individuation, because attunements 'reach more primordially back into our essence . . . in them we first meet ourselves'.[40] He then adds that in attunements, we 'awaken' into being, but this awakening should be understood in the passive sense of '*letting it* [i.e. being] *be awake, guarding against it falling asleep*'.[41] The initial situation is therefore that of passive withdrawal, or 'profound indifference', which determines the minimum threshold of receptivity towards the world, in the sense that it negotiates the structure of engagement and disengagement with being's temporality.[42] To illustrate how this threshold is calibrated, Heidegger turns to the experience of boredom (*Langeweile*), which he considers to be an experience of temporality, and differentiates between two types of boredom: the *ordinary boredom* of being bored *by*, as when one passes the time while waiting for a train at a railway station and feels bored by what surrounds one, and the *fundamental boredom* of being bored *with*, where no particular thing is boring, but where we nevertheless feel oppressed by something, as in the leisurely circumstances of an enjoyable party. In both types of boredom, the dominant sensation is that of inhibition: we feel as being '*held in limbo*' and '*being held empty*', that is, we feel poised, indolent and drained of vitality. However, Heidegger argues, the structure of the experience of inhibition in each case is different. And as his analysis unfolds, inhibition turns out to have less to do with a feeling of being bored than with a certain comportment, a bodily inertness through which we 'give in' to being.

This is evident already in the analysis of ordinary boredom. In this case, what holds us in limbo and leaves us empty are the things that bore us: we are bored by that which 'comes from the outside'.[43] If we find a thing boring, it is not because of its intrinsic quality but because of the way in which it '*concerns us*', and this *concerning* is felt as oppressive weight because it is not something that happens 'of our own accord'.[44] However much we try to assert our rules by inventing ways of passing time at the railway station, this will only expose our intention to confront, to overcome the *'vacillation'* of time which *'drags'*. It is this *dragging* of time that is oppressive, in the sense that it weighs us down and holds us in limbo.[45] This is because the time of boredom at a railway station is always imposed by some schedule; the dragging of the interval to which we are condemned, while passing the time, weighs on us in such a way that although there are many things to do, they *'leave us empty by abandoning us to ourselves'.*[46] It follows that being left empty denotes a feeling of being burdened by the surrounding reality, in the sense of making us aware but not engaged with the world. How does this heaping under the burden of being manifest itself? In what manner does it weigh us down?

Both questions refer us to the issue identified by Catherine Malabou as the general problem of form in Heidegger's *Stimmung* theory. In *Fundamental Concepts of Metaphysics*, Malabou says, the question of form, of how attunement imprints itself on the fabric of the flesh, is continuously set into occlusion, as if attunement was itself its only articulation. Consequently, in Heidegger's discussion of boredom, the body is replaced with 'the existential fontanelle', a meeting point of all attunements, 'where the beating of exist-ence occurs' but which is not 'made of bony membrane but of . . . movement'.[47]

It is precisely this omission, or sidestepping, of the anatomical aspect of perception in Heidegger that Levinas wants to rectify in *Existence and Existents* when he describes the perceptive level of feeling weighed down by the burden of one's being. For Levinas, the idea of being weighed down in Heidegger's *ordinary boredom of being held in limbo and leaving empty* implies an external source of the feeling, and therefore needs to be supplemented with some-thing that will reconnect the sense of burden to the material body, which is its primary, non-external source. The idea that the role of this supplement should be played by the notion of *paresse* seems to derive from Heidegger's definition of the second type of boredom.

At the beginning of chapter 3 of *Fundamental Concepts*, Heidegger is troubled by the connection he has established earlier between being held in limbo and leaving empty. 'What is the link?' he asks, for there must be a 'structural link' between the two – they are 'not simply stuck together'.[48] Perhaps, he speculates, we should imagine a 'more original form of boredom' such as the situation of finding oneself at a dinner party. While at the railway station the sense of oppression came from the sense of being stuck in some time span, the context of the party is entirely different. In the latter case, we choose the time, that is, we have it, and without feeling stuck we enjoy our conversations, the food and the leisurely atmosphere. In other words, there is no idea of having to pass the time that drags. That unpleasant feeling, Heidegger says, is entirely 'repressed', that is to say, 'transformed' into a pose of laxation (*Lässigkeit*).[49]

If there is one moment in the analysis of attunement where the body is not an existential fontanelle but an ontic object, it is precisely at this point, as Heidegger proceeds from *inhibition* to *laxation*. In laxation, passing the time becomes trans*form*ed into 'our entire comportment and behavior', says Heidegger, as we lean back on the chair and loosen the joint of the hand holding a cigarette.[50] Because we are relaxed, we do not feel as if we were being held in limbo – there appears to be no sense of leaving empty. The only thing felt is a sense of what Heidegger calls the 'I know not what' that reminds us about ourselves, as we casually become 'swept away by chatting away'.[51] And so, Heidegger asks: 'What is it about this *casualness?*'

> Can we say that in contrast to being left empty, the casualness of joining in is a being satisfied, because we let ourselves be swept along? Or must we say that this casualness (*Lässigkeit*) is a being left empty (*Leergelassenheit*) that is *becoming more profound*? To what extent? Because as this [German] term is meant to indicate – in this casualness we abandon ourselves [*uns ürberlassen*] to our being there along and part of things . . . our seeking nothing more from the evening [than 'restful relaxation'] is what is decisive about our comportment. With this 'seeking nothing more' something is *obstructed* in us. In this chatting along . . . we have . . . left our proper self behind in a certain way . . . we slip from ourselves.[52]

In this passage we find the thread connecting Heidegger's and Levinas's version of prior position with regard to existence, for apparently the threshold of receptivity of Heidegger's fundamental attunement is established under the circumstances of laxity and effortlessness of *Lässigkeit*, that is to say, in a pose of unrestrained-ness. In the 'peculiar casualness' of *Lässigkeit*, we leave behind and abandon ourselves. The sense of emptiness – rather than being imposed from the outside – '*forms* itself . . . this emptiness is being left behind of our proper self . . . weighs on us', in the sense that although we have given ourselves time, time as such did not leave us, and instead of 'flowing' it just 'stands.'[53]

But in the moment of greatest proximity between Heidegger's and Levinas's conceptualisations of prior position as inhibition-through-laxation, there also emerges a crucial dif-ference. While for Levinas the figure of inhibition captures the perceptive awareness of bodily matter, in Heidegger's discourse, the representation of the lax body's 'objectness' via the figure of inhibition is also the gesture of its dismissal: Heidegger's time-that-stands occasions inhibition in that it restrains us, 'cuts us off' and 'seals us off' from ourselves.[54] Notwithstanding this difference, both Levinas and Heidegger seem to agree on the philosophical function of the lax disposition.

The '*standing of time*', Heidegger says, 'is a *more originary holding in limbo*, which is to say, *oppressing*', as it immobilises us in terms of possibilities of transition from the no-longer of our past to the not-yet of our future.[55] Because the inhibition characteristic of *Lässigkeit* creates a 'rupture' between the world and individuation, it thus occasions what Heidegger calls a 'receptivity' to time and the world, a separate kind of receptivity altogether, which establishes the condition for fundamental attunement.[56] Otherwise put, the self-withdrawal actualised in *Lässigkeit* 'attunes us to the freedom of *Dasein*'.[57] It attunes us to *Dasein*'s essential non-oppressiveness with regard to ourselves revealed by the rupture: 'This liberation of the *Dasein* in man does not mean placing him in some arbitrary *position*, but loading *Dasein* upon man as his *ownmost burden*. Only those who can truly give themselves a burden are free.'[58]

The position for attunement, and thus for reaching the condi-tion of possibility, is not an arbitrary philosophical stance, but an instance of experiencing the burden of *Dasein*. Before *Lässigkeit* becomes a state of preparedness for philosophical reflection it is first a pose of receptivity. The gesture we first identified in Levinas's literal use of the word 'position' is thus present in Heidegger's assertion that attunement ultimately is first a bearing of the body, and only later a philosophical position.

A comparison of Heidegger's *Lässigkeit* and Levinas's *paresse* foregrounds the problematic status of the body in philosophical discourse. Or rather, in the context of contemporary reclamations of the body in New Materialism and Object-Oriented Ontology as a 'matter that matters', the juxtaposition highlights a crucial aspect of the 'body issue' that the new philosophical discourses fail to deflect, namely the tenability of the dialectic of life and vitality as opposed to lifelessness and inanimateness, and the valorisation of liveliness presupposed in this dialectic.[59] Levinas's figure of lifeless inhibition as an elemental position with regard to existence and Heidegger's attempt to enliven inanimateness in giving in to the burden of *Dasein* expose how this dialectic normatises our thinking about the conditions of possibility. By effacing the opposition between life and lifelessness that underpins the normative association of being with vitality, Levinas's and Heidegger's conceptualisations of the liminal threshold of perceptivity through somaesthetic vocabularies of *Lässigkeit* and *paresse* offer an alternative to thinking about the limits of being as limits of possibility understood as potency, vitality. To suggest that certain bodily states give us insight into the 'fundamental event of our being' – a desire to be able to put it in suspension – is to orient the problem of vitality towards the question of freedom.[60] The point highlighted by Agamben in Aristotle's idea of *sterēsis*, that the essence of freedom is in the dual nature of power, seems to linger at the horizon of Levinas's and Heidegger's arguments, as both the discussion of *paresse* and the analysis of *Lässigkeit* progress towards the problem of freedom.

Sterēsis, Paresse, Lässigkeit and the Limits of Freedom

In the final passages of his discussion of fundamental attunement in *Fundamental Concepts*, Heidegger wages an attack on the Enlightenment vision of individual freedom. He says that the only way to feel free is to place upon oneself a burden, which is to say, 'not to counteract' it, and clarifies that such suspended reaction has nothing to do with weakness or servitude.[61] The acceptance of the burden is not a gesture of 'a paralyzing lack of courage [or] resignation', Heidegger says; on the contrary, it is a moment of 'assuming' *Dasein* via perception to bring one into touch with the essence of time and finitude. In other words, rather than obstructing the inquiry into the limits of being, the laxness of *Lässigkeit* makes this inquiry possible, as we assent to the freedom of *Dasein*'s immanence.

Not to act counter, which means not to actualise the dissent towards the burden of being, is what brings us closest to being free, in the most basic sense of freedom, by giving us insight into the scope of man's potency as both power to act and not to act. If Heidegger's idea is read in the light of Agamben's interpretation of 'this amphibolic vocation of power' in Aristotle, it becomes clear why the insight brought about in 'giving in' is not necessarily an act of resignation. What it does instead is assign to man 'the consciousness of privation . . . as the fundamental secret of his every knowledge of every action'.[62]

The dual character of human power is a source of its greatness as well as its misery. Agamben derives this conclusion from Aristotle in three steps. First, he explains Aristotle's analysis of the faculty of vision while our eyes are closed.

> When we do not see (that is when our sight remains in potential) we nevertheless distinguish darkness from light, seeing, in other words, the darkness as the color of vision in potential . . . This signifies that to feel seeing is possible because the principle of vision exists more as a power to see than as the power to not see, and this latter is not a simple absence but something existing, the *hexis* of privation.[63]

Power to see does not work at the expense of the power to not see, rather they coexist in the act and are contingent upon one another. Agamben points out that the accuracy of Aristotle's observation is corroborated by the claims of modern neurobiology, which says that absence of light activates the so-called *off-cells* that work to produce a reflection of the retina that we have learned to simplistically refer to as darkness. What Agamben deduces from Aristotle's theory of vision is the idea that acts of seeing do not consist in an expenditure of power whose reservoir might one day be wholly spent, but that power to not see remains 'conserved' in the act.[64] Agamben supports his argument by recalling Aristotle's ambiguous passage from *Metaphysics*, 'Power is that for which it so happens that in the act of which it is said to have power, nothing will be of the powerless.'[65] In Agamben's translation this means the following:

> If a power [*potenza*] to not be belongs originally to every power [*potenza*], only that will be truly powerful [*potente*], which, in the moment of passage to the act, will not simply annul its own power [*potenza*] to not nor leave it behind in respect to the act but will make it pass integrally in it as such; it will be carried, that is, not–not pass to the act.[66]

The act neither exhausts power, nor leaves it behind, but preserves it, therefore preventing its waste. The power to not is conserved in the act – every act is its actualisation.

The same applies to the faculty of thinking and acts of passive contemplation. Since an act of power consists in its conservation, an act of thinking also conserves power, and thus perfects and enhances it. The power to (or to not) contemplate is to the faculty of thought an 'extreme gift'.[67] The quotation from Aristotle in 'The Power of Thought' puts it as follows: 'to be passive is not a simple term, but, from a certain angle, it is a certain destruction of the action by its contrary, from another it is rather a conservation of that which is in power'.[68]

Viewed from this angle, Heidegger's concept of giving in to being in *Lässigkeit* might be interpreted as a version of the doctrine of the dual nature of power: the passive act of not acting counter, when thoughts pass into acts on their own, is an act that conserves consciousness of privation, and thus gives access to the essence of freedom. One is most free when one does not counteract the burden of existence, because in this passive act of thinking one enhances one's capacity for awareness of one's power as both *dunamis* and *sterēsis*.

Heidegger says that the act of thought occasioned in *Lässigkeit* is a 'moment of vision' which 'brings us to the brink of the possibility of restoring to *Dasein* actuality'.[69] In Agamben's terms, this is to say that thought in its capacity to pass into act on its own is at its closest to resembling the self-sustained perpetuity of Being. It is the passivity and laxness in the comportment that attunes us to a unique way of thinking, or, as Heidegger calls it, to 'conceptual questioning', unconstrained by any prohibitions, but which is also not a form of 'enchantment'.[70] It is a unique way of thinking, because its power resides in 'thinking thinking itself'.[71]

In the light of Agamben's theory, Levinas's concept of *paresse* initially may seem to differ from Heidegger's *Lässigkeit*. The arguments of the latter do not share the lamenting tone that permeates Levinas's assertions of man's imprisonment in being, whose 'brutal' fact 'assaults' man's freedom.[72] Levinas is more extreme in his insistence on the corporeal barrier. His theory of *paresse*, aimed at isolating the exact instance of the experience of un-freedom from being, eventually associates it with the proprioceptive sensation of the body limits, that is, with an experience when refusal to be and do registers itself prior to any reflection on that refusal, in a state of paralysis of the faculty. For this reason, the refusal is always hopelessly impossible. However, there is also a moment in Levinas's argument where by reference to philosophy's capacity for thinking, he aims to transcend the level of physiological determinism. This happens when he confronts his concept of *paresse* with the notion of kinaesthesia, which by denoting a type of proprioceptive awareness of the position and movement of body parts brings into his theory the sense of passivity as suspension of the faculty which all the while remains available. Levinas finds it necessary to differentiate between scientific and philosophical interpretation of this process. As regards fatigue with the burden of existence as a kind of kinaesthesia he says:

> Conceived as muscular exhaustion or toxicity by psychologists and physiologists, it [weariness] comes to the attention of a philosopher in an entirely different way. A philosopher has to put himself in the instant of fatigue and discover the way it comes about. Not its significance with respect to some system of references, but the hidden event of which an instant is the effectuation and not only the outcome.[73]

Fatigue is therefore an act which actualises the hidden event that can only be accessed via philosophical inquiry. The hidden event is, as Levinas argues from the beginning of *Existence and Existents*, the power to refuse being, an impossible, impotent power to not be, *sterēsis*. While science can describe the symptoms and the outcome of this event, the only way to discover the way passivity comes to pass into act, as inhibition of muscular activity, is by philosophical reflection. As Levinas will clarify many years later in *Otherwise Than Being* (1981), this reflection has little to do with applying totalising philosophical dogmas, but consists in putting those dogmas into question. Thus, like Heidegger, who associates states of laxation with unrestrained conceptual questioning, a unique manner of thought manifesting its power as both the power to be and act and the power not to be and act, Levinas seems to consider kin-aesthetic stasis as an act of effectuating and conserving privation in the bodily pose. Consequently, his assertion that the body 'is *only* a means of location, but not the way a man engages with existence' could be understood as a manner of specifying that it is the form (the way) rather than the material that is important in the act.[74] This corresponds with Agamben's conclusions about *sterēsis*, of which he writes that it is 'a form, a presence of that which is not in the act, and this privative presence is power'.[75]

To conclude, *Lässigkeit* and *paresse* are notions by means of which Heidegger and Levinas conceptualise the dual nature of human power, and the significance of *sterēsis* as the essence of that power and as the limit of freedom, in its nascent state. This being said, however, we must bear in mind, as Agamben warns us on several occasions in his essay, that both theories challenge in a certain way rational theories of subjectivity. The doctrine of the dual nature of power, he writes, contains an 'archeology of subjectivity; it is the way in which the problem of the subject is announced to a thought that does not yet have this notion'.[76] Both Heidegger and Levinas consider their respective forms of attunement and dis-attunement as prior and fundamental to subjective differentiation in the sense that the processes of the latter are on hold. But it is precisely this suspension that conserves and enhances the energy without which subjectivation could not go on. Thus, against all negative cultural stereotypes about idle states subsumed under the category of laziness, the philosophical inquiries of Heidegger and Levinas suggest that, far from being destructive, laziness offers a unique possibility of nurturing self-awareness. By letting go and allowing oneself to 'give in' to inactivity, one gains unique access to the consciousness of *sterēsis*.

In the light of all the above, the words of John Steinbeck from the epigraph that opens *The Labour of Laziness* – 'only in laziness can one achieve a state of contemplation which is a balancing of values, a weighing of oneself against the world, and the world against itself' – are no longer as baffling as they appeared initially. For given the uniqueness of the prior position that Levinas associates with *paresse* or the access to freedom that Heidegger finds in fundamental boredom, the assertion that in laziness one can 'achieve a state of contemplation which is a balancing of values, a weighing of oneself against the world, and the world against itself' seems to confirm the distinct role of inactivity for our sense of self.[77] Perhaps laziness is not the only state by which one gains access to the consciousness of privation, but I would argue that it is Western culture's only secular figure for the meditative pursuit of equilibrium. In any case, it is certainly exceptional in that suspension transpires simultaneously on the level of reflection or pre-reflection, as well as on the level of the body.

The Psychoanalytic Perspective

If we say that laziness is a corporeal expression of one's potency-in-suspension, we intimate, as do Heidegger and Levinas, that it is an aesthetic figure by means of which the ability not to be or do is articulated in the fabric of the body. Consequently, we may also say that so long as laziness is a figure, it represents art's relation to its impotentiality. It is a figurative form through which art – visual or literary – tells the story of its relation to the creative faculty's power to not-create. In modernist painting and sculpture, it may come across as gestures of suspended capacity to paint and sculpt, as in Kazimir Malevich's white squares or Marcel Duchamp's *objets trouvés*. In literature, as a trope of creative standstill, it is apparent in the existentialist dilemmas of Franz Kafka's *Metamorphoses* and Jean-Paul Sartre's *Nausea*.

Yet to put it in this way is to occlude the question of the subject. After all, the gestures of suspended ability are always somebody's gestures. We must return therefore to Agamben's assertion that *sterēsis* is 'the way in which the problem of the subject is announced to a thought that does not yet have this notion', and focus on this 'way', that is, manner or style, from the perspective of subjectivity processes.[78] Assuming that the aesthetics of impotentiality is expressed as the field of experiences we ordinarily call laziness, it seems worthwhile to devote specific attention to what psychoanalysis has to say about laziness as opposed to all the other numerous behaviours it has associated with inhibition or suspension of individual potency, especially as this is an important conceptual and historical context for approaching twentieth-century literary expressions of laziness.

The Squiggle

Few theorists of subjective differentiation have addressed laziness as a distinct psychological category, and even fewer have connected it with the idea of a capacity to not and the question of the body. Sigmund Freud, for example, frequently complained about his own 'attacks of laziness' in private letters, but he never gave it the scientific attention that he devoted to what was then called hysteria (though as we shall see the notions are not entirely unconnected).[79] Carl Jung, in his theories, occasionally drifted towards the concept via analogies to the cosmic law of inertia, but he never conceptualised laziness as such. One of the more direct reflections on the mechanism of laziness came from Donald Winnicott. In a 1964–68 essay 'Squiggle Game', which introduced his pioneer method of child analysis on the basis of spontaneous sketches, Winnicott linked laziness to the issue of self-expression:

> Often the result of a squiggle is [for the child] satisfactory in itself. It is then like a 'found object', for instance a stone or piece of old wood that a sculptor may find and set up as a kind of expression, without needing work. This appeals to lazy boys and girls, and throws light on the meaning of laziness. Any work done spoils what starts off as an idealised object. It may be felt by an artist that the paper or the canvas is too beautiful, it must not be spoiled. Potentially, it is a masterpiece. In psychoanalytic theory we have the concept of the dream screen, a place into or onto which a dream might be dreamed.[80]

As is often the case with Winnicott's writing, this short passage makes several complex claims, the relations between which are in no way as simple as the author's style renders them. What Winnicott discovers in his little patients' reluctance to draw (or draw with precision) is a resemblance to the artistic method of *objets trouvés*, of objects that are stumbled upon and appropriated as a form of subjective expression. In other words, the withdrawal of creative capacities does not express itself as total absence of expression but is congealed in the act.

The movement of the child's hand when producing a squiggle is neither controlled nor precise – the hand does not really draw – but the child nevertheless treats the drawing as a satisfying representation of herself. Like an artist who uses external objects as means of self-articulation, the child feels adequately expressed by an act of creation into which, in a certain sense, she did not really put herself. Winnicott links the satisfaction to the child's desire to preserve her own idealised image in potentiality: as long as she does not make an effort to draw a representation, the internal image of the self remains a hypothetical masterpiece. But at the same time, it is not that the page remains blank: the squiggle, like a found object, sits there and expresses the ability of the subject to not not-express herself, the ability which is conserved in the wavy line or contour. So, when Winnicott says that the result of a squiggle is like a found object, he indicates that its form is special in that it is a creative representation of, and a solution to, internal powerlessness. Solution, from the Latin *solvere*, meaning 'to loosen, dissolve, untie, release, detach, depart, unlock, scatter, dismiss, accomplish, fulfil, explain, remove', captures the ambivalence of the squiggle act, which is an undoing of the connection between the self and representation as well as its fulfilment. The squiggle is a performance of simultaneous vacillation and resolve.

Noting the appeal of squiggling to lazy boys and girls, Winnicott realises that laziness in general may be a paradigmatic form of such self-(in)expression. Laziness, it seems to him, has something to do with one's relation to one's own idealised image that one simultaneously wishes to retain in potentiality *and* mediate in an already existing object form. This brings Winnicott to make a reference to the 'dream screen', a concept psychoanalysts use to denote a background canvas on to which the content of fantasies is projected in sleep, and which sometimes is dreamed alone, as an empty dream, in the earliest or most regressive stages of subjective differentiation. Thus, by comparing a child's reluctance to spoil a page with a squiggle to a dream screen, Winnicott conveys the idea that lazy doodling gives us insight into similar regions of unconscious processes that are revealed in empty dreams.

The question in child analysis then becomes: what causes this peculiar form of creative inexpression? For Winnicott, the answer lies in the relation between mind-psyche and soma, or, more precisely, in the distortion of this relation. Indeed, the body and its epidermic shell play a crucial role in Winnicott's theory of differentiation. The perception of one's own skin as the 'limiting membrane', which so eluded Heidegger in his concept of attunement, is fundamental to the primary sense of the self as a separate unit, as it pre-determines all future contacts with the external world.[81] Hence, what Winnicott observes in the gestures of his squiggling patients is a way of getting in touch with that primary mode of receptivity. The effortless drawings re-enact the primary experimentation with the proprioceptive boundary and its continuity with the realm of psyche. In the re-enactment, a patient tests not so much what her hand can draw, but rather whether the hand remains one's own when it cannot do so, when it suspends the ability to draw. Perhaps, it dawns on Winnicott, laziness should not be looked at as a temperamental trait or a defence mechanism, but rather as a symptom presented by a subject when her sense of the body–mind coherence is lost and a desire to re-establish it emerges. That which in Agamben's terms was described as an expression of the capacity to not create, and in Levinas and Heidegger as a position with regard to the limits of existence, in Winnicott's language is defined as a performance of recreating psychosomatic collusion. In short, Winnicott's interpretation situates laziness on the continuum of psychosomatic disorders.

In his 1964 paper 'Psycho-Somatic Illness in its Positive and Negative Aspects', presented to the Society of Psychosomatic Research, Winnicott explores the idea of drawing the psyche back from the mind to its original intimate association with the soma.[82] As the title of the lecture suggests, psychosomatic disorders have a negative side in that the conversion of psychological trauma into its physical manifestation leads those who suffer from the disorder to partition their treatment into many fragments, distributing symptoms among multiple medical professionals, who then work on single ailments without being aware of the broader picture of the illness:

> Many patients do not split their medical care into two; they split it into many fragments, and as doctors we find ourselves acting in the role of one of these fragments. I have used the term 'scatter of responsible agents' to describe this tendency. Such patients . . . also exploit the natural splits in the medical profession.[83]

In this way, Winnicott continues, the psychosomatist is like a skilful circus performer who 'prides himself on his capacity to ride two horses, one foot on each of the two saddles, with both reins in his deft hands'.[84]

However, this peculiar arrangement of partitioned treatment actually offers the key to what is the core of the problem with psychosomatic disorders in general, namely that the insistence on separating the somatic from the psychological aspects runs concurrent with an equally strong desire to be cured.

> The bodily symptoms do not constitute the illness but are, rather, signifiers of the intrapsychic dissociation . . . It is the persistence of a split in the patient's ego-organization, or of multiple dissociations, that constitutes the true illness.[85]

While the 'forces' that maintain this split are 'tremendously strong', Winnicott explains, their powerfulness curiously manifests itself in a remarkable impotence of the patient, who resists analysis, in the sense that he is 'only too ready to understand something about himself on the intellectual plane', which in turn only strengthens the 'intrapsychic dissociation' from his physical self.[86]

This observation leads Winnicott to conclude, in a classically psychoanalytic fashion, that the split in the subject is maintained by the very same forces that in a 'good-enough environment' would normally integrate the psyche with the body.[87] One implication of Winnicott's conclusion is that even if the not-good-enough environment had facilitated the development of psychosomatic symptoms, the integrative forces are still *in* the subject, dormant in potentiality:

> psycho-somatic illness implies a split in the individual's personality, with weakness of the linkage between psyche and soma, or a split organised in the mind in defence against generalised persecution from the repudiated world. There remains in the individual ill person, however, a tendency not altogether to lose the psychosomatic linkage . . . Psychosomatic illness . . . has this hopeful aspect, that the patient is in touch with the possibility of psychosomatic unity . . . even though his or her clinical condition actively illustrates the opposite of this through splitting, through various dissociations, through a persistent attempt to split the medical provision, and through omnipotent self care-taking.[88]

To stay 'in touch' with the potentiality of integrity means that the communication between the potential and the actual is active but suspended. Winnicott adds that this state is 'the negative of the positive', the visual allusion pointing to the fact that the dark, disorderly form of integrity manifested in symptoms is not the absence of integrity but instead its other, suspended form. This is why, Winnicott says at the end of his lecture, therapy of a psychosomatist requires tremendous patience of the analyst, who has to resist the temptation to lead and correct the patient, but rather withdraw his power and wait for the patient to resolve the split on her own.

Relaxation and Catharsis

Winnicott was not the first to praise the therapeutic benefits of suspending analytic rigour. The palm of honour in this respect, as far as psychoanalysis is concerned, should be given to Sandor Ferenczi, whose famous paper 'The Principle of Relaxation and Neocatharsis', delivered in 1929 at the Eleventh International Psycho-Analytical Congress in Oxford, stirred the psychoanalytic community with a proposition that the method of free association is not really free, nor productive, unless the 'psychological atmosphere' during the analytic session is more relaxed. The paper, which, as it turned out, led to a profound and unresolved conflict between Freud and his promising Hungarian disciple, in many ways anticipates Winnicott's reasoning in both 'Psycho-Somatic Illness' and 'Squiggle Game'. For Ferenczi is also interested in how to deal with the cases when therapy goes on for too long, and no amount of analyst's effort eases the symptoms.

Ferenczi begins 'The Principle of Relaxation' on an autobiographical note, with remarks about his fascination with the cathartic treatment method for hysteria, his own 'too strict' attachment to the principle of frustration, and finally, his doubts about the 'objective reserve and scientific observation which Freud recommends' in order to vouch his belief in the principle of relaxation.[89] No use can be made in the case of certain patients, Ferenczi argues, of the attitude of 'the rigid and cool aloofness' of the analyst, because, as his therapeutic experience tells him, much better effects can be achieved if one mixes frustration with loosening of the rules: 'I decided on the phrase "economy of suffering", to express what I have realized and am trying to convey – and I hope it is not far-fetched – namely, that the principles of frustration and indulgence should both govern our technique.'[90] Ferenczi realises that his idea is somewhat blasphemous with regard to Freud's doctrine: 'Softly, ladies and gentlemen!' he begs his audience, before you interrupt me 'by a general uproar and clamour'.[91] But he explains that his own therapeutic experience has proven the benefits of allowing relaxed freedom of expression on patients whose 'analytical insight had gradually closed to him all avenues of resistance', so that 'he would be cornered':[92]

The way in which patients improved when I employed this relaxation therapy as well as the older method was in many cases quite astonishing. In hysterics, obsessional neurotics and even in persons of nervous character-types the familiar attempts to reconstruct the past went forward as usual. But, after we had succeeded in a somewhat less superficial manner than before in creating an atmosphere of confidence between physician and patient and in securing a fuller freedom of affect, hysterical physical symptoms would suddenly make their appearance, often for the first time in an analysis extending over years.[93]

In an attempt to illustrate what the technique of securing freedom of affect should look like, Ferenczi brings into the picture the *casus* of child analysis, prompted to him by Anna Freud's remark: 'You really treat your patients as I treat the children whom I analyse',[94] and pairs it with Georg Groddeck's psychoanalytic approach to organic illnesses, to propound his final argument that certain symptoms would manifest themselves in the atmosphere of relaxation, often without the conscious awareness of his patients, but their physical actualisation would fuel the process of their 'neocathartic' purging and withdrawal. The idea that Winnicott would pick up three decades later is, in other words, that some disorders cannot be treated without a simultaneous mobilisation of the mind and the body, whose intimate collusion can only be restored by the patient herself. Neocatharsis, in which Ferenczi so strongly believes, is a specific form of restoring power balance to what Winnicott called the negative and the positive aspects of the conversion disorder.

The bone of contention that the principle of relaxation placed between Ferenczi and Freud seemed to come from the implications that the method carried for the status of psychoanalysis as a science. Freud's original concern, as expressed in his *Studies on Hysteria*, was that case stories are more literary than scientific; they are like experiments that happen only once. As Adam Phillips puts it in 'Freud's Literary Engagements':

> Freud wants to be writing with the 'serious stamp of science'; and his case stories he insists are at least 'intended to be judged like psychiatric ones.' Yet they 'read like short stories,' in part because, Freud suggests, the subject matter itself dictated the form the writing took. Freud took consolation in 'the reflection that the nature of the subject is evidently responsible for this, rather than any preference of my own' . . . The patient's story of his suffering is somehow inextricable from his symptomatology. Indeed the symptom is itself a story, or a story kept at bay . . . about a quest for a new kind of story . . .
>
> When Freud comes to write his case histories, he remembers himself as a reader of short stories; it is a reading past that informs his work. If the so-called hysterical patient is dying not to remember and the psychoanalyst is trying not to write short stories, the question arises: What, for the psychoanalyst as writer, is wanting not to write short stories wanting not to do?[95]

In Phillips's reading of Freud, the hysterical symptoms are stories kept at a distance, suspended in their potentiality. They are figurative expressions of searching as well as delaying the quest for new scenarios. They follow, in other words, the ambivalent Stoic formula of 'A no more than B' (*ou mallon*), along the lines of which certain kinds of passivity or suffering are forms of empowerment. Indeed, in their self-annulling quests for expression, the psychoanalyst and the patient both suffer 'from languages that are buried alive in them, from censored alternative accounts'. Hence, when Phillips asks, 'what is the wanting not to remember or not to write wanting not to do', he refers to that which Agamben calls the essence of human power, that is, the ability to not not-want, remember or create stories – restraining oneself from abandonment of desires, memories and story writing.

Ironically, perhaps, Freud's correspondence from the period of *Studies on Hysteria* suggests that the realisation of this remarkable ambivalence came to him under the conditions of what Ferenczi would call neocathartic relaxation. In an 1898 letter to Wilhelm Fliess, Freud reports: 'I am now living in comfortable laziness and am harvesting some of the fruits of familiarity with the hysterical things. Everything is becoming easy and transparent . . . For once I am free from pain; when I am well, I am terribly lazy.'[96] But comfort and clarity of insight are not the only feelings Freud experiences in idleness. Another letter to Fliess two years later reveals the dark side of the experience: 'I cannot work. I am permeated with laziness; the kind of work I have been doing from October until now is very unlike that which leads to writing, and very unfavorable to it . . . I would like to disappear for a few weeks to someplace where nothing like science exists.'[97] Contradictory as they are, however, both confessions revolve around the same issue, the issue of creativity. Freud defines laziness as a relation to one's (his in this case) creative faculty. When he enjoys being lazy, the writing seems clear and fluent; when he does not, he daydreams that he could disappear into the world of creative writers, where science is denied admittance. The figure of laziness thus marks the horizon of his creative capacities as both their catalyst and hindrance. It is, to use William James's phrase, an 'efficacious obstruction'.[98]

Energies and Relaxation

In psychoanalytic register, the notion of a useful obstacle, of something that both blocks the way and opens it at the same time, is the definition of a symptom. A symptom is that which intervenes between the self and the hidden desire, in the sense that it obstructs as well as gives access to that desire. Symptoms are, to borrow Adam Phillips's phrase, 'unconscious mnemonics' of unrecognised wishes.[99] This mnemonic operation involves an aesthetics. In the case of hysterical symptoms, as Freud explains in the first of his *Five Lectures on Psycho-Analysis*, this aesthetics consists in 'hysterical conversion', that is, the transformation of 'strangulated' emotions into somatic disturbances. The hidden feelings remain 'a permanent burden upon the patient's mental life and a source of constant excitation for it; and in part they [undergo] a transformation into unusual somatic innervations and inhibitions, which manifest themselves as the physical symptoms'. Freud makes it clear that while all emotions are 'normally directed along the paths of somatic innervation and produce what we know as "expression of emotion"', the hysterical conversion is different in that it 'exaggerates this portion of the discharge'.[100] If hysterical conversion is a form of exaggeration, it is, aesthetically speaking, a hyperbole, an amplification, heaping up, overdoing. Freud's metaphorical illustration for the process is that of an overflowing stream: 'When the bed of a stream is divided into two channels,' he says, 'then, if the current in one of them is brought up against an obstacle, the other will at once be overfilled.'[101] The metaphors of overfilling and heaping up on the one hand, and of being burdened and strangulated on the other, reiterate the idea of ambivalence of human potency captured by the notions of *potenza*, *paresse* and *Lässigkeit*, discussed above. The figurative representations of the philosophical concept of suspension as position of inhibition, a pose of being overburdened by being or impotence, locate in figures of apparent lifelessness the element of potency to confront life, and thus closely correspond to the figurative language of psychoanalytic descriptions of states of 'absence', as Freud calls them, such as paralysis, fatigue and resignation. Those somatic figures mediate, by way of psychosomatic conversion, the overabundance of what Winnicott identifies as 'enormous internal forces'.

Hence, when Winnicott describes laziness as a form of longing for an idealised, masterpiece image of oneself, he situates it within the spectrum of psychosomatic conversion mechanisms as, precisely, an empowering obstacle. The idea of laziness as a mnemonics of the desire for self-integration (the 'I am', as Winnicott puts it in 'The Capacity to be Alone'), which also transpires from Freud's letters and Ferenczi's principle of relaxation and neocatharsis, is greatly illuminated by the notion of exaggeration. For hyperbole, we must remember, does not only consist in amplifying the expression. It also involves theatricality. To exaggerate, in other words, is to inflate the form while retaining a degree of distance from the performance, to have a double consciousness. In *Studies on Hysteria*, Josef Breuer recalls the words of his most famous patient, Anna O., who 'even when she was in a very bad condition – a clear sighted observer sat, as she put it, in a corner of her brain and looked on all the mad business'.[102] The trait of dramatic mastery can also be traced in Winnicott's metaphor of a circus stunt artist riding two horses at once, as well as in Ferenczi's neologism of neocatharsis – catharsis to the second power; a purer form of purification. Exaggeration here is a mask of a repressed stability (that of a clear-sighted observer in the corner of the brain), and the thread of contiguity between them is never broken. What Winnicott calls the positive aspect of disorders in psychosomatic collusion is expressed in laziness in its most generic form, whose theatricality is less overt that in, say, paralysis. Laziness is a figure of the desire for the balancing of the body's relation to psyche, which conserves in the act one's wish to refrain oneself from abandonment of the desire of equilibrium. It is, in other words, the trope of the dual nature of power in the narrative of one's subjectivity.

William James realised this all too well, when in *On Vital Reserves* he asked the questions: What are the limits of human faculty? How to protect this faculty's potency.[103] His answer was that if we ever stop, loosen up and reconnect with the 'slumbering energies' inside ourselves, the faculty will only grow in potency. What to some looks like laziness and fatigue, James says, is a 'mask' for 'levels of new energy' that help rebuild the equilibrium of power:

Let no one think, then, that our problem of individual and national economy is solely that of the maximum of pounds raisable against gravity, the maximum of locomotion, or of agitation of any sort, that human beings can accomplish. That might signify little more than hurrying and jumping about in inco-ordinated ways; whereas inner work, though it so often reinforces outer work, quite as often means its arrest. To relax, to say to ourselves . . . 'Peace! be still' is sometimes a great achievement of inner work. When I speak of human energizing in general, the reader must therefore understand that sum-total of activities, some outer and some inner, some muscular, some emotional, some moral, some spiritual, of whose waxing and waning in himself he is at all times so well aware.[104]

If one thinks that James has in mind only a very productive kind of 'arrest' of movement, à la meditative trance, one could not be more mistaken. James lists a colourful variety of disorders – hysteria, neurasthenia, dipsomania, dromomania and finally psychasthenia – to say that even there the balancing of power is achieved through stillness. When 'victims of a chronic sense of weakness, torpor, lethargy, fatigue . . . impossibility, unreality, and powerlessness of the will' express their states through laxation of the body, the expression, 'deleterious though it be', temporarily 'raises the sense of vitality' and makes the sufferers 'feel alive again'.[105]

Being a pragmatist philosopher, James includes practical advice on how to perform acts of relaxation. In the second essay in *On Vital Reserves*, entitled 'The Gospel of Relaxation', James formulates an important recommendation. There is some truth, he says, in manuals for young ladies about how to behave in church even when faith has abandoned their souls: if this be the case, the manuals tell them to perform the physical gestures of kneeling and folding hands, hoping that spirituality will soon fill those empty gestures. In a like manner, one who does not know how to relax or get in touch with one's sense of agency should assume the pose of passive relaxation. The release of energies thus incurred will bring one freedom and access to as well as 'great enlargement of power'.[106]

The Political Perspective

In the first part of this chapter, I focused on the philosophical potential of the concept of laziness. My conclusion that the concept overlaps with the definition of *sterēsis* in that it puts us in contact with the dual nature of power and the essence of freedom needs, however, to be examined for its ethical and political implications. For this figure of power poses a challenge to how we think about the relations between individuals and constituted structures of power, about possibilities of emancipation, in short, about the consequences of the doctrine concerning the conservation of potency-to-not-do in the socio-economic context.

Therefore, this section attends to the possible scenarios of rethinking power relations through the prism of the concept of laziness as position of *sterēsis*, with special emphasis on two types of social structures: the system of education and knowledge management and the system of work and employment. Answering Agamben's call to consider the concept of *sterēsis* and its role in the doctrine of power in the real, social context, I use the affinity between power-as-privation and the notion of laziness established earlier in this chapter in order to see whether laziness, besides being a philosophical position, can also function as an oppositional strategy.

'The Right to Be Lazy'

Something of the kind is suggested by Roland Barthes in the question from the epigraph to my Introduction: 'I wonder if here, in the modern Occident, *doing nothing* really exists.'[107] Barthes wonders if doing nothing is at all thinkable by the Western mind, and therefore if demanding the right to it makes any sense. Yet Barthes was not the first to posit the question of the right to be lazy, as far as the French tradition was concerned. The demand for the right to *paresse* was one of the undercurrents of Enlightened thought in France, 'repeatedly contesting the universality of labor and activity', with *homo otiosus* as the underlying ideal of Rousseau's model of a free thinker.[108] Following this tradition, the end of the nineteenth century featured an explosion of texts celebrating idleness, the most popular of which was the scandalous anti-work manifesto *The Right to Be Lazy*, published in 1883 by Marx's son-in-law, Paul Lafargue.[109] In the pamphlet, Lafargue employs the word *paresse*, somewhat provocatively, in the service of a political demand to shorten the average workday, but the particular way in which he introduces the idea of not-working in his anti-capitalist argument indicates that *paresse* is a philosophically loaded concept that bears a relation to the notion of freedom. It is this relation that Barthes alludes to in his question about the right to be lazy from 'Osons être paresseux'. Let us therefore examine some of the affinities between Barthes's modern conceptualisation of laziness and Lafargue's provocative pamphlet.

The Right to Be Lazy begins with a psychological diagnosis of life at the end of the nineteenth century, which, as Lafargue puts it, is governed by the mania of work:

> A strange delusion possesses the working class of the nations where capitalist civilization holds its sway. This delusion drags in its train the individual and the social woes which for two centuries have tortured sad humanity. This delusion is the love of work, the furious passion for work, pushed even to the exhaustion of the vital force of the individual and his progeny. Instead of opposing this mental aberration, the priests, the economists and the moralists, have cast a sacred halo over work . . . In capitalist society work is the cause of all intellectual degeneracy, of all organic deformity.[110]

Lafargue's affirmation of laziness relies on a radical reversal of the opposition between labour and idleness. In his optics, it is work, not laziness, that must be stigmatised as a mental disorder, a degenerative illness and a complete waste of life energy. Work is the modern *daemon* that slays the minds and bodies of individuals and leads them to death. What may seem a mere provocation appears to have nevertheless quite a coherent philosophical genealogy, which transpires from the image by means of which Lafargue introduces his conception of laziness: '[One] rejoices in his admiration for the hardy Andalusian . . . straight and flexible as a steel rod; and the heart leaps at hearing the beggar, superbly draped in his ragged *capa*, parleying on terms of equality with the duke of Ossuna.'[111] From the philosophical perspective, Lafargue's image of a beggar who treats the duke as an equal bears a striking likeness to the figure of the ancient philosopher Diogenes the Cynic, known for having famously replied to Alexander the Great's 'I am the king' with an unruly 'I am Diogenes, the dog.' What Lafargue's image communicates is not simply a loafing pose, but a pose of resistance that has a Cynical air of indomitability. This correspondence makes all the difference as to whether we treat *paresse* in Lafargue's text as a rhetorical provocation or as a serious political option.

For there is, Michel Foucault argues in *The Government of Self and Others* (1982–83), a great political potential in the Cynic's confrontation of authority. As he puts it, the importance of Diogenes' response to Alexander the Great was that it established in philosophical tradition a unique model of performing *parrhēsia* (truth telling) as political action, whose form of speaking truth to power is that of 'exteriority, challenge and derision'.[112] Lafargue's figure of the Andalusian beggar who does not shy away from speaking to the duke represents the Cynical paradigm, since it articulates the same *parrhēsiastic* position as the one embodied in Diogenes' challenge to the sovereign. It is a position that enables the performative enunciation of one's individual agency *vis-à-vis* the apparatuses of biopower, what Barthes calls, in his lectures *The Neutral*, the 'sentiment de puissance'.[113]

The affinity between Lafargue's vision and the Cynical paradigm is particularly apparent in Lafargue's depiction of the beggar's pose as 'straight and flexible as a steel rod'.[114] While the English translation of the original French phrase 'droit et elastique comme une tige d'acier' communicates the idea of flexibility and amenability, the original uses the word 'elastique' in the technical sense of resistance to pressure and strain.[115] For the body to be elastic as a rod of steel thus means to be unbendable, indomitable and resistant. Strictly speaking, then, Lafargue's definition of *paresse* does not denote any kind of doing nothing, but a very particular attitude of steel-like indomitability and resistance to the changes in labour organisation brought about by the Industrial Revolution. In addition, its philosophical grounding in the *parrhēsiastic* model of parleying with power lends the notion of *paresse* concrete conceptual contours. As Marina Van Zuylen observes, one of the reasons that *paresse* is such a bold and sane alternative to work is that it can never become part of any organized faith. Unlike indoctrinating labor-worship, it is a condition that is private, not public. It can only be the consequence of one's own (ir)responsibility. This is why it is much wiser, Lafargue suggests, to bask in philosophical *paresse* – to engage in the type of work that produces only what one needs, adopting a style of life that requires only the immediate fruits of one's labor.[116]

According to Van Zuylen, Lafargue recognises that the power of laziness lies in singular, individual acts of conserving one's power and resisting its co-optation by public rhythms of productivity. It is the ultimate guardian of privacy, because, tied to individual performance of indomitability, it can never transform into a pedagogy. In other words, the conception of freedom inherent in this model of resistance stands in sharp contrast to the French model of liberty shaped by the Revolution in that it locates revolutionary potential in the withdrawal from power-struggle rather than in its theatrical display.

To make sure that his affirmation of laziness does not appear ridiculous, Lafargue situates *paresse*-as-indomitability on a spectrum of lazy attitudes, and distinguishes it from both physical fatigue and gluttonous rottenness. *Paresse*-as-fatigue, that is, a laziness born out of physical exhaustion and inurement to labour, represented in the image of 'pale, hollow-eyed, emaciated bodies of mechanical workers', occupies one end of his spectrum.[117] The other belongs to *paresse absolue* ('absolute laziness'), imagined as an abject, overfed body of the capitalist nation-state: 'an enormous female, hairy-faced and bald-headed, fat, flabby, puffy and pale, with sunken eyes, sleepy and yawning . . . stretching herself out on a velvet couch'.[118] Characterised in terms of a loss of *élan vital*, both fatigue and *paresse absolue* mark the extremes of Lafargue's spectrum of lazy attitudes, which ought not to be pursued by any means. The one type of laziness Lafargue really calls for is *parrhēsiatic* laziness-as-indomitability, located right in the middle of this spectrum, at its null point. Only this kind of laziness is capable of generating the sentiment of puissance.

The Neutral

It is this idea of a null point that terminates Roland Barthes's reflections on laziness in 'Osons être paresseux'. Throughout the text, Barthes's thoughts wander in search of an emotional definition of laziness through an examination of his own experience of being lazy, which oscillates between, on the one hand, the painfulness of being out of touch with one's will (which refuses to be forced to work) and, on the other, a euphoric pleasure of being/feeling free to do nothing. What Barthes eventually decides upon is that laziness, as a mixture of blissfulness and pain, is the purest form of *jouissance*, a state between the depressive sense of 'marinading' in one's thoughts and the exuberance with this 'most glorious form of philosophizing'.[119] Having located the emotional structure of laziness in the middle of this spectrum, between thoughtless marinading and thoughtful reflection, Barthes turns away from intimate confession towards a more sustained idea about the possibility of *paresse* as an ethico-political position. The idea of doing nothing, of withdrawing from work and action, he argues, reveals something very important about the modes of resisting social pressure to participate in socio-economic reality. For Barthes, true laziness is not just about not doing anything; instead, it is about leaving the choice between doing and not-doing open. In short, it is a state that opens up the question of ethics.

True laziness would be basically a laziness about 'not deciding' whether or not 'to be there'. Much like the class dunce sitting at the back of the classroom who has no other trait than being there. They don't participate, nor are they excluded. They're there, period, like a sort of heap . . .

To be there, but not to decide anything. There we could find certain tenets of Tolstoy's ethics. To the degree in which we might ask ourselves if we have the right to be lazy in the face of evil. Tolstoy said that yes, indeed, this would still be the best possibility left, since answering back to evil with another form of evil is not acceptable. Needless to say that, today, such a form of morality has been completely discredited. And if we went even further, laziness might seem like a high philosophical solution on the side of evil. Not answering back, though once again, today's society doesn't really put up very well with neutral attitudes. Laziness is intolerable then, as if this were the basic principal evil.[120]

Western thought offers no means of thinking about 'withdrawal from action' outside of the registers of moral stigmatisation. The possibility of a limit mode of ethical neutrality, however, is what Barthes finds most intriguing. This interest finds reflection in his 1977–78 lectures at the Collège de France entitled *The Neutral*.

In the lectures, composed in the spirit of Adorno's idle thoughts, notes and free associations, Barthes gradually constructs his concept of the neutral. One of the first definitions involves the physical sensation reminiscent of *paresse*; as Barthes explains, echoing Levinas's proprioceptive logic, the neutral is the strongest, 'minimal' bodily feeling of 'autoexistence', a sense of 'adhesion to inner reality', experienced as 'derailment' or loosening of mental associations, 'bifurcation' or dissemination of thought, and 'rerouting' of thought in the most uncanny or enigmatic direction towards the horizon of thought's potentiality.[121]

From a rational perspective, Barthes's glorification of unfocused mental states is very difficult to accept. One is much more inclined to side with John Locke's condemnation of laziness in *Of the Conduct of the Understanding*, where similar symptoms are listed as errors in thinking. Locke calls them desultoriness, fatigue and despondency, thus anticipating with remarkable accuracy the modern neuroscientific accounts of our brain's work. Desultoriness, from Latin *desultorius*, 'hasty, casual, superficial', is one of the obstacles in the proper conduct of understanding. 'Skipping from one sort of knowledge to another', Locke writes, is a 'fault of ill consequence' that stems from laziness mixed with vanity: 'Some men's tempers are quickly weary of any one thing. Constancy and assiduity is what they cannot bear: the same study long continued in is as intolerable to them, as the appearing long in the same clothes or fashion is to a court lady.'[122] With the exception of the genderisation of desultoriness in the passage, Locke seems to be absolutely right that it is an attention disorder.

But when Barthes argues against this condemnation, he does so less in order to deny the diagnosis than to highlight the possibility dormant in loose, bifurcated thinking to move in between and destabilise conventional modes of reasoning.[123] The mind's escape from the disciplining conventions is Barthes's ideal of philosophical practice.

Of course, this is as far from Locke's Enlightenment observations as one can possibly get, for Locke is certain that the discipline of thinking is the mind's only correct destination. Vagabond thoughts wandering around the mind in 'lazy recumbency and satisfaction on the obvious surface of things' are to the British philosopher a serious educational problem.[124] In the section titled 'Practice', for example, Locke approaches idleness of thought from the angle of what today we would call behavioural reactions, as a negative response to the aversive stimulus of extensive mental effort, that is, as a cessation to respond to stimulation, to move and show signs of life when faced with an intellectual task. His solution is gradual training and habituation of unaccustomed brains to correct reasoning. For even though 'such slow progress will never reach the extent of some sciences', it is nevertheless the only path to intelligence.[125] Again, however, what Locke treats as a problem to be eradicated, Barthes recognises as a possibility. To withhold judgement and conclusions is for him of the highest axiological value. As he puts it, the *puissance* of the neutral lies precisely in the attitude of 'a-correction': in other words, 'abstention from correcting', opining and formulating dogmas.

Education as the disciplinary formation of mental habits is thus the bone of contention between Barthes and the Enlightenment tradition. While Locke praised intellectual training monitored by superior authorities, Barthes insists on its limitations. Compare Locke's description of correct education with the response of the French thinker. Locke says:

> It is not strange that methods of learning, which scholars have been accustomed to in their beginning and entrance upon the sciences, should influence them all their lives, and be settled in their minds by an overruling reverence, especially if they be such as universal use has established. Learners must at first be believers, and, their masters' rules having been once made axioms to them, it is no wonder they should keep that dignity, and, by the authority they have once got, mislead those who think it sufficient to excuse them, if they go out of their way in a well beaten track.[126]

Barthes's response is:

> School is a structure of constraint, and laziness is a means for the pupil to dupe this constraint. The classroom inevitably includes a repressive force, if only because the student has no real interest in the things that are taught there. Laziness can be a way to answer back to this repression.[127]

Barthes's image here is reminiscent of Adorno's vision of missing a mathematics lesson for the sake of a blissful morning in bed, during which a truly original thought has a chance to be born. For Barthes, as for Adorno, being a believer in one's master's rules is to repress and deny one's own intellectual capacities and participate in nothing more than the reproduction of academic capital.[128] Because laziness activates itself so naturally in situations of scholarly oppression, Barthes considers it to be a useful strategy of intellectual insubordination to the inuring conversion practices inherent in pedagogical rituals, fully embracing Adorno's idea that 'the value of a thought is measured by its distance from the continuity with the familiar'.[129] In a sense, however, this sentiment is already inscribed within Locke's repudiation of idle thinking, when he compares it to 'stepping off the well beaten track' away from dogmatism and duty, and thus unwittingly proves the persistent presence of laziness at the margins of normalisation. Barthes's laziness, as redefined in his 1977 lectures, is thus not a state of self-marinading, but a radically 'active' and 'productive' neutrality: it is attention without arrogance, participation without involvement, and resistance without violence.[130]

It is hardly surprising therefore that Barthes's examples of perfect neutrality are Pyrrho, the father of the doctrine of suspension – 'he created the Neutral, as if he had read Blanchot!'[131] – and Diogenes, 'the Cynic, the man of Im-pertinence', whose figure, while 'not the least in the service of power, doesn't stay permanently in the service of contestation'.[132] Pyrrho illustrates for Barthes the position of ethical neutrality born out of weariness and a sense of being burdened by the weight of life, that is, a position loaded with potentiality but insistent on suspending judgement and identity for the sake of its truer understanding. The figure of Diogenes, on the other hand, exemplifies the indomitable pose of loafing that conserves the political puissance of *parrhēsia*. It cultivates the potency to preserve oneself, one's sense of agency and sovereignty against structures of institutional power.

All perspectives on laziness presented in this chapter indicate that the idea of laziness promises to conceptualise the elusive intersection of the biological, or the bodily, and the symbolic in theories of oppositional strategies as well as aesthetic representations thereof. From Locke to Levinas, thinking about laziness mobilises two sets of issues: first, issues of the body (its haptic arrangements such as laxity or elasticity; its putatively impedimental states such as weariness or fatigue) and, second, issues of agency, whose spectrum ranges from the generic vitalist idea of individual power as self-generating *sterēsis* (Agamben), through the existential notions of refusal (Levinas) and reconciliation (Heidegger) with the materiality of life that find their reflection in the psychoanalytic interpretation of symptom exaggeration or symptom withdrawal, to the political conceptions of boycotting, abstention from engagement or work (Barthes), or confrontation (Foucault). In this way, the conceptual field demarcated by the meanings of laziness helps us to reconstruct the language of docility.

Where Foucault's work focused on disciplining practices towards the docile body – on how power relations 'invest it, mark it, train it, torture it, force it to carry out tasks, to perform ceremonies, to emit signs' – I concentrate on the gestures that oppose this mode of subjectivation.[133] 'New things are born out of lassitude', Barthes concludes in *The Neutral*.[134] In this spirit, the aesthetic experiments of Herman Melville, Ernest Hemingway, Donald Barthelme, David Foster Wallace and others, described in the following chapters, undermine Foucault's pessimistic diagnosis that the body is 'a useful force only if it is both a productive body and a subjected body'.[135] It is also, biologically as well as symbolically, the site for cultivating the value of self-preservation.

Notes

1. Giorgio Agamben, 'The Power of Thought', *Critical Inquiry* 40.2 (2014), 480.
2. Ibid., 486–7.

3. Kalpana Seshadri, 'Agamben, the Thought of Sterēsis: An Introduction to Two Essays', *Critical Inquiry* 40.2 (2014), 476, 479.

4. Agamben, 'The Power of Thought', 487.

5. Ibid., 487; Seshadri, 'Agamben, the Thought of Sterēsis', 478.

6. Giorgio Agamben and Daniel Heller-Roazen, *Potentialities: Collected Essays in Philosophy* (Stanford: Stanford University Press, 1999), 256.

7. Gilles Deleuze and Félix Guattari, *What Is Philosophy?* (New York: Verso, 1994), 8.

8. Agamben, 'The Power of Thought', 482.

9. Emmanuel Levinas, *Existence and Existents* (The Hague: Nijhoff, 1978), 24.

10. John Locke, *The Philosophical Works and Selected Correspondence of John Locke. Of the Conduct of the Understanding*, 5th edn (Charlottesville, VA: InteLex Corporation, 1995), 83.

11. Immanuel Kant, *Lectures on Anthropology* (1772–98) (Cambridge: Cambridge University Press, 2012), 503, 456.

12. Pierre Saint-Amand, *The Pursuit of Laziness: An Idle Interpretation of the Enlightenment* (Princeton: Princeton University Press, 2011).

13. Maurice Blanchot, *The Infinite Conversation* (Minneapolis: University of Minnesota Press, 1993), 196.

14. Martin Heidegger, *The Fundamental Concepts of Metaphysics: World, Finitude, Solitude* (1983) (Bloomington: Indiana University Press, 1995), 17, 67–8.

15. Locke, *Philosophical Works and Selected Correspondence*, sec. 28, 62.

16. Catherine Malabou, *The Heidegger Change: On the Fantastic in Philosophy* (Albany: State University of New York Press, 2011), 236.

17. Levinas, *Existence and Existents*, 24.

18. See Bettina Bergo, *Levinas between Ethics and Politics: For the Beauty that Adorns the Earth* (Dordrecht: Kluwer Academic, 1999); Tina Chanter, *Time, Death, and the Feminine: Levinas with Heidegger* (Palo Alto: Stanford University Press, 2001); John E. Drabinski and Eric Sean Nelson (eds), *Between Levinas and Heidegger* (Albany: State University of New York Press, 2014); David J. Gauthier, *Martin Heidegger, Emmanuel Levinas, and the Politics of Dwelling* (Lanham, MD: Lexington Books, 2011); Reginald Lilly, 'Levinas's Heideggerian Fantasm', in *French Interpretations of Heidegger: An Exceptional Reception*, ed. David Pettigrew and François Raffoul (Albany: State University of New York Press, 2008), 35–58.

19. Levinas, *Existence and Existents*, 25.

20. Ibid., 24, 25.

21. Martin Heidegger, *Being and Time*, trans. J. Macquarrie and E. Robinson (New York: Harper and Row, 1962), 184.

22. Levinas, *Existence and Existents*, 25.

23. Ibid., 24.

24. John Llewelyn, *Emmanuel Levinas: The Genealogy of Ethics* (New York: Routledge, 1995), 33.

25. Levinas, *Existence and Existents*, 26.

26. Ibid., 25.

27. Ibid., 27.

28. Ibid., 25.
29. Ibid., 70.
30. Ibid., 70.
31. Ibid., 70.
32. Ibid., 70.
33. Ibid., 71.
34. Ibid., 71.
35. Charles Scott Sherrington, *The Integrative Action of the Nervous System* (New Haven, CT: Yale University Press, 1947), 132.
36. Andy Hamilton, 'Proprioception as Basic Knowledge of the Body', in *Basic Belief and Basic Knowledge: Papers in Epistemology* (Frankfurt: Ontos, 2005), 273.
37. Levinas, *Existence and Existents*, 72.
38. Ibid., 28.
39. Llewelyn, *Emmanuel Levinas*, 37.
40. Heidegger, *The Fundamental Concepts of Metaphysics*, 68, 80.
41. Ibid., 79.
42. Ibid., 77.
43. Ibid., 83.
44. Ibid., 84, 93.
45. Ibid., 101.
46. Ibid., 103.
47. Malabou, *The Heidegger Change*, 239.
48. Heidegger, *The Fundamental Concepts of Metaphysics*, 107.
49. Ibid., 112.
50. Ibid., 112.
51. Ibid., 114.
52. Ibid., 17–19.
53. Ibid., 120, 122.
54. Ibid., 124, 125.
55. Ibid., 122, 126.
56. Ibid., 170.
57. Ibid., 166.
58. Ibid., 166.
59. I take this idea from Elizabeth A. Povinelli's yet unpublished critique of new materialist discourses, presented as a lecture 'The Fossils and the Bones' at the 'EcoMaterialisms: Organizing Life and Matter' conference, held at the University of California, Irvine on 15 May 2015.
60. Emmanuel Levinas, *On Escape: De l'évasion*, trans. Bettina Bergo (Palo Alto: Stanford University Press, 2003), 60.
61. Heidegger, *The Fundamental Concepts of Metaphysics*, 161, 174.
62. Agamben, 'The Power of Thought', 485.
63. Ibid., 485.
64. Ibid., 490.
65. Ibid., 488.
66. Ibid., 490.

67. Ibid., 491.
68. Ibid., 90. In Seshardi's translation of Aristotle's passage, 'to be passive' (*paschein*) is translated as 'to suffer'. My alteration of this translation is prompted by Agamben's use of *paschein* in the entire essay, which is as 'passivity'.
69. Heidegger, *The Fundamental Concepts of Metaphysics*, 173.
70. Ibid., 174.
71. Agamben, 'The Power of Thought', 491.
72. Levinas, *On Escape*, 49.
73. Levinas, *Existence and Existents*, 30.
74. Ibid., 72.
75. Agamben, 'The Power of Thought', 483.
76. Ibid., 482.
77. John Steinbeck, *Log from the Sea of Cortez* (New York: Viking, 1951), 81.
78. Agamben, 'The Power of Thought', 482.
79. Sigmund Freud, 'Letter from Sigmund Freud to Karl Abraham, November 25, 1914', in *The Complete Correspondence of Sigmund Freud and Karl Abraham 1907–1925* (London: Routledge, 2002), 285–6.
80. Donald W. Winnicott, 'Squiggle Game', *Psycho-Analytic Explorations*, ed. Clare Winnicott, Ray Shepherd and Madeleine Davis (Cambridge, MA: Harvard University Press, 1989), 302–3, 299–317.
81. Donald W. Winnicott, 'Ego Integration in Child Development', in *The Maturational Processes and the Facilitating Environment: Studies in the Theory of Emotional Development* (London: Hogarth Press, 1965), 59.
82. Donald W. Winnicott, 'Psycho-Somatic Illness in its Positive and Negative Aspects', *International Journal of Psychoanalysis* 47 (1966), 510–16.
83. Ibid., 510.
84. Ibid., 513.
85. Ibid., 513.
86. Ibid. 516.
87. Ibid., 513.
88. Ibid., 513–14.
89. Sandor Ferenczi, 'The Principle of Relaxation and Neocatharsis', *International Journal of Psycho-Analysis* 11 (1930), 433, 435.
90. Ibid., 436–7.
91. Ibid., 435.
92. Ibid., 436.
93. Ibid., 437.
94. Ibid., 440.
95. Adam Phillips, 'Making the Case: Freud's Literary Engagements', *Profession* 11 (2003), 10–20, 11, 12.
96. Sigmund Freud, 'Letter from Freud to Fliess, July 7, 1898', in *The Complete Letters of Sigmund Freud to Wilhelm Fliess, 1887–1904* (Cambridge, MA: Belknap Press of Harvard University Press, 1986), 319–20.
97. Sigmund Freud, 'Letter from Freud to Fliess, May 20, 1900', in ibid., 415–16.
98. William James, *On Vital Reserves: The Energies of Men. The Gospel of Relaxation* (New York: Henry Holt, 1911), 4.

99. Adam Phillips, *On Kissing, Tickling, and Being Bored: Psychoanalytic Essays on the Unexamined Life* (Cambridge, MA: Harvard University Press, 1993), 83.

100. Sigmund Freud, *Complete Psychological Works* (London: Hogarth Press and the Institute of Psycho-Analysis, 1973), vol. VII, 2207.

101. Ibid., 2207.

102. Josef Breuer and Sigmund Freud, *Studies on Hysteria*, trans. James Strachey (New York: Basic Books, 1891), 46.

103. James, *On Vital Reserves*, 11.

104. Ibid., 6, 9–10.

105. Ibid., 23.

106. Ibid., 33.

107. Roland Barthes, 'Osons être paresseux', in *Oeuvres Complètes*, vol. 3 (Paris: Seuil, 2002), 760.

108. Saint-Amand, *The Pursuit of Laziness*, 10.

109. Paul Lafargue, *The Right to Be Lazy* (1883) (Chicago: Solidarity Publications, 1969).

110. Ibid., 21–2.

111. Ibid., 23–4.

112. Michel Foucault, *The Government of Self and Others: Lectures at the Collège de France, 1982–1983* (London: Macmillan, 2011), 287.

113. Roland Barthes, *The Neutral: Lecture Course at the Collège de France (1977–1978)*, ed. Thomas Clerc and Éric Marty, trans. Rosalind E. Krauss and Dennis Hollier (New York: Columbia University Press, 2005), 79.

114. Lafargue, *The Right to Be Lazy*, 23.

115. Paul Lafargue, *Le Droit à la paresse: réfutation du droit au travail de 1848*, ed. Henry Oriol (Paris: 11 Rue Bertin-Poireé, 1883).

116. Marina Van Zuylen, 'The Importance of Being Lazy', *Cabinet* 11 (2003), http://www.cabinetmagazine.org/issues/11/paresse.php (accessed 25 January 2019).

117. Lafargue, *The Right to Be Lazy*, 31.

118. Lafargue, *Le Droit à la paresse*, 33; Lafargue, *The Right to Be Lazy*, 50, 67.

119. Barthes, 'Osons être paresseux', 761.

120. Ibid., 763.

121. Barthes, *The Neutral*, 112.

122. Locke, *Philosophical Works and Selected Correspondence*, 59.

123. Barthes, *The Neutral*, 85.

124. Locke, *Philosophical Works and Selected Correspondence*, 81.

125. Ibid., 80.

126. Ibid., 81.

127. Barthes's original words are 'c'est une donnee fondamentale et comme naturelle de la situation scolaire'; Barthes, 'Osons être paresseux', 760.

128. Pierre Bourdieu, *Homo Academicus*, trans. Peter Collier (Palo Alto: Stanford University Press, 1988).

129. Theodor Adorno, *Minima Moralia: Reflections from Damaged Life*, trans. E. F. N. Jephcott (London: Verso, 2006), 80.

130. Barthes, *The Neutral*, 81.

131. Ibid., 21.

132. Ibid., 121.
133. Michel Foucault, *Discipline and Punish: The Birth of the Prison* (1975), trans. Alan Sheridan, 2nd edn (New York: Vintage, 1995), 25.
134. Barthes, *The Neutral*, 21.
135. Foucault, *Discipline and Punish*, 25.

CHAPTER 2

Laziness in American Literature:
The Inaugural Moment

> Our natural powers would be overextended and severed if nature had not
> placed a counterweight in the human being, that is, such a propensity to
> repose and inactivity.
>
> Immanuel Kant, *Lectures on Anthropology*

This chapter is a historical overview of the preliminary stages in the
development of the trope of laziness in the American literature of
the Puritan colonies and early Republic. It presents how the idea
functioned in the American cultural context long before it evolved
into a distinct trope of protest in the twentieth century, when its
aesthetics as well as its ethico-political rationale became uniquely
its own. While the birth of laziness as a figurative device may be
said to coincide with the formation of the American pastoralist
paradigm, its gestation period stretches way back to the times of
the early colonies. For it is in the colonial period, when laziness
barely emerges on the poetic horizon of American letters, that we
find the inaugural moment of the complicated relation between
laziness and the American ethics of labour, which will later inform
nineteenth- and twentieth-century counter-systemic uses of the
trope of doing nothing.

Laziness in the Puritan Colonies

The Protestant separatists who left Europe in search of religious
freedom by no means associated laziness with righteous dissent.

In 'A Modell of Christian Charity', delivered on board the *Arbella* in 1630, John Winthrop equated it with apostasy. And although he used the theological term 'sloth' rather than 'laziness', the sense he gave to the word exceeded its standard religious references. In Winthrop's usage, sloth was not only an offence against God but also a transgression of the law, worse than the crime of ideological treason. '[He] is worse than an infidel who through his own sloth and voluptuousness shall neglect to provide for his family', Winthrop intimated, implying that it is a lesser crime to renounce religion than to be negligent in economic pursuits.[1] Thus, by inserting the discourse of law and economy into the motivational address to his fellow travellers, Winthrop articulated the interrelatedness of the financial and the religious dimensions of the early colonial experience. Indeed, the vision of a community developed in 'A Modell of Christian Charity' consisted for the most part of detailed instructions on money lending and debt forgiving, while the religious motif on which Winthrop based his instruction was the divine origin of socio-economic division into the rich and the poor: 'God Almighty', the first sentence of the sermon declared, 'hath so disposed of the condition of mankind, as in all times some must be rich, some poor, some high and eminent in power and dignity; others mean and in submission.'[2] Not only was there nothing to be done about this distribution of means and power, Winthrop said, but one was obliged to follow Scripture as regards the rules for controlling the flow of capital and maintaining this social hierarchy.

Enumerating dangerous threats to this balanced structure, Winthrop ranked 'sloth and voluptuousness' as offences graver than the denial of God's sovereignty. Their combination indicated that the harmfulness of sloth derived mainly from its economic aspect: both laziness, defined as negligence of work, and voluptuousness, that is, immoderate consumption of goods, would lead to poverty. Therefore, while one should always be diligent in labour and avoid poverty, one also had a 'duty of mercy' towards those who were poor, which was to assist them in maintaining financial balance. Mercy was to be exercised, very specifically, 'in the kinds: giving, lending and forgiving (of a debt)'.[3] One was supposed to lend resources to those who ask: 'From him that would borrow of thee turn not away.'[4] And when one did so 'by way of commerce or in mercy', one was obliged to 'forgive' – 'except in cause where thou hast a surety or a lawful pledge' – those debtors who could not pay one back.[5]

The conflation of economic and religious concerns in the discourse of the early American colonies has been high on the agenda of criticism since the turn of the twenty-first century. Authors such as Hugh Dawson and, more recently, Michelle Burnham have pointed out the 'interpenetration' of the financial and spiritual rhetoric in Winthrop's sermon specifically, as well as more generally in the entire colonial discourse of New England.[6] According to Dawson, the 'pervasive legal tenor' of Winthrop's 'Modell' renders it more akin to legal documents than to the format of religious didacticism.[7] Burnham, the author of *Folded Selves: Colonial New England Writing in the World System*, goes even further than Dawson in applying the economic filter to her view of Puritan discourse. She decisively contests the tradition inaugurated by Perry Miller of reading early colonial rhetoric through the prism of religion, and claims that the entire ideological structure of colonial aesthetics is grounded much more firmly in the principles of mercantile and monetary dissensus with regard to world capitalism than in the principles of religious dissent.

The example of another founding text of New England's moral system, John Cotton's 1630 'God's Promise to His Plantation', provides strong evidence for Burnham's point. The sermon relies on terminology related to the laws of land property: Cotton explains to his people that, as the Bible says, they are blessed to dwell in this 'vacant' land, 'like Free-holders in a place of their owne', those whom God promised 'firme and durable possession'.[8] Can't you see, Cotton asks, that God made room for you here, 'either by lawfull descent, or purchase, or gift, or other warrantable right?' If you don't, he adds, you 'are but intruders upon God'.[9] The rules of occupying the new property are phrased by Cotton in terms of repayment for the debt of 'removing' the 'company' from their former, unsatisfactory dwelling. They can repay the debt, for example, by transplanting their trade to the new place, like bees who, when one hive is full, seek a new one elsewhere, for tradesmen who live 'one by another' will 'eat up one another', while 'our Saviour approveth travaile for Merchants'.[10] In return for the new location, the company should also employ their 'Talents and gifts'. If they left the old place with earthly 'debts and miseries', they will have to seek opportunities 'to discharge their debts and satisfie their Creditors'.[11]

Underpinning the new rules of conduct and lawful dwelling was the opposition between two inclinations: the godly 'travaile' and the ungodly 'idleness', which differentiated between those who could partake in the new company and those who could not. Someone who was naturally predisposed to work, but followed the 'vaine inclinations ' to 'live idly', 'see fashions' and 'deceive his Creditors' was not a good fellow in the plantation business.[12] On the other hand, 'if his heart be inclined upon right judgement to advance the Gospell, to maintaine his family, to use his Talents fruitfully, or the like good end', one was a valuable society member.[13] Apparently, for Cotton, a man 'more solicitous not to be found idle' than Calvin himself, sloth was primarily conceivable in economic terms, on the spectrum of financial misconduct alongside extravagance and fraud.[14] In a curiously secular manner, it signified a waste of resources that ought to be multiplied rather than spent.

While the accumulation of financial references is perhaps more baffling in the case of Cotton's properly religious 'God's Promise' than in the case of Winthrop's lay sermon, its recurrence clarifies the enigmatic assertion of Winthrop's 'A Modell of Christian Charity' that it is in the end better to be infidel than idle. Of course, the argument that the reformed Protestant worldview positions sloth and idleness in economic perspective as negligence in business and excessive expenditure has been a part of the Weberian thesis about Puritanism as the cornerstone of the capitalist work ethic. However, contemporary scholars such as Burnham or Stephen Innes go further than Weber in the direction of an economic reading of the early colonies, focusing exclusively on the nuances of the financial and legal context and the accompanying complex technologies of affect management that governed the lives of those who participated in what the preacher Samuel Danforth called 'an errand into wilderness'.[15] For no less were the settlers' religious ambitions intertwined with mercantile ones than with the legal constraints on individual freedom and private strategies for alleviating the want of that freedom, or accommodating its excess *vis-à-vis* power structures at the level of the emerging nation-state.

As far as legal constraints were concerned, the criminalisation of laziness in poor and vagrancy laws and financial documents went hand in hand with its demonisation in religious literature. The figure of bodily lethargy was a synecdoche for all violations of divine law, as if the idea of idling alone captured the very essence of disobedience. This view was taken to its extreme in John Cotton's 1654 *Brief Exposition with Practical Observations Upon the Whole Book of Ecclesiastes*, which famously begins with the biblical exhortation of everydayness as 'vanity of vanities' in order to instil in his readers the unusual idea that by doing nothing one can break the first five commandments. For example, one violates the commandment against using God's name in vain, because spending one's time and talents in vain is idleness. As for the commandment against working on the Sabbath, one obeys it not by resting on that day but by labouring for the other six. The commandment to honour one's parents, supported by Proverbs 10:5 which warns that a prudent son gathers in summer, also boils down to obeying the rule of practicality and industriousness. The commandment against adultery, derived from Ezekiel 16:49, where Sodom is described as a place of 'prosperous ease', is a commandment against idle expenditure of one's energy. Finally, the condemnation of idleness is also operative in the restriction against stealing, because Proverbs 19:15 proclaims that an idle person will suffer hunger and Proverbs 10:4 says that a slack hand causes poverty.

Social and religious problems as well as fears about the impending calamities of King Philip's War, depicted in such texts as Increase Mather's *The Day of Trouble is Near, A Brief History of the War with the Indians* and William Hubbard's *Narrative of the Troubles with the Indians*, were too significant to be remedied by means of religious indoctrination unsupported by legal regulations. The motif of the idle poor who deserve charity temporarily disappeared from the orbit of interest, while idleness and slothfulness became transparent categories in the rhetoric of economic threat. Mather's *The Day of Trouble is Near* coincided with the first dramatic upsurge in vagrancy in New England related to King Philip's War, which shook the territorial stability of the inhabitants of Massachusetts and Rhode Island. As the Indian uprising 'forced settlers from their farms and into coastal towns', their inhabitants complained that the migration did indeed 'increase the sin of idleness', which led to the institution of new tramp regulations and Settlement Acts.[16] The need to strengthen community ties, in the wake of the war-related migration in the colonies, renewed the demand for vigilance against those who, in one way or another, posed a threat: Indians, vagrants, rebels and heretics. One way of solving migration problems was via stricter application of the poor and vagrancy laws, which had to be supported by stricter religious stigmatisation of laziness. This stigmatisation consisted in the elaboration of its economic references: in his 1676 *Earnest Exhortation*, for instance, Increase Mather subsumed under the category of sloth such financial misconducts as 'the sin of Oppression' or 'the sin of Usury'.[17] In the 1674 *The Day of Trouble is Near*, he condemned any action, however laborious, whose ends were private rather than communal. The sense of security derived from one's work, rest and 'Freedome from hard Bondage' were lumped together under one category: the 'obnoxious' sin of idleness.[18]

Although the deviantising rhetoric, including condemnations of pleasure and restrictions on security and freedom, dominated public discourse, its reign was occasionally subverted in poetry. In the writings of Anne Bradstreet, for example, the original debt rhetoric is intertwined with the sentiment of longing for rest. On the one hand, Bradstreet's famous verses upon the burning of her house – 'Yea so it was, and so 'twas just. / It was his own: it was not mine' – echo the rhetoric of financial reparation to the divine creditor. The idea that there might not be enough time to pay back the debt also resounds in some of her 'Meditations' upon the nature of life. Destined to be spent in getting 'bread with pain, and sweat of face',[19] life is dangerously slowed down 'in eating, drinking, sleeping, vain delight'.[20] The result of succumbing to those delights is, as the harsh logic of vagrancy laws has it, to end with nothing, like 'vagabonds to Land of Nod'.[21] In Bradstreet's image of a homeless vagabond immersed in oblivious slumber, the sentiment of fear is communicated by abject images of the body as a 'lump of wretchedness, of sin and sorrow' or a 'weather-beaten vessel wrackt with pain'.[22] A slothful body is thus a disfigured, lifeless mass, like the biblical lump of clay or a wearied beggar; it is the form of the abject.

On the other hand, inasmuch as the restfulness of one who engages in vain delight is presented as lifelessness, death and abjection, Bradstreet constructs other images of inaction, and tries to breach the moral divide between carnal and heavenly rest. In the collection of meditations, set in prose, entitled 'Meditations When my Soul Hath been Refreshed with the Consolations which the World Knowes Not', Bradstreet is no longer a proponent of restless toil: 'Much Labour wearys the body . . . and many thoughts oppresse the minde; man aimes at profit by the one, and content in the other; but often misses of both, and findes nothing but vanity and vexation of spirit.'[23] Like the body, the mind needs repose from constant engagement, otherwise it will become blunt and confused, Bradstreet thinks, thus intimating that obsessive obedience to the dictum of constant action is stupefying and limiting. The poet imagines states of inactivity as necessary in both work and restless self-examination. For the seventeenth-century meaning of vexation, the *OED* has 'the action of troubling or harassing by aggression or interference, specifically by unjustifiable claims or legal action', which may indicate that apart from pondering that non-stop labour brings unnecessary weariness and meaningless lifestyle, Bradstreet also suspects that life where intense intellectual (self-)scrutiny is never suspended is a form of harassment.

In the next meditation in this series, she complains about 'slanderous tongues' that all too readily 'kill the good name' of those who are different, fatigued or oblivious. The meditations lead her to also let her own imagination loose to dream of freedom from earthly toil. In 'Longing for Heaven' she begins with the hopeful image of the 'weary pilgrim, now at rest':

> His wasted limbes, now lye full soft
> That myrie steps, haue trodden oft . . .
> The burning sun no more shall heat
> Nor stormy raines, on him shall beat.
> The bryars and thornes no more shall scratch
> Nor hungry wolves at him shall catch[24]

As is typical for Bradstreet's oscillation between the correct Puritan mindset and the sensible meditation upon the precarious dimension of material existence, this blissful vision of rest and relaxation is ironically pictured as attainable only in death, for as the weary pilgrim 'bids farewell' to the earthly dwelling, the body at rest becomes a 'Corrupt Carcass'.[25] In between shifts of tone, however, Bradstreet manages to articulate the fantasy of escaping earthly toil. Safely suspended between the dream vision of a resting vagabond and the image of a corrupt dead carcass, the wish is enunciated with unique clarity and earnestness: 'Oh how I long to be at rest'.[26] It is revealed in the next line of her poem that, like Shakespeare's Hamlet, she is imagining an experience she has never had before, and so, like Hamlet, she has to imagine it as another unknown experience, namely, that of death: The whole sequence is 'Oh how I long to be at rest / and soare on high among the blest'. Like death, therefore, rest, that is, cessation of mental and bodily activity, is both the end of life and the beginning of a new one. Once freed from the labour contract, one soars on high – to 'soar' meaning here 'ascension' in an easy, 'loose' manner, as the dictionary for the early seventeenth century has it.

In this way, by masquerading the wish to evade the toilsome life of constant fatigue with the official image of heavenly rest, Bradstreet articulates what cannot be openly stated by a diligent Puritan, especially by a woman who was already dubbed the muse of the migrant population, namely, the fantasy of repose from the physical and intellectual regime of religious existence and the regime of colonial economics. What the fantasy also articulates is a down-to-earth, subversive wish to be able to let go of the robust identity of a pilgrim and espouse a more relaxed manner of living.

Towards Abstraction: the American Enlightenment

As Bradstreet's century ended, the legal war on idleness, whose beginnings can be traced back to the poor and vagrancy laws of the Colonial Empire, gradually replaced economic categories with psychological ones. If we accept the Foucauldian thesis about the evolution of biopolitics by way of steps in the process of norm-interiorisation by individual subjects, and the particular acceleration of this process at the time of the Enlightenment, it comes as no surprise that in eighteenth-century American letters the meaning of laziness was infused with new references. On the one hand, the shift ran along the lines of John Locke's rational classification of laziness as an inherent vice of the mind – an attention disorder and an intelligence deficit that requires correction through mental discipline. On the other, however, it still made use of the residual metaphors of divine debt and amoral time expenditure. An illustration of such conceptual revalorisation can be found in the sermons and philosophical thought of Jonathan Edwards, which predates the equation of moral value with productivity that Weber famously detected in the works of Benjamin Franklin. However neck-breaking the task of combining Cartesian logic with religious doctrine, the Revd Edwards managed to redefine sloth in a way that combines its spiritual, financial and psychological meanings as a form of time expenditure. It is the concept of wasting time that Edwards sets out to examine, eventually concluding that there is no such thing as 'free' time that one can own and use to one's private ends.

In the 1734 sermon 'On the Preciousness of Time and the Importance of Redeeming It', Edwards inserts the familiar Puritan conception of life as debt to be paid off: not only should one devote one's entire time to the task of repaying one's debt of life 'for one's own advantage', but whenever possible, also work to repay the debts of others and 'redeem time' from the threat of it being reclaimed by the almighty creditor:

Christians should not only study to improve the opportunities they enjoy, for their own advantage, as those who would make a good bargain; but also labour to reclaim others from their evil courses; that so God might defer his anger, and time might be redeemed from that terrible destruction, which, when it should come, would put an end to the time of divine patience ... [The] corruption of the times tends to hasten threatened judgments; but your holy and circumspect walk will tend to redeem time from the devouring jaws of those calamities. However, thus much is certainly held forth to us in the words; viz. That upon time we should set a high value, and be exceeding careful that it be not lost; and we are therefore exhorted to exercise wisdom and circumspection, in order that we may redeem it. And hence it appears, that time is exceedingly precious.[27]

Time is the currency in the contract with God. The time people withhold from repaying the debt of life qualifies as 'corrupt' – its moral disorderliness stemming from economic destabilisation. Time is a 'precious value' whose worth is legitimated by the amount of effort required to redeem it, that is, the work invested in paying it back.

First, time is costly, because

> a happy or miserable eternity depends on the good or ill improvement of it. Things are precious in proportion to their importance, or to the degree wherein they concern our welfare. Men are wont to set the highest value on those things upon which they are sensible their interest chiefly depends.[28]

The interest depends on the amount of work we perform, because otherwise 'we shall be in danger of coming to poverty and disgrace', and consequently to 'death' and 'everlasting misery'. On work, Edwards asserted, 'depends our escape from an infinite evil, and our attainment of an infinite good'. In other words, labour time is the only currency by means of which the wicked man may negotiate the rules of the covenantal contract.

Second, time is precious, because its resources are scarce:

> Time is very short, which is another thing that renders it very precious. The scarcity of any commodity occasions men to set a higher value upon it, especially if it be necessary and they cannot do without it . . . Time is so short, and the work which we have to do in it is so great, that we have none of it to spare. The work which we have to do to prepare for eternity, must be done in time, or it never can be done; and it is found to be a work of great difficulty and labour, and therefore that for which time is the more requisite.[29]

Spending time and labour on the work of great difficulty is the way of accumulating capital which is requisite: that is to say, considered necessary in the rules and conditions of the covenant. It is a commodity to which one cannot claim rights as to a bargain because it is not a private good but a universal currency in which the debt of life can be redeemed.

Third, time is precious because we cannot be certain of its continued availability. We do not know how much life we have left, when it will end, and thus do not know the date of the final call. The time when the law will claim the unpaid debt is uncertain, and therefore, says Edwards, we should hurry in accumulating the currency with which to get even with the divine creditor. Especially since, as Edwards's fourth reason has it, every moment that passes and cannot be recovered increases the value of time. In that, time is unlike any other resource or commodity and thus must not be squandered. But if the third reason for the preciousness of time has it that time is uncertain, it follows that apart from devoting one's life to settling the exchange rate for time in relation to hard work, one should also consent to the fact there is actually no way in which this rate can be settled by the mortal individual. One must consent, in both economic and religious senses, to the unfair rules of the contract without the possibility of negotiating it. If 'we refuse, it [time] is immediately taken away, and never offered more', while man becomes 'bankrupt'. Therefore, one should improve well 'time of leisure from worldly business . . . [s]pend not such opportunities unprofitably . . . [w]aste them not away wholly in unprofitable visits, or useless diversions or amusements. Diversion should be used only in subserviency to business.'[30]

At one point in the sermon Edwards says that some personality types are particularly prone to violate these rules and suffer bankruptcy. As the first and most obvious group, Edwards lists 'those who spend a great part of their time in idleness, or in doing nothing that turns to any account'.[31] Somewhat surprisingly, therefore, the greatest dissenters are not those who openly deny the covenant, but those whose denial concerns the productive use of time. Wasting it unproductively, or 'doing nothing', is pictured by Edwards in exclusively economic terms, as a form of possessiveness (towards time) and consumerist short-sightedness:

> There are some persons upon whose hands time seems to lie heavy, who, instead of being concerned to improve it as it passes, and taking care that it pass not without making it their own, act as if it were rather their concern to contrive ways how to waste and consume it; as though time, instead of being precious, were rather a mere encumbrance to them.[32]

Similarly to Locke, on whose work Edwards modelled his own understanding of the human mind, and who described the unbrilliant learners as those who are naturally burdened by intellectual effort, Edwards considers some human beings unfit for the business of living, thus tracing their disobedience to the imperative of industriousness to some innate deficit – a 'hurtful ill' or a 'madness'.[33] Especially for those who are 'suffering' in this way, every misstep on the path of life, such as a wasteful expenditure of time, is fatal. Its short-term effects are material barrenness, poverty and bankruptcy, while in the long run it brings bodily as well as spiritual death.

'The Preciousness of Time' is not Edwards's only sermon on productivity. In 'The Manner in Which the Salvation of the Soul is to be Sought' from 1740, Edwards says that men 'have no reason to expect to be saved in idleness, or to go to heaven in a way of doing nothing. No; in order to it, there is a great work, which must not only be begun, but finished.'[34] Similarly, in 'Perpetuity and Change of the Sabbath' from the same period, he takes care to distinguish between legitimate and illegitimate forms of rest. While sabbath is a time of rest, rest should not be confused with freedom to do what one desires. It was 'not designed to be a day of idleness' but a day of spiritual exercise where there is no room for wandering thought or passion.[35] The economic rationalisation of unfreedom from spending one's time and life-energy as one wishes dominates also 'Directions for Self-Examination', where Edwards prepares the ground for the Franklinian method of daily self-examination:

> Inquire whether it be not our manner to *loiter away the time* of the sabbath, and to spend it in a general measure in idleness, in doing nothing. Do you not spend more time on sabbath-day, than on other days, on your beds, or otherwise idling away the time, not improving it as a precious opportunity?[36]

That Edwards's advice is immediately followed by the question about sinning against obedience to the 'institutions of God's house' finds explanation in Foucault's assertion of continuity between the forms of pastoral governmentality, founded on the Christian principle of the leader as shepherd, and the evolution of biopolitical forms of governmentality which peek behind the doors of a house

on a Sabbath to control private life.[37] The pastoral missionary rhetoric during the second wave of the Great Awakening, captured in the
journals of such of Edwards's contemporaries as David Brainerd,
whose legacy Edwards promoted, and thoroughly documented in
postcolonial criticism within Native American Studies, enriched
the Protestant ideology with yet another meaning of idleness, as a
savage, disorderly disposition of 'ungratefulness'.

Brainerd's logic that missionary preaching was a document of an
inborn Christian 'kindness' against which some are naturally, that
is to say, temperamentally, inclined to be 'ungrateful' was grounded
in the transparency of the idea of laziness as a disease. Christianity,
the popular argument ran, might not 'cure' the savages 'of their
ungrateful tempers', or not cure them 'at *once*', before a long-term
treatment is administered, because 'they are in general unspeakably
indolent and slothful . . . bred up in idleness, and know little about
cultivating land, or indeed of engaging vigorously in any other
business'.[38]

In conclusion, the idea of 'doing nothing', as far as Edwards's
Enlightened version of Calvinism is concerned, serves as a busy
category in the rationalisation of the religious doctrine at a time
of progressing secularisation. It connects the economic discourse
driven by the category of debt to spiritual stigmatisation of
sloth and to scientific discourses on the processes of the mind.
Associated with a lack of life-energy, it becomes a blanket term for
any existential position or behaviour that opposes the principle of
individual and collective obedience to the norm of productivity
derived from the concept of divine debt. Moreover, because 'doing
nothing' is qualified as an atavistic, inborn illness of temperament,
it legitimates both the eugenic doctrine of predestination and the
colonialist rhetoric of civilising the wilderness. As a savage vice of
ungratefulness, the concept of laziness has lent much-needed transparency to the discourses of Manifest Destiny, Great Awakening
and economic progress.

Ever since Weber's *The Protestant Ethic and the Spirit of Capitalism*,
the prime role in the consolidation of the norm of productivity
has been attributed mainly to Benjamin Franklin. However, the
religious writers of the Great Awakening seem to have been just as
vocal about the conflation of moral and economic value. Franklin's

Advice to a Young Tradesman on the value of productivity employs the same abstract category of time that one finds in Edwards's sermons:

> Remember, that *time* is money. He that can earn ten shillings a day by his labour, and goes abroad, or sits idle, one half of that day, though he spends but sixpence during his diversion or idleness, ought not to reckon *that* the only expense; he has really spent, or rather thrown away, five shillings besides.[39]

But the reference to the abstraction of time also helps Franklin to detach the idea of capital from its understanding as a material form of wealth. Capital thus acquires the characteristics of an abstract entity in an unstoppable process of accumulation for its own sake. It is thus inextricably linked – by the logic of irredeemable time – to an impossible desire of final satiation and a competitive anxiety.[40] In short, Franklin's revision of the Puritan understanding of idleness abstracts it from the materiality of labour, situating it among more indefinite categories of satiation and rivalry, thus anticipating such concepts as Thorstein Veblen's conspicuous consumption or Pierre Bourdieu's symbolic capital.

Franklin makes this contribution to the ethos of capitalism by not so much condemning time expenditure for the sake of industriousness as recognising how it influences one's public image. *Poor Richard's Almanack*, *The Way to Wealth* and *Autobiography* offer advice on constructing the *image* of a productive individual rather than teaching productivity itself, and reiterate the formula that to appear industrious is a way of gaining social recognition. The importance of social image transpires from Franklin's aphorisms, such as the disarmingly straightforward 'if one cannot or doesn't want to work, one should at least keep his nose close to the grindstone' – a maxim Franklin definitely found useful in his own life, when taking air-baths, delaying ambassadorial duties and handing the famous book-laden wheelbarrows to his workers as soon as the door to the street closed behind him.[41] Leaving these biographical trivia aside, however, one thing that is definitely present in Franklin's writing on the preciousness of time and the virtue of industry is that it is the appearance of productivity, in other words a specific repertoire of gestures and behaviours, rather than productivity as such that fulfils the norm. As the image of keeping one's nose close to the grindstone aptly captures, idleness is a hindrance to achieving or maintaining noble social status:

> Do you imagine that sloth will afford you more comfort than Labor? No! For as Poor Richard says *trouble springs from idleness and grievous toil from needless ease. Many without labor, would live by their Wits only; but they'll break for want of Stock.* Whereas industry gives comfort, and plenty, and respect.[42]

Didactic Literature of the Early Republic

As the historian Sarah Jordan observes in *Anxieties of Idleness*, parallel to this valorisation of the industrious lifestyle as an affirmation of social status at the turn of the eighteenth and nineteenth centuries ran two apparently contradictory affective pedagogies. On the one hand, there was what Berlant calls the affective technology of compassion, which under the guise of charity promoted an attitude of indifference towards class-related injustice, poverty and delinquency.[43] On the other, there was the corrective pedagogy of the poverty doctrine, which discouraged those forms of industry that aimed to alleviate the hardships of the underprivileged.[44] The anti-charity logic of the doctrine stated that the poor – the labouring classes, immigrants and children – should not be entitled to any leisure time, any pauses in work, nor any intellectual or material rewards for their activity. Instead, the labouring groups were to be 'inured' to hard labour by experiencing 'the pain of overwork so early' in their lives and so often that it was no longer recognised as pain or fatigue.[45] The recommended cure for their idling, often out of fatigue and exhaustion, was real physical exertion and the habituation of constant effort.

Within the genre of didactic literature of the new nation, the two affective structures were strongly intertwined – the narratives appealed to the sense of compassion as well as disgust, to which end they borrowed from the repertoire of religious literature. The tone of corrective fictions and educational literature such as children's primers was no longer openly devotional, although some elements of the colonial worldview and rhetoric persisted, so that the didactic stories now served the double function of sermon and jeremiad, which is to say that they were oriented towards regulating the private conduct of American citizens as well as being a source of entertainment. The pedagogical impulse to promote the virtues of industry and productive growth included the figure of laziness as the epitome of destructiveness, wastefulness and stagnation. But the very same impulse that led to the perversification of lazy behaviour also made it a trope of forbidden pleasures, by means of which popular audiences could enjoy scopophiliac glimpses of the outlawed obscenities of negligent life. Ironically, it is in the discourse that so relentlessly pilloried laziness as an obstacle to individual growth and the common good that one can detect the first traces of the trope's counter-normative potential.

The double-edged sword of this disciplining rhetoric is aptly illustrated by 'The Instructive Story of Industry and Sloth', which after its debut in 1796, was frequently reprinted in the first decade of the nineteenth century. As with all didactic material produced to influence the private lives of young audiences, the 'Instructive Story' was addressed primarily to parents, thus intertwining educational messages with popular entertainment. The combination was, to a large extent, possible due to the narrative device of the panoptical, policing gaze, inherited from the colonial tradition of mutual watch.

In a manner characteristic of the genre, the narrative of the 'Instructive Story' invites the reader to join the investigative gaze of a benevolent home-visitor, who, one fine day, calls on two houses in his neighbourhood – one run by the family of Industry and the other, by the family of Sloth. From the outset, the pretence of charity and equity masks and legitimates the intrusive character of the peeping gaze, for from the perspective of the narrator there is nothing wrong with disturbing the privacy of another's home, as long as it is done in the service of communal well-being. His glimpse into the house of Industry is quick, cursory and lacklustre. Here the humble and diligent daughter of the family, Nancy, keeps herself busy in the kitchen, the household being quiet, tidy and well maintained. Keeping the account of the house to the minimum, the narrator speedily lists all of Nancy's virtues, most of which could not have been spotted during his visit: the girl is an embodiment of prudence, for not only is she modest and chaste, but she also learns very fast and excels at everything she touches. The didactic lesson of the tale, that one ought to be 'virtuous and to your virtue join prudence and perseverance; so shall you not fall into want, nor feel the envenomed stings of guilt and remorse', could not be illustrated any more plainly.[46] In fact, this is perfectly obvious before the narrative even begins – the reader receives no guidance on how to reach the Franklinian ideal that one should get up early, keep one's dwelling in order and keep one's nose close to the grindstone – to the point that we may doubt whether instruction is the real goal of the story.

The qualities that are associated with the socially desirable virtue of productiveness are not as exciting as those to be illustrated by the behaviour of the Sloth family, which is why, having pre-empted the duty of moral guidance, the scopophiliac gaze of the narrator travels to the 'miserable abode' of the Sloths, revealing it to be the real object of interest. In the house of the Sloths, the narrative suddenly gains momentum, and laziness becomes a code word for all possible obscenity. Upon opening the door, the eye of the narrator encounters the shocking sight of an undressed boy, Richard Sloth, lying in an indecent pose on his bed, while his sister Susan – Nancy's clumsy and neurotic negative – unsuccessfully tries to light a fire under the kettle. The distress of the narrator at what he sees is as great as his obliviousness to having trespassed upon private property, and he reports that this 'shameful situation' as well as the sequence of events that it unleashes force him, albeit temporarily, to flee from the Sloths' premises. As the half-naked boy shamelessly 'stares' the narrator 'full in the face', Susan drops the kettle, an act that puts her mother 'in a passion' and the whole house 'in an uproar'.[47]

Given that the shameful situation is also the only event in the story to be illustrated by a drawing, one might intimate that the narrative tactic inaugurated here uses disgust in order to conceal the effort to satisfy the adult readers' scopophiliac desire with images of the forbidden. The very same tactic, however, ensures that the perversity of their pleasure and the guilt derived therefrom will be even more readily transformed into a vigorous implementation of the values of prudence and perseverance unto their offspring. Accordingly, the panoptical gaze of the narrator does not cease to register every sinister excess in the Sloths' lives. It follows the delinquent Mr Sloth to the 'buckster's shop', where he is 'almost too drunk to swear' (though, as escapes the narrator's attention, he is sober enough to point out the wrongfulness of a home visit), and then returns to the house, where in the flash-forward mode, he witnesses Richard's and Susan's gradual moral corruption: the boy becomes a drunkard like his father, to then join the army, 'full of deprived' people like himself, and occasionally brings home his comrades, who become 'intimate' with his sister.[48] Susan, who suffers the disrepute of being a local harlot, is eventually 'induced' by one of the soldiers to follow the army, as a result of which she becomes 'ruined – cast off – and die[s] a beggar!'[49]

The abundance of obscenities that the reader of the didactic tale is invited to envisage – 'dear young reader, please pause and reflect on it', the narrator begs in his final words – suggests that the moral lesson about the destructiveness of being lazy and the benefits of diligent work serves as a cover story for a collection of perverse images designed to deliver adult entertainment. This seems rather ironic, given that, as Karen Weyler argues, the epoch's didactic tales, primarily addressed to poor audiences, praised the virtue of honesty higher than they did industriousness.[50]

When 'Instructive Story' is compared to a classic representative of the didactic genre, such as Maria Edgeworth's 'Lazy Lawrence', also published in 1796, the sensationalist undertones of the story of the Sloths become even more ostensible. Unlike the anonymous author of 'Instructive Story', whose rhetoric spelled out the culture's unconscious, Edgeworth was fully aware of those undercurrents and wary of how industriousness ought to be promoted so as not to become another form of excessiveness: the orgy of consumerism that plagued the middle-class population in Edgeworth's native England as well as in the United States, where her work was frequently reprinted.[51] Hence, 'Lazy Lawrence', the lead story of Edgeworth's *The Parent's Assistant*, was addressed explicitly to grown-ups, featuring detailed accounts of which industrious behaviours should be encouraged (in children as well as in adults), and how this encouragement should be effected.[52] Rather than praising hard work as such, Edgeworth's educational programme was to teach readers how to resist the pursuit of productiveness for its own sake, and instead invest oneself in 'other-oriented' activities that would foster the development of 'networks of good-will'.[53]

In contrast to the narrative about the Industries and the Sloths, 'Lazy Lawrence' devotes substantial attention to examples of correct conduct: Jem, a hyperactive, cheerful and industrious boy who works from dawn to dusk at his mother's strawberry plantation, decides to gain extra money in order to save his horse from being sold in exchange for rent money. Even though Jem's days are already filled with labour, he is determined to expand the work-day to acquire the necessary sum. Undeterred by his initial lack of success, Jem impresses several people in the village with his selflessness and his entrepreneurial perseverance, and as a result builds social capital which eventually helps him achieve the goal that he pursues. The networks of good-will established as a result of Jem's kindness immediately begin to work to the boy's advantage, as he finds clients for his products (fossils found on the beach) and receives a well-paid job offer as a gardener. In this way, the story reveals another cultural role of the norm of productivity: to strengthen community ties. Edgeworth's narrative is punctuated by the exact moments when Jem's industrious attitude is reinforced by others, to indicate the ways in which communal collaboration can be achieved.

The role played in this lesson by the titular lazy Lawrence is to instruct about bad networking. This ever-lounging, apathetic boy is a 'good natured poor fellow enough, and would never do anyone harm but himself', but he just happens to have acquired the bad habits of stableboys and postilions.[54] As Lawrence confesses to Jem in prison, where he is taken for stealing Jem's money, 'the wicked-ness in his head' was implanted by 'idleness' that led him to 'bad company'. In short, and importantly, if industriousness is the glue that holds societies together, then idleness is that which ruins this adhesion.

The hierarchising element of the idea of bad networks is particularly evident in Robert Grant White's popular sketches entitled *Law and Laziness; or, Students at Law of Leisure* (1846), which have recently been proposed as a potential intertext of Melville's short story 'Bartleby, the Scrivener' (1853).[55] In White's stories, the role of bad company is played by the modern caste, or 'class' of lazy lawyers, an emerging social group that misuses justice and ignores the Franklinian codes for respectable behaviour. But what starts in White's text as a critique of the American 'new Aristocracy' who 'just when they have it, with much pain, become adept in the profession of idleness' quickly becomes its opposite, that is to say, a version of class determinism.[56] There would be no bad networks, the sketches insist, were it not for the contagious disease of idleness:

> There is no place like a law office for making a fashionable acquaintance, and doing the least work with the greatest ease . . . The sons of doubtful families, or even of mechanics, must be fashionable too; that *they* determine on; they must learn a trade . . . that their fathers determine on. So *they* enter the office; and the habits of this last class soon assimilate to those of the other, with which they thus mingle at an early age, for the vulgarity which is natural to low birth, is more akin to the acquired vulgarity of fashion that is usually imagined.[57]

Laziness spreads like a virus, infecting everyone who enters the legal profession, its openness to new members being precisely the source of its corruption. In a familiar gesture of voyeurism posing as moral concern, White's narrator peeps into one law office in the morning and, travelling from room to room, witnesses 'men dying of ennui' who 'catch at any straw in the way of pastime'.[58] With disgust he reports that their pastimes lack any refinement – a scrivener will strain 'unearthly whispers out of an octave flute' rather than play the instrument, while an attorney will turn pieces of coal in the fireplace 'with an aptness which would have made him eminent as a stoker, had he not devoted himself to the law'.[59] In short, White's students of law are nothing 'but bad copies' of dandies from Edward Bulwer Lytton's *Pelham* (1828), who 'lose sight of [Pelham's] refinement, and are only bullies'.[60] Vulgarity by birth is apparent in their physiognomies – noses shaped like whitewashing brushes pressed against the wall – and is amplified by their lack of intellectual sophistication. When one student starts a conversation about the British social theorist Thomas Carlyle, finding 'an obscure depth about him' which, he speculates, is assumed 'to hide his shallowness', his companions become so bored as to threaten to leave the office unless the 'bell letters' are left alone. White's reference to Carlyle is calculated as an ironic allusion to Diogenes Teufelsdröckh's condemnation of modern consumerist life in *Sartor Resartus* (1836), though less to its Romantic-socialist aspect than to Carlyle's view that dullness and laziness would eventually be features of a popular man, whereas an interesting man would never share this fate.[61] Indeed, White's students indulge in the obscenely plebeian by spending their free time in corrupt ways. They receive packages with new fashion items, and visit taverns – acts through which they become entirely unsuited to their role as guardians of justice. White's final condemnation of idleness as that which dissolves structures that hold society together features emphatically in the closing scene, where upon receiving their first legal job, young lawyers turn out to be incapable of handling the simplest of cases or dealing with regular professional correspondence.

The Inaugural Rupture: Washington Irving's 'Rip Van Winkle'

It was at the time of the early American Republic that the restrictive corset of the productivity norm began to burst at its seams. If there is any one text in which a rupture in its divisive paradigms is captured, it is Washington Irving's retelling of the European folktale 'Rip Van Winkle', published in *The Sketchbook of Geoffrey Crayon, Gent.* (1819–20). I would argue that Irving's story of an unproductive vagabond inaugurates the trope of laziness and rehearses its counter-normative potential.

In the critical paradigm established by American literary critics of the 1950s such as Leslie Fiedler and Leo Marx, Rip inaugurates the Romantic model of a character who presides over the pastoral imagination of American letters as its 'fundamental archetype' of heteronormative protest and evasion.[62] Rip seizes the American imagination, the familiar argument goes, because he is 'a symbol of misplaced innocence' – a failed husband and citizen, whose maladjustment to social norms makes him a master storyteller.[63] However, the multi-levelled satires of Irving's narrative undermine this interpretation as much as they support it. Indeed, Rip is a parody of a dreamy, nature-inspired poet as well as a romantically tragic dissenter from the culture of marital contracts, thriving business and industry. The economic sphere of evasion is particularly relevant to the model of idleness that Rip so captivatingly epitomises. On the one hand he is idle, but his 'insuperable aversion', it turns out, is directed solely against 'all kinds of profitable labor', while work in general is not something that he avoids at all:

> he would never refuse to assist a neighbor even in the roughest toil, and was a foremost man at all country frolics for husking Indian corn, or building stone-fences; the women of the village, too, used to employ him to run their errands, and to do such little odd jobs as their less obliging husbands would not do for them. In a word, Rip was ready to attend to anybody's business but his own.[64]

In short, useless, lazy and evasive as he appears to his Dame, Rip is a hard-working guardian of the deteriorating community ties of Sleepy Hollow, whose demise is threatened by the spirit of prosperity and wealth. Rip's apparent laziness is a way of protesting against the imperative of productivity upon which those ties are secured, and a form of emancipating himself from their grip.

The question of community ties is crucial to Irving's critics. Some, like Donald Pease, Donald Anderson, Howard Horwitz and Sarah Wyman, interpret 'Rip Van Winkle' as Irving's 'dangerous critique' of the values of the American Revolution and the ideological transformation it brought about, as an 'instrument of self-knowledge and social cohesion for a nation abruptly split from its past history and identity'.[65] The Fiedlerian critics, on the other hand, focus on the theme of evasion. Interpretations of Rip's retreat from the community to the Catskill Mountains describe it in terms of despair with heteronormativity, which makes immaturity and withdrawal to a paradise of bachelors the only way to protest against patriarchal norms.[66] Finally, historicist readers locate 'Rip Van Winkle' on the spectrum of didactic literature on alcohol abuse in early nineteenth-century America, demanding that Rip's so-called protest be read as an act of delinquency, and the story as a whole as an instruction on social rehabilitation.[67] But the problem that all those interpretations eventually face is that the message of the tale is uncomfortably heteroglossiac: in other words, the story questions too many values while withdrawing from all judgement.

It seems therefore that by introducing a delinquent, unproductive, wasteful literary character, Irving inserts into the cultural imaginary of the new nation a trope of longing for unrestrained freedom from the norm of collective labour, a figurative mode of questioning the patterns of inclusion and exclusion within the consensual frameworks of social participation. As Fiedler puts it, Rip's story 'represents a projection, entertained *without final faith,* of a way of life hostile to the accepted standards of the American community'.[68] Though uttered without conviction, this image of a private realm, where free time is spent as one desires, would capture the imagination of the American writers of the following generation such as Henry David Thoreau and Herman Melville, precisely because it so radically appealed to the possibility of suspending commitments and finding a private heterotopia of individual sovereignty. Significantly, Irving's 'framing of freedom' relied as much on the high Romantic aesthetics of the pastoral as it did on the low and unrefined motifs of vagabondage and delinquency.[69] In the central image of the story, the idyllic, tableau-like stasis of the mountain amphitheatre, with its uninterrupted 'stillness' and 'profound silence' as 'in an old Flemish painting', mixes with the displeasing and blurry images of the disfigured faces of the Hudson crew drunkards. To the generation of writers inspired by Irving, this mixture was an entirely deliberate, ingenious invention. To use a metaphor from Melville's late poem 'Rip Van Winkle's Lilac' (published posthumously in 1924), the trope planted by Irving was both 'fair' and 'ungainly'. It was a dream of a limit, in a Nietzschean sense: a heterotopic realm of total freedom from life, from time and from all commitment that would not be otherworldly but immanently material.

When Richard Henry Dana set out to recreate the same idea in his 1821 editorial project *The Idle Man,* the effect was not quite the same. Even though Dana pictured idleness in terms of such ordinary phenomena as infancy or illness, intimate domesticity and the like, his reliance on the Romantic pastoral sensibility rendered his project less inspiring to writers such as Whitman or Melville than Irving's heterotopic vision. *The Idle Man* survived only four volumes, never matching Irving's success nor the success of Samuel Johnson's serial *The Idler* on which it was modelled. In theory, Dana's vignettes depicted the work of idleness in everyday life. Idle contemplation was described in his preface to be the very condition of creative writing; domestic relaxation allowed time to 'shake ourselves loose of [the] hypocrisy of life', and to achieve 'harmonious union of our feelings and fancies', forgetting about the toils of the day.[70] In practice, however, as Raymond Williams would put it, Dana's images never transgressed the logic of pastoral repression. His idleness was always civilised and well-groomed, as in 'Letter from Town' in the second volume of *The Idle Man*, in which the narrator confesses to a sophisticated gentleman in an inn: 'I prefer the country, inasmuch as a man sees there less of the frivolities of his species, and more of nature, than in town, and stands a better chance to have a more equable temper, and a better turn of mind.'[71] The reply of his genteel interlocutor is a similarly packaged pastoral bias: 'Look you around', he says; most men you see here 'have been all their lives industriously making up for themselves false characters'.[72] But while Dana's characters exchange their critiques of inauthenticity, their vision of unrestrained leisure itself lacks honesty.[73]

Of course, with all credit to Irving for inaugurating the trope of radical idleness, much was yet to be accomplished in terms of nurturing its counter-normative potential in the American literature that was to follow. The route towards Rip's lilac, paved with norms to be questioned and subverted, was pursued most boldly by three writers of American Romanticism: Ralph Waldo Emerson, Walt Whitman and Herman Melville.

Laziness in American Romanticism

When Theseus asks his innocent question in *Midsummer Night's Dream* – 'How shall we beguile / The lazy time, if not with some delight?' – he is certainly unaware that it is a performative act of language that introduces the word 'lazy' into the English language. Interestingly, modern versions of the play omit the adjective, as if it threatened to bring into play the ancient and Judeo-Christian associations with moral vice, spiritual death, *acedia*, *tristitia* or melancholia, even though the way Shakespeare uses the word appears to bear no negative connotations. Enunciated as an invitation to repose, 'lazy' apparently denotes a time of relaxation. Or does it? After all, *Midsummer Night's Dream* is a classical text of the Renaissance bucolic tradition, which anchors laziness in a very specific cultural and ideological context of pastoral aesthetics. It is only logical that the aesthetics of laziness would emerge in the time of Shakespeare, for his century was also an epoch of the institutionalised proscription of all forms of 'beguiling lazy time' as delinquency or mental disorder, at the same time as it allowed for the flourishing of the ethos of *oisiveté*, or idle leisure, among the upper classes.[74]

The modern understanding of laziness owes a lot both to the category of delinquent passivity as documented by Foucault's historical archive and to the category of leisurely joy depicted in pastoralist images, which have always maintained a relation to the class distribution of labour and leisure and the affective structures that express this distribution. Perhaps the most succinct theory of this relation is Raymond Williams's *The Country and the City* – its well-known argument being that images of pastoral idylls, with their languorous atmosphere and plentiful geography, always stand in contrast to the rough realities of the rural landscape and the miserable, labour-driven temporalities of the inhabitants that they conceal.[75] In Williams's optics, the figures of individuals who beguile lazy time serve as 'objects rather than the subjects of the pastoral' – the latter being the beneficiaries of the socio-economic inequalities whose fantasies and fears the pastoral metaphorises.[76] *The Country and the City* sketches the evolution of the pastoral metaphor in British literature from the sixteenth to the eighteenth centuries and the onset of the Industrial Revolution, when, according to Williams, the pastoral metaphor mutated to the point of absorbing 'a moral attitude with social implications'.[77] As the eighteenth century was coming to an end, the reverie of easy repose among nature expanded to represent 'an alternative to ambition, disturbance, and war'.[78] According to Williams, it is in this guise of the pastoral that we may find the nucleus of the affective dynamics of class relations – the 'structure of feeling' characteristic for the epoch of Romanticism and all its future reincarnations.[79] Ever since the Romantic pastoral, images of tranquil nature have served as the locus of charitable sentiments of the 'responsible' part of civilisation. The elaborate artifice of this poetics became thinkable and representable as a result of the 'extraction' from the artistic image of the labouring groups who should be the potential recipients of compassion or charity. As Williams argues, by erasing from the artistic vision all traces of the underprivileged others, the privileged artist of the late eighteenth and early nineteenth centuries manages to eliminate as well his actual, shameful sentiment of condescension and indifference towards the labourers' toilsome fate. What completes the erasure is the artist's rhetorical gesture of redirecting the compassionate gaze at himself, and thus adorning the image of leisurely repose among nature, or amid his fantasies, with the aura of a metaphysical experience.

Developing the concept of extraction in *Marxism and Literature*, Williams associates it with the demise of revolutionary instinct in early nineteenth-century Romanticism. The Romantic aesthetics, which initially had been 'the most important expression in modern literature of the first impulse of revolution', definitely separates 'humanity from society', becomes irrational, and ends up 'denying its own deepest impulses or even reversing them'.[80] Extraction, separation or as Rancière would call it 'discernment' of humanity from society (of human subjects from political subjects) is therefore the one aesthetic gesture of the Romantic pastoral that apparently buries its potential for dissensus. If so, I would argue that pastoralism should be interpreted as the inaugural moment of consolidation of a laziness aesthetics that framed its relation to labour, leisure, freedom, responsibility and the environment. The echoes of this inaugural moment resound strongly in the literature of the leisure class at the end of the nineteenth century, in the reinvention of nature's experience in modernist Imagism, post-pastoral science fiction utopias and dystopias, as well as in eco-poetry of the 1970s through to the present.

If, as Lawrence Buell observed, Williams's insight 'applies with even greater force to the American pastoral tradition', so does its theorisation of idleness.[81] What we should bear in mind though is that American pastoralism has always differed from the Continental European version. Its technophiliac specificity, spelled out by Leo

Marx, and revised by Jane Tompkins, Myra Jehlen and others, highlights a whole new dimension of the pastoralist aesthetics of laziness.[82] Whereas outside of the cultural and historical context of the United States, laziness is clustered with the concept of nature, the American machine-in-the-garden convention (as identified by Leo Marx) foregrounds its relation to technology.[83] As a result of the inclusion of technology in its idyllic frame, American pastoralism may be said to have produced aesthetic forms of laziness even more coterminous with technological progress than its British counterpart.

If it seems somewhat precarious to invoke the now obsolete concept of pastoralism in the discussion of laziness, it is certainly not because of those politically problematic issues. Even the critics who question the pertinence of the pastoralist label, such as Terry Gifford, would agree that as far as structures of feeling are concerned, an inquiry into the origins of pastoralism may benefit our understanding of contemporary forms of affect, especially those involved in the performance of otiosity and repose.[84] It might, for example, makes us re-reflect upon such post-pastoral sentiments as the 'cruelly optimistic' desire for a 'good life', because this form of affective attachment relies on an extraction from its formula of such elements of reality as labour exploitation, human rights violation and surveillance of privacy that maintain its appeal.[85] The extraction concerns also the right to liberate oneself from the economy of the good life, which is replaced by the ethos of self-care and self-betterment. Recognising it as a valid desire, the biopolitical *dispositif* 'coopts it, stimulating the desire, or even prescribing it as sort of new categorical imperative'.[86]

The structure of Berlant's cruel optimism is identical with that of the pastoralist extraction of the dimension of foulness and misery as described by Williams. For just as the pastoralist fantasy of idyllic self-fulfilment amid nature exalted the pleasure principle at the expense of the reality principle, the affective paradigm of the pursuit of happiness identified by Berlant also establishes itself upon a similar fallacy. Therefore, against those who consider pastoralism an obsolete critical category, one might repeat after Scott Hess that, as a mode of experience and of fantasy, pastoralism 'has become central to our contemporary society' in the form of 'consumer pastoral', which projects the idea of fulfilment not just on to the economic elites but also on to underprivileged groups, as it 'refracts back at us' the dream of secular and sensual utopias 'through the massive proliferations of new technologies' which exclude the human from the social.[87] In that, however, the new pastoral refracts back at us also the anachronic conception of leisurely temporality which it renders ambivalent. On the one hand, idleness is something desirable and attractive; on the other, due to a centuries-long tradition of normativising forms of social uselessness and unproductivity, it is perceived as abject and degrading. In short, due to the paradigm established in pastoralism, the modern ways of thinking, representing and experiencing idleness continue to reveal 'deep and habitual forms of false consciousness'.[88]

But let us come back to Romanticism. I singled out above Irving's experiment with pastoral poetics in 'Rip Van Winkle' as inaugurating into American literature the vision of total withdrawal through the trope of laziness. Irving's gesture, I argued, seemed so particularly inspiring for other writers because it articulated the idea that literature, more than anything else, was the heterotopic space for the experience of privacy and freedom from all norms; that, as Donald Winnicott put it a hundred years later, it was a space for nurturing the empowering 'capacity to be alone' with oneself and experience this aloneness.[89] What Irving imagined was different from the pastoralist notion of a book as an 'asylum', a retreat from reality *as well as* from the space of ethical responsibility.[90] In the tranquillity of his repose, the artist acquires higher consciousness and communicates it to his readers who, finding the same tranquillity in the leisurely immersion in the imaginary world of the text, retrace the path from relaxation to sense elevation.

But it was precisely this recipe for transforming literature into a 'moral tonic', to borrow Buell's term, that Irving's vision of asylum tried to contest. The problem was, however, that in the nineteenth century – the time of the consolidation of middle-class values of industriousness and productivity, and of the subsequent waning of the institution of literary patronage that granted some degree of artistic liberty to writers – aesthetic standards were being redefined in terms of their moral value. The pastoralist mode fitted these conditions so perfectly that it became necessary for some writers to search for ways out of its paradigm. In the forthcoming pages I focus on three examples of such exploratory effort by Ralph Waldo Emerson, Walt Whitman and Herman Melville. What I wish to demonstrate is how, by returning to the Rip Van Winkle archetype and pursuing the trope of doing nothing, those writers put the all-encompassing norm of productivity into question; how they expose and dissect the flawless façade of industrious moralism; and finally, how they challenge the deceptive optimism of the concept of pastoral leisure. In different ways, Emerson, Whitman and Melville recognise in the trope of doing nothing the conceptual and poetic capacity to destabilise nineteenth-century socio-economic norms and their underlying dichotomy of productivity and unproductivity, and thus co-create the 'prototype for a revolutionary kind of citizen', a loafer 'governed by the necessity of repose'.[91]

Ralph Waldo Emerson's Philosophy of Inaction

What in Raymond Williams's terms was a moment of establishing a new affective paradigm, Jacques Rancière calls an act of *aisthesis*, which he defines as a scene of establishing a new order of the sensible. In 'The Poet of the New World (Boston, 1841–New York, 1855)', Rancière traces the inauguration of the pastoral paradigm to two texts: Ralph Waldo Emerson's 'The Poet' and Walt Whitman's *Leaves of Grass*, whose aesthetic power comes from the fact that they also transgress the paradigm of which they partake.[92] Rancière's reading ignores Lawrence Buell's admonition that pastoralism 'ought to be looked at as conservatively hegemonic rather than as dissenting from an urbanizing social mainstream', thus calibrating the pastoral perspective to illuminate the distinction between leisure and laziness.[93]

Rancière's political reading of Emerson's 'The Poet' and 'The American Scholar' focuses on the question of time and how Emerson radicalises the importance of living the present moment in the geography of the fisheries, including the spaces of Oregon and Texas, which are 'yet unsung', rather than in the paradigm of history of Troy and Delphos. In Emerson's vision of America as 'a poem in our eyes; its ample geography dazzles the imagination', Rancière sees a formulation of the 'modernist ideal, in the strong sense . . . of a new poetry of new man', which has to do with a changed perception of temporality:

> [the formulation] defines change in the poetic paradigm: the poetry of the present time breaks with a certain idea of time, one regulated by great events and rhythms inherited from the past. It finds its material no longer in historical succession, but in geographical simultaneity, in the multiplicity of activities distributed in the diverse spaces of territory. It finds its form no longer in regular meter inherited from tradition, but in the common pulse that links these activities.
>
> But one must not be mistaken: the common pulse that the new poet must make sensible in the material activities of the new world is itself entirely spiritual. The ideal of the new poet can reject refined muses, and the norm of the 'American Scholar' to call for 'the single man [who] plant[s] himself indomitably on his instincts' . . . The task of the American poet is to restore the vulgar materialities of the world of work and every-day life to the life of the mind and the whole.[94]

In other words, the new temporality is established upon the symbolic use of nature, geography and the ordinary materiality of life in order to abolish 'the distinction of low and high, honest and vile', to redeem 'all ugliness and all vulgarity'.[95]

Rancière's intervention is to highlight the distribution of unproductive activities that fashion the poetic imagination. Rereading 'The Poet' from Rancière's perspective, one discovers that the activities that stimulate poetic imagination are not necessarily farming, peddling or keeping a school, but those of disengaged relaxation. Since Emerson believes that stimulation of the instinct of imagination will open the flows 'into and through things hardest and highest', he does not seem to condemn 'any manner' of achieving this 'metamorphosis', not even the most 'vulgar' and dissipating one:

> This is the reason why bards love wine, mead, narcotics, coffee, tea, opium, the fumes of sandalwood and tobacco, or whatever other species of animal exhilaration. All men avail themselves of such means as they can, to add this extraordinary power to their normal powers; and to this end they prize conversation, music, pictures, sculpture, dancing, theatres,

travelling, war, mobs, fires, gaming, politics, or love, or science, or animal intoxication, which are several coarser or finer quasi-mechanical substitutes for the true nectar, which is the ravishment of the intellect by coming nearer to the fact. These are auxiliaries to the centrifugal tendency of a man, to his passage out into free space, and they help him to escape the custody of that body in which he is pent up, and of that jail-yard of individual relations in which he is enclosed. Hence a great number of such as were professionally expressors of Beauty, as painters, poets, musicians, and actors, have been more than others wont to lead a life of pleasure and indulgence; all but the few who received the true nectar; and, as it was a spurious mode of obtaining freedom, an emancipation not into the heavens, but into the freedom of baser places, they were punished for that advantage they won, by a dissipation and deterioration. But never can any advantage be taken of nature by a trick. The spirit of the world, the great calm presence of the creator, comes not forth to the sorceries of opium or of wine. The sublime vision comes to the pure and simple soul in a clean and chaste body. That is not an inspiration which we owe to narcotics, but some counterfeit excitement and fury.[96]

So, one way to attain imaginative powers is 'animal intoxication' and indulgent life, which so many artists ('professional' artists for that matter) practise; but even though a life of indulgence endows the mind with a sense of liberation, it eventually brings upon the artist 'dissipation and deterioration'. What deteriorates is the internal power, which instead of being conserved in the self for the sake of its 'ravishment' is expended beyond necessity. On the one hand, Emerson assents to the fact that many expressors of beauty achieve higher states of consciousness in this way, as everybody avails 'to such means as they can' – his later poem 'Bacchus', for example, delivers a straightforward affirmation of such exuberance. On the other hand, however, he would like to see the same ends achieved without the 'sorceries of opium', for fear that the sense of freedom and empowerment achieved in this way is illusory. Intoxicated languor does not really energise the 'mental flow' of imagination, because the rhythms of fake 'excitement and fury' are not in tune with the circuits of nature. The latter are more, as Emerson puts it, 'ethereal' and 'flowing'.[97] Imagination, then, has the rhythm of a 'chant', not of hyperpneic panting.[98] This Zen-like concept of imagination as a flux of sensations is developed by Emerson in 'Experience', which establishes a direct link between the experience of freedom through imagination and the idea of self-reliance (as auto-relation of the self to itself), and situates the pedagogical impulse in the experience of chant-like disengagement.[99]

Emerson writes: 'in times when we thought ourselves indolent, we have afterwards discovered, that much was accomplished, and much was begun in us', thus identifying what Anton Ehrenzweig a century later would call the power of 'unconscious scanning' and Giorgio Agamben 'the conservation of power as potentiality'.[100] In other words, according to Emerson, the work of imagination and a sense of liberation derived therefrom come from passive immersion in the 'trivial' world, which manifests itself as privation of faculty:

> By persisting to read or to think, this region [of 'trivial particulars'] gives further sign of itself, as it were in flashes of light, in sudden discoveries of its profound beauty and repose, as if the clouds that covered it parted at intervals, and showed the approaching traveller the inland mountains, with the tranquil eternal meadows spread at their base, whereon flocks graze, and shepherds pipe and dance. But every insight from this realm of thought is felt as initial . . . I do not make it; I arrive there, and behold what was there already.[101]

But perhaps the most direct assertion of passivity's power is when Emerson says that, unfortunately, neither the artist nor the scholar nor even the farmer understand that power actualised in activity is but a '*dis*-ease', a form of bodily and intellectual rigidity.[102] True power of imagination originates with a resistance to this rigidity in ease, repose and passivity.

In the standard pastoralist reading of Leo Marx and Lawrence Buell, this passage captures the characteristically liminal position of the literary subject who, poised between nature and civilisation, observes it from a distance and thus partakes of the sublime. However, Emerson's emphasis on the affective register of passivity and inaction does not necessarily suggest the amount of sensory engagement and attention that the threshold position demands. If there is any kind of pedagogical moment in 'Experience' and

'The Poet', it does not happen in the artist's appropriation of the shepherds' leisure, but in the withdrawal from it and minimalism of performance, because only in such suspension of active power does the potency of imagination manifest itself.

This poetic emphasis, according to Eve Kosofsky Sedgwick, is perhaps the closest approximation of a non-violent pedagogical position one can possibly strive for.[103] Emerson does not preach in a conventionally pastoral manner; he does not *pretend* to teach, projecting the artistic illusion of idyllic comfort on to those readers who are excluded from the order of comfortable life. Instead, he anchors the pedagogical impulse in the experience of passive inertia as a mode of reconnecting oneself with one's inner sense of freedom, which is to be differentiated from any class-determined leisure practice. Passivity is of 'extremely high value' because of rather than in spite of its 'economy of means'.[104] In this way Emerson achieves, as Rancière insists, 'a mode of presenting common things that subtracts them both from the logic of economic and social order and from the artificiality of poetic exception'.[105] There is, in Rancière's opinion, an element of political dissensus in Emerson's pedagogical logic of passivity. But how can dissent flourish from disengagement? As Gilles Deleuze and Félix Guattari would say, it would flourish by fleeing and eluding – following the trajectory of 'lines of flight' – with creativity unleashed in the state of passivity causing cracks in the system of norms and rupturing subjectivisation processes. If this is the case, then it would be interesting to juxtapose Emerson's dissent-breeding passivity with that of Charles Baudelaire, since, as has been argued, there exists a structural similarity between their views on the self *vis-à-vis* modernity.[106] Where Baudelaire proposes a mode of 'vigilant consciousness', which serves as a protective shield against stimuli, Emerson situates the opposite: a withdrawal of sensuous vigilance.[107] In other words, Baudelaire's aesthetics is the aesthetics of hyperpneic panting, which is precisely what Emerson dismisses in favour of a stabilised breath of chant-like immersion. In contrast to Baudelaire, therefore, Emerson's aesthetics of passivity hints towards the ethical-affective sphere of inactivity as the more sustainable source of self-emancipation of 'the new man' than any form of direct engagement with the newness of modernity.

Sedgwick reads Emerson's privation-based logic of self-emancipation through the lens of its direct and indirect involvement with Buddhist and Hindu teaching – a powerful impulse among many anti-Protestant Transcendentalists with a penchant for Orientalisation, such as Henry Thoreau and Elizabeth Peabody.[108] Indeed, when in 'Experience' Emerson emphasises the potential of passivising one's psychological faculties, Zen references are impossible to ignore. 'We must hold hard to this poverty', says Emerson, for the experience guarantees the 'proportion' between the two elements of human life: 'power and form'.[109] However, as Agamben demonstrates in 'The Power of Thought', the embracing of privation does not have to be understood only within a Buddhist framework. For Agamben, a similar definition of power is found in the concept of *sterēsis*, which constitutes the core of Aristotle's theory of power in *Metaphysics* and *De Anima*. In Agamben's reading, Aristotle defines 'power' not in terms of *dunamis* (the potency that becomes actualised as evidence of one's faculty), but in terms of *sterēsis*: a privation of potency whose force results precisely from it being withheld from actualisation. The essence of power, in other words, lies in the capacity *not* to pass to action. Agamben says that the potency of power comes from:

> the specific ambivalence of every human power that in its original structure maintains itself in relation to its own privation; it is always – and with respect to the same thing – power to be and not to be, to do and not to do. It is this relation that constitutes, for Aristotle, the essence of power. The living being that exists in the mode of its power is capable of its own powerlessness and only in this way possesses its own proper power . . . In power, sensation is constitutively anesthesia, thought non-thought, work worklessness . . . The greatness of [man's] power is measured against the abyss of his powerlessness.[110]

Anaesthesia, non-thought, worklessness, powerlessness – the states that offer immersion in the capacity not to do things – this is where power finds its apotheosis. True power is the condition of having the faculty but withdrawing from its usage, which is exactly what Emerson seems to have in mind when he says that power 'keeps quite another road than the turnpikes of choice and will, namely,

the subterranean and invisible tunnels and channels of life', implying that access to power is in the economy of sensual engagement
with the world with which the senses nevertheless remain in a
relation.[111] As I demonstrate below, it is precisely this understanding of power that, after Emerson, will illuminate Whitman's loafer
demeanour in *Leaves of Grass* and its aesthetics of freedom.

As for Emerson, his idea of freedom and emancipation as a product of passive attunement with the world seems remarkably consist-
ent with Aristotle's idea of power-as-privation. It is possible, says
Agamben, 'to glimpse in [Aristotle's] doctrine, in the amphibolic
nature of every power, the place in which the modern problem of
freedom may be discovered at its foundation'.[112] For the very idea
of 'freedom as a problem' is born precisely with the emergence of
the possibility of being capable to act or not to act. However, this
particular kind of freedom is more elemental than freedom in the
sense of the right to choose; it is not 'a right or a property'[113] that
one owns and/or performs. Rather, it is 'an experience that puts the
entire being of the subject in play' and 'a way of being in relation
to a *sterēsis*'.[114] Just as power is essentially based on the modality
of availability/inactivity, the idea of freedom it gives rise to simultaneously accommodates both a potential for exerting and for not
exerting power.

It is perhaps this ambivalence within the structure of power that
explains the contradictions of Emerson's idea of self-reliance. To
invoke Sedgwick again, the dominant, affirmative interpretations of
self-reliance as synonymous with self-management – and of 'Self-
Reliance' as a type of self-help manual – capture only one aspect of
the amphibological concept of power that emerges from Emerson's
writing, while ignoring the significance of passivity. Set against the
background of the idea of power-as-privation, of Foucault's power
as both *puissance* (potency) and *pouvoir* (state power), Emerson's
oscillation between the claims that power/freedom originates in
inertia and indolence and the claims that it registers in the 'plasticity' of movement and rapidity of 'transitions' does not appear to
be entirely self-defeating after all.[115] For only as long as power is
first understood as *sterēsis* can it be considered power at all, while
the vigour of *dunamis* is only the expenditure of 'steresiac' privation. The concept of power-as-privation illuminates the meaning of

Emerson's statements in 'Self-Reliance', such as 'to talk of reliance is a poor external way of speaking. Speak rather of that which relies, because it works and is', because to say that the auto-affection of the self's reliance on itself consists in active *doing* as well as in passive *being* draws attention to the importance of the privative suspension of faculty in the process of generating and maintaining power. In 'Self-Reliance' Emerson illustrates this phenomenon with an image of the excessive motion of a cat chasing its tail as opposed to motion-resisting cosmic bodies in Kepler's principle of least action, and concludes that all action, like the cat's chase, comes down to 'solitary performance', whereas attention to intrinsic resistance makes things eventually 'fall into place'.[116]

This brings us to the last observation about Emerson's idea of power and freedom in passivity, namely, his vision of the affective kinetics of contemplative repose. Emerson says that art and artists have 'no power of expansion' when they lack 'elasticity'.[117] Furthermore, however, he says that 'absence of elasticity' is accompanied by an 'immobility'.[118] Because immobility is something that thwarts the passage to power, one may speculate that the passivity of insightful repose in Emerson is somehow *not* immobile. Apparently, elasticity presupposes a mobility, as the pose of a resting body (for example, a shepherd in the field) enunciates the mobility of the mind, which 'flows' underneath the skin of the motionless corpus. Just as earlier in 'Experience', when Emerson argued that much is accomplished when the thought wanders, here too, he posits that relaxation of the muscles in the passive pose is contiguous with the flow of mental processes.

But in what does this mobility of the mind consist? According to Emerson, it involves keeping the 'proportion' between form and power: 'Human life is made up of the two elements, power and form, and the proportion must be invariably kept.'[119] In this way, elasticity denotes the manner of balancing life-energies. It is not joyous exuberance and intellectual voraciousness: in fact, it is closer to the technical meaning of elasticity in physics, where the notion, perhaps counter-intuitively, denotes resistance to change and deformation. On the one hand, therefore, the elastic nature of passive languor in Emerson evinces the technological dominant of his pastoral poetics, but on the other hand, and more importantly, it indicates the mode of power-as-resistance that passivity activates.[120] It is in this definition of power that Stanley Cavell came to recognise the locus of Emerson's ethics, which seems to echo closely the Stoic idea of ethics as *epimeleia heatou*, the 'care of oneself'.[121] In Cavell's view, Emerson's philosophy of self-reliance is all about 'the mode of the self's relation to itself' in pursuit of superpersonal wisdom.[122] Therefore, from the perspective of pastoral pedagogy, to read Emerson's aestheticisation of resistance as passive-elastic repose as an ethical formula is to challenge the views of Williams and Buell about the reactionary ideology of the pastoral frame. For in the instances of Emerson's vision of passivity, the encouragement to access resistance through ease – to 'plant' oneself 'indomitably' on one's instincts – gestures towards an aesthetics of dissensus, a situation where two conflicting regimes of sense, the trivial and the pedagogical, are brought together in a way that ruptures their cause and effect relation, unlocking the potential of social change.[123] To approximate an aesthetic of dissensus is not the same as to actualise its potential, but Emerson's vision spells out the affective region which needs to be nurtured in pursuit of dissensus.

Walt Whitman's Poetics of Loafing

In the context of the American Renaissance, the connection between dissensus and passivity instantly brings to mind Henry David Thoreau's 'Civil Disobedience' (1849) and *Walden* (1854). But it may be argued that Thoreau's entire project – however militant against the norms of productivity and bourgeois morality and supportive of the vision of private freedom – bypasses the aesthetic dilemma of his contemporaries, in that Thoreau literally builds a heterotopic realm rather than exploring the trope. In that he is a true dissenter, of course, but not necessarily a contributor to the trope of idleness. Furthermore, as some critics argue, *Walden* does not render dissent in terms of withdrawal of life-energies: Thoreau may be watching bullfrogs all day or report having done a lot of sitting, but he will never admit to lassitude, associating it with insensibility that obstructs the ethical process of self-development.[124]

The one writer who decidedly foregrounds the connection between passive laxation and indomitability, who brings together

Emerson's ideas of life's trivialities, elasticity and power to resist, and does so without being afraid to subsume them under the barbaric name of 'loafing', is Walt Whitman. That loafing serves as the conceptual core of Whitman's performativity was affirmed by the poet himself at the end of his career, when in 'Backward Glance On My Own Road' (1884) he wrote that the most important trait of the poet is 'the spirit he brings to the observation of humanity and nature – the mood out of which he contemplates his subjects'.[125] Whitman's mood, as he would define it, would be that of 'physiological', 'leisurely absorbency', a sensuous immersion which would have to be 'suggestive' enough to 'dominate in the reader as it does in the book', to make the reader re-enact the mood.[126]

'Glancing backward' at Leaves of Grass, Whitman's critics, especially in the gay-identitarian interpretations of his body politics, certainly emphasise his effort at suggestiveness.[127] However, the passage from sexuality to politics in those readings leaves out the dissensual potential of the lazy mood and its 'uniform hieroglyphic'. By way of omission, the slippage in body-political readings nevertheless maps the conceptual terrain of passive repose as a 'gap in the fabric of common experience that changes the cartography of the perceptible, the thinkable and the feasible'.[128] In Rancière's terms, Whitman's aesthetics of loafing is the aesthetics of dissensus, for it stages the conflict inherent in the very idea of democracy while working within the convention of democratic discourse. Echoing Foucault on self-governance and Adorno on mediation, Rancière claims that although the conflict, or paradox, of politics in general and democracy in particular is that its idea of freedom excludes the possibility of (democratic) government of free people, aesthetic forms enable a transformative intervention into politics, because their performance of the conflict creates the possibility for a redistribution of ways of thinking and feeling within the operating norms of the sensible.[129]

In the case of Leaves of Grass, the redistribution takes on a very literal form of catalogues and ellipses as well as the rearrangement of parts, additions and changes in the subsequent editions of the book. Whitman pins down what Rancière calls the paradox of democracy with remarkable frankness, all in one breath: 'I speak the password primeval . . . I give a sign of democracy / By God! I will accept nothing which all cannot have their counterpart of on the same terms', thus enunciating the position of disagreement *vis-à-vis* the order of politics.[130] Finally, the disagreement and the new mode of the sensible is partitioned among the poem's contradictions: while in 'The Song of Myself', democracy is the 'password primeval', and in the later added 'Calamus' poem, 'For You O Democracy' (1860), democracy (with a capital D) is a 'femme' whom the speaker 'serves', in 'Great are the Myths' (1900) Whitman celebrates the 'throes' and 'falls of democracy'.[131] The passage at the end of this section aptly captures those contradictions:

> Great is Law . . . Great are the old few landmarks of the law . . . they are the same in all times, and shall not be disturbed.
> Great are marriage, commerce, newspapers, books, freetrade, railroads, steamers, international mails, and telegraphs, and exchanges.
> Great is Justice;
> Justice is not settled by legislators and laws – it is in the soul,
> It cannot be varied by statutes, any more than love or pride or the attraction of gravity can,
> It is immutable . . . it does not depend on majorities . . . majorities or what not come at last before the same passionless and exact tribunal
> . . .
> Great is wickedness . . . I find I often admire it just as much as I admire goodness:
> Do you call that a paradox? It certainly is a paradox.[132]

But whereas these lines terminate *Leaves of Grass*, the general frame for Whitman's ethico-political project is established in the opening pages of the book. On the one hand, there is the image of the poet with his arms folded. On the other, there stand the famous 'suggestive' lines: 'I loafe and invite my soul, / I lean and loafe at my ease . . . observing a spear of summer grass'.[133] The gestural economy of loafing thus unfolds as a sequence of crossing the arms, leaning and sauntering, which is to be 'assumed' by Whitman's readers. The folding of the arms, soon to be taken up by the socialist and anti-work movement's poster art at the end of Whitman's century, does not simply represent abstention from work and going on strike, so to speak. It also harks back to one of the oldest Judeo-

Christian renditions of laziness as simultaneous auto-protection and auto-destruction: 'the fool folds his arms together and eats his own flesh'.[134] As Nili Wazana points out, the gesture of the folding of arms in the biblical tradition combines the opposites of self-protective, even affectionate embrace and the abject, auto-cannibalistic impulse to abstain from labour and thus starve oneself to death.[135] This combines the stigmatising warning against laziness as well as the advice to protect oneself against excessive work.

There is, therefore, an inherent immanence in the gesture of folding the arms between the impulse to disengage from activity and the impulse to test the limits of one's endurance in passive withdrawal. While the biblical script may underlie Western culture's proscription of laziness as obscenity – auto-cannibalism being its most drastic representation – and while it may have incited accusations of indecency and vulgarity among Whitman's readers, it certainly does not operate in his poem on any direct intertextual level[136] – or at least, not in the manner in which it is employed in Melville's pastoral visit to the valley of the leisurely cannibals in *Typee*, which I discuss in the next section, where the immanence of the auto-cannibalistic gesture becomes the central pastoral trope.

Whitman's own interpretation of the picture of 'Me-Myself' is as follows:

Apart from the pulling and hauling stands what I am,
Stands amused, complacent, compassionating, idle, unitary,
Looks down, is erect, bends an arm on an impalpable certain rest,
Looks with its sidecurved head curious what will come next,
Both in and out of the game, and watching and wondering at it.[137]

Thus, whatever the cultural script that controls the perception of loafing in Western culture, Whitman disables it with an invitation to unfold the arms and rest at ease. As a result, his 'Me-myself' is not the only one to 'lay' on the grass or in bed, or to have his 'elbows rest in sea-gaps'.[138] The unfolding of arms recurs in a succession of arms embracing his comrades and hugging lovers, arms protecting families and pointing to landscapes, arms stretching out in salutation, swimmers' arms leisurely ploughing water, as well as arms receiving a newborn child. The gesture is also reiterated in the image of the farmer contemplating his oats or when 'the girl and the wife rest the needle a moment and forget where they are'. In the manner of 'an impalpable certain rest', says Whitman, bodies become *un-disciplined*, in the Foucauldian sense of the term:[139]

> My ties and ballasts leave me, my elbows rest in sea-gaps,
> I skirt sierras, my palms cover continents,
> I am afoot with my vision.[140]

In other words, not only does the suspension of faculty in the experience of loafing release this faculty from the disciplining regime of labour and reunite the self with its surrounding environment, but it also unlocks the potential for power-as-*puissance*. Whitman's 'vision' is of the availability of power – the power to counteract and be free from *pouvoir* – to all: the lunatic, the express-wagon driver, the prostitute and the child.[141] But given Whitman's ambivalent representations of democracy, the expression 'availability of power to all' may not be entirely synonymous with the affirmation of democratic forms of government. If *Leaves of Grass* is read as an instance of the aesthetics of dissensus, a staging of a conflict, and if dissensus is the primary form of political thinking, then Whitman's politics of loafing can be compared to the politics of philosophical truth telling (*parrhēsia*) practised by the Ancient Cynics.

Explaining the concept of *parrhēsia* in the context of politics in his 1983 lectures on *The Government of the Self and Others*, Foucault paraphrases Epictetus's passage on the Cynics from *Discourses*. The Cynic:

> is someone who detaches himself from all artifice and ornament. He is someone who detaches himself from everything pertaining to the passions. Above all, he is someone who does not seek to conceal his desires, passions, dependencies, etcetera, but who presents himself naked, in his destitution . . . He will display his indecency in his nudity and in the open . . . The second characteristic of the Cynic . . . is the fact that to tell the truth he is ready to address even the powerful . . . Epictetus comments: 'In reality, the Cynic is a scout for men, finding out what is favorable to them and what is hostile . . . without letting himself be . . . paralyzed by fear.'[142]

An example of this attitude is Diogenes, whom Whitman resembles in his bold acts of loafing and singing himself. One instance of Diogenes' philosophical *praxis* is the famous story of him addressing the powerful king Alexander the Great with fearless self-confidence. Responding to Alexander's words 'I am Alexander, the king', Diogenes said 'And I am Diogenes, the dog', thus performing what Foucault understands as an enunciation of political power in the act of philosophical truth-telling:

> The philosophical *parrhēsia* of Diogenes basically in showing himself in his natural nakedness, outside all the conventions of and laws artificially imposed by the city . . . That is to say, with regard to the power that on one side he accepts, he feels free to say frankly and violently what he is, what he wants, what he needs, what is true and false, what is just and unjust. [It is] a game of philosophical *parrhēsia* . . . a mode of connection of philosophical truth-telling to political action which takes place in the form of exteriority, challenge, and derision.[143]

In the context of Foucault's reading of the Cynical stance, Whitman's embracing of his passions, his loafing – or 'buoyancy' and 'animality' as the poet retrospectively calls it in 'Backward Glance' – reciprocate Diogenes' *parrhēsiatic* assertion of indomitability with respect to organised power structures.[144] Just like Diogenes, the subject of Whitman's poem is a 'scout for men' who celebrates himself and asserts the truth of his emancipated self by performing the contradictions of the discourse he inhabits. That the form of this performance is the lounging pose is only logical insofar as dissensus can only be asserted and transmitted via affects that do not normally find their place in the social frame. In Rancière's terms, it is only by activating such deviant affects that the field of the sensible may be open for the creation of dissensual subject positions. As he puts it in *Disagreement*, dissensual subject positions are produced 'through a series of actions of a body and a capacity for enunciation not previously identifiable within a given field of experience, whose identification is thus a part of the reconfiguration of the field of experience'.[145] Whitman's buoyant loafing does precisely that: it identifies the potential of loafing which has not been previously intelligible, and via aesthetic means changes the parameters of the field of experience. While in his piece from the Brooklyn *Evening Star* of 10 October 1845 he scorns his tobacco-chewing, obscenity-speaking, loafing readers,[146] in *Leaves of Grass* he recalibrates the aesthetic lens to expose the emancipatory potential of the loafing pose.

'I pronounce openly for a new distribution of roles', says Whitman in 'Respondez!', a poem added to *Leaves of Grass* in the 1871–72 edition. In his post-Civil War lexicon, the rule for dissensus (or what Foucault calls the game of philosophical *parrhēsia*) becomes fully articulated as (re)distribution and 'transposition'. Not only does 'Respondez!' play with Diogenes' legacy: 'Let us all, without missing one, be exposed in public, naked, monthly, at the peril of our lives! / let our bodies be freely handled and examined by whoever chooses!' – but it also expands the legacy with an invitation to a mass carnival of social roles:

> Let judges and criminals be transposed! let the prison-keepers be put in
>   prison! let those that were prisoners take the keys! Say! why might
>   they not just as well be transposed?
> Let the slaves be masters! let the masters become slaves!
> Let the reformers descend from the stands where they are forever bawling!
>   let an idiot or insane person appear on each of the stands![147]

With its anarchic claims, 'Respondez!' may well fit the 'genre of manifesto art' whose distinctiveness, according to Martin Puchner, is measured by the 'preposterousness' of its claims.[148] However, in the context of 'Backward Glance', Whitman's poetics of excess calls for a different reading, which assumes a different vision of politics than the discernment-based logic assumed in manifestos. Whitman's transpositions appear to be exercises in emancipation, testing the status of equality and the rules of social discernment. All in all, therefore, and unlike manifesto art, *Leaves of Grass* is not a political programme, nor a rational pedagogical stance, but rather a performance of puissance *in relation* to political action, a generic form of the aesthetics of dissensus. If the idea of manifesto can be invoked in relation to Whitman at all, it is perhaps only because of the appropriation of his figure of the Cynical loafer by Paul Lafargue in *The Right to be Lazy* (1883).[149] After all, the opening image of Lafargue's pamphlet features a Whitmanesque reinvention of the Cynic, an indomitable beggar who 'straight and flexible as a steel rod . . . and superbly draped in his ragged *capa*, parley[s] on terms of equality with the duke of Ossuna'.[150]

Herman Melville's Haptic Style in *Typee*

In a lecture 'Against Self-Criticism', the psychoanalyst Adam Phillips revisits Freud's reading of *Hamlet* and the concepts of conscience and superego to talk about their mutilating and deforming impact on our identity. As Hamlet's eloquent and subtle battle with his conscience and the consciences of others in Shakespeare's play illustrates – 'thus conscience does make cowards of us all / And thus the native hue of resolution / Is sicklied o'er with the pale cast of thought' – conscience 'obscures self-knowledge' and 'this allows us to think it is complicitous not to stand up to the internal tyranny of what is only one part – a small but loud part – of the self. So frightened are we by the super-ego that we identify with it: we speak on its behalf to avoid antagonising it (complicity is delegated bullying).'[151] In short, we lose our agency. Arguing against this kind of relentless self-reproach, Phillips says that we should turn to literature, which is perhaps *the* place where, through 'dialogues with and around self-criticism', conscience can be 'caught', for catching conscience is one of the most imaginative things we can do. Phillips insists on the importance of 'catching', for which the OED has 'to seize or take hold of, to ensnare, to deceive, to surprise, to take, to intercept, to seize by the senses or intellect, to apprehend'. If literature can do that, then it can also expose the cowardly conscience that poses itself as a tyrant king. It can be a place of regaining and redefining the sense of agency.

One way of doing this, as exemplified by Hamlet, is to think about experiences one has never had before: suicide and death. Another may be to address those limit experiences about which the voice of conscience is equally if not more decisively vigilant, such as the experience of laziness. When Herman Melville debuted in 1846 with his novelistic fantasy about repose entitled *Typee*, he might have been motivated by precisely this impulse: to catch and expose his epoch's conscience and its modes of stigmatising unwanted and counter-productive behaviour. This fictionalised account of Melville's own voyage[152] to the Marquesas archipelago is summarised by the narrator in the following words:

> Now, when the scientific voyager arrives at home with his collection of wonders, he attempts, perhaps, to give a description of some of the strange people he has been visiting. Instead of representing them as a community of lusty savages, who are leading a merry, idle, innocent life, he enters into a very circumstantial and learned narrative of certain unaccountable superstitions and practices, about which he knows as little as the islanders do themselves. Having had little time, and scarcely any opportunity, to become acquainted with the customs he pretends to describe, he writes them down one after another in an off-hand haphazard style . . .
>
> For my own part, I am free to confess my almost entire inability to gratify any curiosity that may be felt with regard to the theology of the valley, I doubt whether the inhabitants themselves could do so. They are either too lazy or too sensible to worry themselves about abstract points of religious belief. While I was among them, they never held any synods or councils to settle the principles of their faith by agitating them. An unbounded liberty of conscience seemed to prevail.[153]

If the narrator of *Typee* only could, he would have described the Taipis and their merry, idle and innocent mode of life without passing judgement. But such a celebratory way of contemplation is somehow unattainable by the literary means at his disposal. They would, as he says in the Preface, 'appear strange, or perhaps entirely incomprehensible'.[154] All he can do is enter a dialogue with his own 'circumstantial' conscience and the 'learned' consciences of others, which warp his initial impressions. Inasmuch as he is bullied by those acquired narrative modes, inherited together with the Protestant work ethic, he holds on to the minimum of freedom to at least abstain from judging the beliefs of the Marquesans, who seemed either 'too lazy or too sensible to worry' about arbitrary laws that would control their mode of living. He may not have captured their customs correctly, but he has at least understood one thing: the only law in the Taipi valley – the one worthy of deep reflection – has been the 'unbounded liberty of conscience'.

It is this fascination with the Marquesan freedom of conscience that underlies the anarchic, multi-genre narrative strategy
of *Typee*, where the pastoral sides with the grotesque, the grim
refrain of the cannibal threat with the satirical exaggeration thereof,
the quasi-ethnographic tone with meditations on its artificiality, the cultural critique of Western imperialism with nods towards
the voyeuristic tastes of the popular public. Put otherwise, *Typee*'s
stylistic 'mess', as John Bryant calls it, might be read as Melville's
quarrel with the Western civilised conscience. Staged in the pastoral
idyll of the island of Nuku Hiva, Melville's literary debate with his
era is aimed at challenging the mid-nineteenth-century normative
restrictions on the freedom of agency and imagining what it would
be like to lift their tyranny.

Should one, Melville seems to be asking, be like the Taipis: lazy
and carefree? Is inactivity the only way to think outside of external norms or their internalised form that we call conscience? Is
it immoral and cowardly? Or does it perhaps inaugurate a radically different, non-normative sort of morality and a radically
non-normative sort of prowess? Laziness, cowardice and norm-
transgression are the themes through which *Typee* explores the limits
of Western conscience. In these topoi Melville discovers a style of
relating to himself and to the readers 'in which praise and blame
are not the only currency', where freedom from conscience can be
approximated and the dogma of univocal morality suspended.[155]

In his review of *Typee*, Nathaniel Hawthorne said that Melville's
writing is unique because it 'has that freedom of view'. D. H.
Lawrence added that what is good about Melville in *Typee* is that
'he never repents', even if that which he has to say stands against
all the values of his epoch.[156] Finally, more than seventy years later,
Myra Jehlen emphasised in her introduction to a 1994 collection
on Melville the 'particularly penetrating way of seeing his world' in
Typee, a way that goes past so many seemingly insurmountable conventions.[157] Indeed, it seems that the exploration of the tabooed
low theme of laziness and its relation to notions of cowardice and
moral ambivalence allowed Melville to create in *Typee* a literary
space in which the ontological problem of self-constraining mechanisms could be explored alongside the political critique of the
Western colonial episteme. Or, to phrase it differently, the theme

made it possible for Melville to perform a self-examination – a dialogue with his conscience, if you will – and capture through its lens the entire spectrum of the nineteenth century's unproductivity. On the one hand, the motif of loafing opens a way to think resistance to nineteenth-century socio-economic norms, but on the other, it denotes a less transformative kind of passivity, namely the intellectual inertness of his Victorian-minded readers, which admits moral beliefs 'merely because it is a custom' and thus serves as 'the preconditions for morality'.[158] In short, it structures *Typee's* aesthetics of laziness, which opens up space for rethinking Western moral norms and the limits of democratic freedom.

The historian of laziness Tom Lutz has dubbed *Typee* 'one of the most significant paeans to slackerdom ever produced'.[159] Paean is probably too strong a word. This appraisal is also much too triumphant, given that the original reception of the novel was not even half as enthusiastic. In terms of genre, *Typee* is a mixture of autobiography and travelogue account of life among the natives of the Marquesan island of Nuku Hiva. It was first published in 1846 in London as the non-fictional *Narrative of a Four Months' Residence Among the Natives of the Marquesas Islands: A Peep at Polynesian Life.* After the book failed to receive favourable reviews, it took the inventiveness of Melville's New York publishers to relaunch *Narrative* as a work of fiction, this time under the title *Typee: A Peep at Polynesian Life,* which was supposed to make the story more attractive to the nineteenth-century public. Using a strategy reminiscent of 'The Story of Sloth', an erotic vignette dressed up as a didactic tale, the publishers wanted to advertise its voyeuristic dimensions. The effort paid off, as *Typee* was popular among the reading public and upset the reviewers, who considered it, to use the words of Horace Greeley, 'unmistakably defective if not positively diseased in moral tone' as well as 'dangerous for those of immature intellects and unsettled principles'.[160] The publishers' strategic emphasis on the scandalous elements of Melville's story, underscored by the voyeuristic 'peep' in the title, brought the novel much-needed controversy as well as popular success, but at the same time it diverted his contemporaries' attention from *Typee's* ethico-political and existential dimensions. For while the novel features elaborate descriptions of naked or half-naked bodies and draws its momentum from the motif of dreading the cannibal Other, it in no way celebrates the 'peeping', Orientalist perspective.

Neither is it a straightforward travel narrative. As has been estab-lished by historians, Melville may not have spent as much time on Nuku Hiva as he declared (it was four weeks rather than four months), and he may have collaged his narrative out of fragments of early nineteenth-century travelogues such as David Porter's *Journal of a Cruise Made to the Pacific Ocean* (1815, 1822); but in the three years that passed between his travel to the Marquesan archipelago in 1842 and the completion of *Typee*'s manuscript, he had enough time and retrospection to devise a narrative which, in the words of Greg Dening, 'was not history or autobiography but significant narrative'.[161] John Bryant's challenge to the archeological approach is even stronger: 'whether Melville fabricated a little or a lot in relating those steps is merely a quantitative question subordinate to the larger problem of where in the text fact blends with fiction, where Melville fabricates and *to what end*'.[162]

By and large, twentieth-century literary critics of Melville tend to embrace Bryant's view and agree that, despite its ambivalences, *Typee* is primarily a postcolonial critique of Western claims to cultural domination, as well as a political meditation on the issue of slav-ery. Within this critical framework, Melville's story of a white man's captivity in the Taipi valley is viewed as an instance of ideological commentary on colonisation, bondage and labour exploitation by means of pastoralist aesthetics. The idyllic setting of the Marquesas admits the runaway sailor who, while never losing the perspective of his 'civilisation', achieves a level of political awareness of his fears and prejudices, and redefines his understanding of culture, barbarity, norm and freedom. In the words of Geoffrey Sanborn, 'the only reason Melville identifies himself with the Orientalist desire of his readers is so that he can bring them to see, in the failure of his voyeuristic desire, the failure of theirs'.[163] Persuasive as they are, however, the political readings of *Typee* sometimes lose sight of the fact that as an aesthetic act it is capable of more than an ide-ological critique of reality and reaches beyond the praise-or-blame paradigm. Part of *Typee*'s aesthetic work in this respect seems to be performed through the narrative tension between unproductivity as the novel's theme and productivity as its textual condition. In this sense, *Typee* is not simply a paean to slackerdom, but an autotelic meditation on the limits of agency and (bio)political pedagogy.

One study in which the significance of unproductivity in Melville's style has been acknowledged is John Bryant's *Melville and Repose*. Bryant's general argument is that Melville's poetics is established upon the concept of passive repose, understood along Emerson's lines as a self-reflexive experience in which the mind suspends awareness in order to achieve 'higher, benevolent authority'.[164] In Bryant's phrasing, repose 'is a halfway sensibility that is conscious of Ideality but nevertheless fatally rooted in Actuality . . . a liminal state which conjoins sensibility and sublime', and therefore affords a high degree of philosophical and political self-reflexivity.[165] As Bryant puts it, *Typee* may well be a self-contradicting, 'formless mess', but through the aesthetics of repose it becomes 'an event' which stages 'a political *cri de conscience* against Imperialism'.[166] As long as Bryant understands an 'event' in Alan Badiou's terms, as a rupture in being, then the claim that an aesthetics of repose may perform a political event resonates with Melville's ironic disclaimer that *Typee* is written 'in an off-hand haphazard style', against the pressures of 'circumstantial and learned narrative' strategies. There is nothing off-hand or haphazard about *Typee*, but the fact that it seems so – that it ruptures both 'authentic' and 'learned' conventions from within – allows us to call it a political event. For, in Badiou's logic, an act or a gesture may be considered an event – a cry of truth, a rupture in being – only if it ruptures as well the very idea of moral and political principality of *cris de conscience*. I would go even further than Bryant to suggest that in *Typee*, Melville imagines a world where the logic of cries of conscience is replaced by cries of desire, in the sense that his ideological reflection on biopolitical norms incorporates a reflection on the biological body – the biological body in terms of its sexuality *and* more generally in terms of its counter-disciplinary potential.

The formless mess of *Typee*, which I would rather call, borrowing Samuel Otter's term, the poetics of 'corporeal excess', is Melville's aesthetic strategy of suspending within the novel's literary subject the disciplining norms and hierarchies that found its identity[167] – the hierarchies of social discernment into those who have conscience and therefore the right to pass judgements and those who seem to live without it: that is, those who subordinate bodies to the norm and those who use them performatively for the sake of norm transgression. The aim of this aesthetic tactic is to explore the intersection of the symbolic, the corporeal and the political within the structure of nineteenth-century social norms.

Unlike Melville's later work, the body in his debut novel is not a symbolic body, but a real, tactile site of agency with a natural impulse to resist the apparatus of social and ideological normatisation. Undeniably, literary attempts to grasp biological corporeality are exercises in impossibility – one of the reasons why texts that do so will always be 'messy' – but as the remainder of this chapter demonstrates, Melville's *Typee* makes this ambitious attempt and succeeds in it by employing the theme of laziness.

Laziness and the Shaming Gaze of the Evil Eye

Laziness begins to permeate the atmosphere of *Typee* from the beginning, for its appearance coincides with the ship's entry into the Marquesan waters. Melville's narrator, Tommo, describes it in the following way:

> What a delightful, lazy, languid time we had whilst we were gliding along! There was nothing to be done; a circumstance that happily suited our disinclination to do anything. We abandoned the fore-peak altogether, and spreading an awning over the forecastle, slept, ate, and lounged under it the live-long day. Every one seemed under the influence of some narcotic. Even the officers aft, whose duty required them never to be seated while keeping a deck watch, vainly endeavored to keep on their pins; and were obliged invariably to compromise the matter by leaning up against the bulwarks, and gazing abstractedly over the side. Reading was out of the question; take a book in your hand, and you were asleep in an instant.[168]

With this description, *Typee* harks back to the Shakespearean pastoral image of lazy time by denoting a delightful, languid temporality, a mood that hangs in the air, putting a spell upon the minds of the sailors, in a vague premonition of the leisurely lifestyle that Tommo will later discover among the Marquesans. The lazy temporality does not spare anyone, even the officers, who do not feel like doing anything whatsoever, having been exhausted by 'the last eighteen or twenty days' of the whale chase.[169]

The opening passage belongs among the aesthetic edifices of Melville's generic recollections of the Marquesas, which is emphasised by the 'purely touristic'[170] gaze introduced in the next sentence: 'Although I could not avoid yielding in a great measure to the general languor, still at times I contrived to shake off the spell, and to appreciate the beauty of the scene around me.'[171] The touristic gaze wanders down from 'the clear expanse of the sky' to 'the long, measured, dirge-like swell of the Pacific', the 'impressive silence', and registers here and there 'the flying fish' or 'the superb albacore'. Its aestheticising lens captures even that which the eye of the lounging sailor would not be able to spot: 'a monster of the deep', 'a whale' and, last but not least, a 'prowling shark, that villainous footpad of the seas, [who] would come skulking along, and, at a wary distance, regards us with his evil eye'.[172]

Innocent or 'touristic' as the opening passage may seem, its juxtaposition of languid laziness on the one hand and predatory shark on the other offers a miniature version, a *mise en abyme* so to speak, of the conflict between peaceful leisure and the danger of being eaten by cannibals, the conflict that will control the entire narrative of *Typee*. In the light of Sanborn's idea that Melville creates and identifies with the pastoral Orientalist gaze only to make his readers follow him towards the failure of the voyeuristic desire that motivates the gaze, we might concentrate for a moment on the ideological optics of that gaze which circumvents the beauty of the Marquesas as well as the evil eye of the shark. The question to be addressed is, if the shark's 'evil eye' is something that the narrator of *Typee* cannot really see, then why does Melville make his narrator fantasise about interlocking gazes with evil? Is there a relation between his fear of the evil eye and his languorous state?

The answer to these questions is prompted by Silvan Tomkins's explanation of the cultural taboo of the evil eye in *Affect, Imagery, Consciousness*. For Tomkins, evil eyeing is all about shame as an affective state, which bears interesting consequences for our understanding of Melville's opening scene as well as the entire affective economy of *Typee*. Tomkins argues that the idea of the evil eye and the fantasy of interocular intimacy are part and parcel of the affective mechanism that governs the expression of shame and the subsequent conscientious behaviour on the part of the subject. Crucially for our reading of the interlocking gazes of Tommo and the shark, Tomkins's discussion of the link between the evil eye taboo and shame begins with an emphasis on the role of the optic system in the formation of one's affective reactions in general:

> No other of [the human] receptor systems provides such continuous and abundant information as the optic system. In this wealth of information it receives and also sends messages concerning the affects. The movements of the eyes and the musculature surrounding the eyes express and communicate joy, excitement, fear, distress, anger and shame. So the eye receives affective displays not only from the face of the other but also from the eyes of the other, and at the same time one's own eyes and face communicate affect to the other. It is this rich, two-way, simultaneous transmission and reception which make man the most voyeuristic of animals.[173]

Since humans are the most voyeuristic of all animals, Tomkins intimates, it is primarily through ocular contact that they become aware of one another. Only in this way can a human being express his affects, register the awareness of those affects in the other, and respond to this awareness. And since the eyes are where mutual awareness originates, the interocular interaction appears to be the most intimate form of contact: 'it is an incomplete intimacy when one is looked at, without seeing the other, or when one looks at the other without being looked at'.[174] And as there is no greater intimacy than the one achieved in interocular exchange, this intimacy 'results in a universal taboo on direct mutual looking', which is primary to any taboo on sexual intimacy.[175]

According to Tomkins, the oldest expression of the taboo on 'shared interocular intimacy' is the idea of the evil eye, that is, the eye whose reflective emanation corrupts, and inflicts diseases and malaise of the soul:

> The most ancient and universal belief is that the eye of an evil one will injure wherever its gaze happens to fall. This force may emanate from

the eyes of animals, demons, even from the painted or sculptured eyes of inanimate objects, as well as from the eyes of human beings.[176]

The persistence of the belief in the evil eye up until the late twentieth century leads Tomkins to assume that the taboo on mutual looking is in fact not only primary to, but also 'more stringent' than the taboo enforced on sexuality.[177] The fact has to do with the affective reaction that activates the taboo on intimacy, namely, the expression of the shame of looking and being looked at:

> Although shame is innately produced by the incomplete reduction of the positive affects of interest and enjoyment, through learning one can be taught to be ashamed of the witnessing or expression of any affect. Since . . . the eyes not only can witness any affect in the face of the other but also express one's own affect to the other, and since this can be a shared experience, interocular intimacy becomes the occasion, for the adult, of experiencing shame about any affect. Given any restraint on the expression of any affect, when such restraint is not completely accepted, then complete interocular freedom must evoke shame, since the residual wish to look, to exchange affect, will also come under inhibition.[178]

The fear of the evil eye is thus an expression of shame derived from inhibiting the enjoyment in looking, from the suppression of a wish to look and be looked at. Tomkins says that we 'are all necessarily would-be both voyeurs and exhibitionists of all those affects we are inhibited in expressing, witnessing, and sharing'.[179]

It is precisely the logic of the voyeuristic–exhibitionist wish to look and be looked at that informs Melville's hyper-aestheticised description of Tommo's fantasy of interocular exchange with the evil-eyed shark in the second chapter of *Typee*.[180] Tommo imagines being observed while enjoying the lazy, languid hours on the ship. Because he feels ashamed and guilty about his languorous disposition, the terrifying consequences of his laziness assume the fantastic form of a predatory animal.

In Tomkins's terms, the source of Tommo's shame is the ambivalence of the 'I want but–' attitude which organises his simultaneous desire to give in to laziness as well as the 'contrivance to shake off [its] spell'. Not only does the wish establish the pattern for

Tommo's responses to the nudity of the Taipis later in the novel, but most importantly it sets the pattern for his relationship with his readers, which from the laziness episode onwards will follow the dynamics of the taboo on shared interocular intimacy. On the one hand, the narrator will wish to be looked at as he partakes of the leisurely life of the Taipis, but on the other, the shame of being observed in this context will dictate his regular, intrusive, moralistic outbursts or self-admonitions about the horror of cannibalism.[181]

That this dynamics of shaming gazes is first established with reference to the lazy time on the *Dolly*, Tommo's worksite, is not a coincidence, because the logic of 'I want, but–' which conditions all expressions of shame is also the logic of normativised responses to laziness in Western culture. Indeed, Tomkins links the two as he observes that one's relation to work and worklessness is one of the most basic contexts for the emergence of shame.[182] In his account of how the taboo of the evil eye has persisted into modern times, he gives numerous instances of this relation – one as late as the example of a 1957 Associated Press dispatch from a labour-racket investigating committee, which mentions hiring a person for the purpose of 'glaring' at the employees at work in order to keep them busy.[183] The impulse to be unproductive, as the example illustrates, appears therefore to be one of the wishes that universally attract the shaming glance of the evil eye.

The Optic versus the Haptic

The interocular exchange with the evil eye of the shark organises the first tension in Melville's *Typee*. On the one hand, there is the intimidating force of the ocular vision; on the other, the liberating force of the haptic as experienced in the pose of laxation. Against the claims of modern affect psychology, which privileges the optic system as the most important mechanism in relating to others and to oneself, Melville associates the sense of vision with normative oppressiveness. A gaze is always essentially a shaming gesture and in that way it is oppressive. If it does bring a sense of awareness and identity, this identity is always already pre-formed, imposing and reductive. Thus, anticipating by over a century Lacan's concept of the self-alienating gaze and Foucault's analysis of power gazes in 'Las

Meninas' (1966), Melville reserves the 'ocularocentric' poetics in *Typee* to represent normativised perception of the Western eye that Tommo desires to escape.[184] From the first scene in the book to the last, looking and being looked at trope conventionality, bigotry and prejudice. And it is by references to looking that the narrator communicates his own biases and sense of imprisonment within the norm as well as puncturing the biases of his audience.

Needless to say, such a totalising tropological scheme causes certain problems on the level of the main character's integrity, inasmuch as he would desire not to, but has to resort to the apparatus of vision. Hence, the confusing accounts of Tommo praising laziness in order to then condemn it, wanting to be freed from the norm that organises the relation between productivity and unproductivity and fearing the loss of identity that such liberation would effectuate, desiring to plunge into 'unrestrained liberty of conscience' but 'satisfying' his 'curiosity by gazing at the scene'.[185] Mitchell Breitwieser associates Tommo's curiosity with 'self-absorption', which delays the description of the Marquesans until the second quarter of the book, thus indicating that the real object of Melville's interest is the Western gaze rather than the Taipis. But what is more interesting to him is his own participation in the gaze, 'the idea that the root of colonialism is so deep that even an apparent rebel may turn out to be an agent'.[186] I will come back to this point in the following pages, but first let me signal the second mode in which *Typee* signifies: namely, the mode of the haptic as it colludes with the ocular.

Significantly, Tommo's cries of desire to go against the moral and political principality of his culture are mediated by references to the sense of touch. Languor signifies his attunement with himself and with his surroundings. Although it is frequently interrupted by the intrusions of the optic, the kinaesthetic mode of lazy passivity is delivered via excessively long descriptions of lax bodies and sprawling landscapes. Melville's idea that the haptic sense is not inferior but equally if not more potent and fundamental to the human sense of self can be confirmed by contemporary scientific findings into proprioception, which prove that skin, the organ of touch, is more than a mere envelope for the sensory system controlled by the brain, but is instead an independently processing structure in its own right, our 'second brain', so to speak, which contributes to our sense of who we are. Consequently, while a body may seem inert or immobile, much is accomplished on the subcutaneous level of the organism, calibrating its attention, threshold of perception, positioning in space and sense of integrity. The intricate and complex haptic system located in the skin appears to be an alternative mode of negotiating our identity, and certainly a way of renegotiating the identity produced optically. Although Melville's scientific imagination may not have been as detailed, the way he employs touch and skin as metaphors of liberation certainly justifies the analogy. The moments in his novel when characters indulge in corporeal laxity, which seems like doing nothing, are the pivotal moments of their self-rebooting and 'weighing oneself against the world, and the world against itself', to use John Steinbeck's memorable phrase. In *Typee*, the concentration on the tactile experiences of inaction transpires on the level of content – with characters using the experience to courageously say or do what they really want – as well as the level of form, through the slowing down and prolonging of action and excessive accumulation of metaphors.

An example of the tension between the optic and the haptic is a scene when Tommo, having made a decision to escape from the ship, dwells on the pleasures of swimming. Significantly, Tommo leaps into the water at 'high noon', the Evagrian hour of *daemon meridianus* which brings upon the mind slowness and *acedia*.[187] This inaugurates the novel's rhythmic sequence of 'noon-tide slumbers' and 'luxurious siestas' that he will enjoy among the Taipis:

What a delightful sensation did I experience! I felt as if floating in some new element, while all sort of gurgling, trickling, liquid sounds fell upon my ear. People may say what they will about the refreshing influences of a cold-water bath, but commend me when in a perspiration to the shade baths of Tior,[188] beneath the cocoa-nut trees, and amidst the cool delightful atmosphere which surrounds them.

How shall I describe the scenery that met my eye, as I looked out from this verdant recess! The narrow valley, with its steep and close adjoining sides draperied with vines, and arched overhead with a fret-work of interlacing boughs, nearly hidden from view by masses of leafy verdure, seemed from where I stood like an immense arbor disclosing its vista to the eye, whilst as I advanced it insensibly widened into the loveliest vale eye ever beheld.[189]

What is striking about this passage is how its first part overflows with numerous references to the sense of touch: the experience of 'floating', 'refreshing' and 'coolness' are so vivid, and even the sound is experienced haptically as 'liquid'. What is also notable about the first part is how audaciously free Tommo feels in that particular moment. Floating in water, he does not care what people may say, and feels unrestrained in his enjoyment. However, in the second part, as he starts looking around, his language ventriloquises the pastoralist convention, with 'verdant recess', 'draperied' valley and 'leafy verdure' being the stylistic elements of an otherwise coarse pastoralist eroticisation of colonialist intrusiveness. In the Western colonial gaze, the land is no longer experienced, but judged for its fertility through the normative lens of productivity. The eye does not really see the valley; it sees prosperity and growth draperied with decorations. In sum, the two paragraphs depict contrasting modes of sensing the world, but their disparity does not necessarily ruin the congruity of the description. For while in the haptic passage, the trope of proprioceptive receptivity wrestles the pastoral sensibility from its ocularocentric convention, in the optic passage the convention implodes via excessive intensification of its poetic means. In effect, the identity built around the narrator's acculturated ocular habit is radically put into question, not to mention that of the reader, whose normativising gaze and its intrinsic colonialist bias are reflected back to her with the full force of its capacity to shame.

Looking may serve to mobilise the dynamics of shame, but in itself it is pictured as productive. Unlike lazy passivity, it is a form of leisure, an activity. The opposition between looking and touching, very much like the dichotomy of work and idleness – a dichotomy into which it is inscribed – serves to support a clear (and very old) societal discernment between those who work with their bodies and those who do not, those whose inactivity registers as laziness and those whose inactivity comes off as *action*. The association of work with vision, noted by Tomkins with respect to the evil eye, may indeed be as strongly embedded in the Western cultural tradition as Melville's aesthetic strategy seems to assert. After all, one of the first symptoms of being possessed by *daemon meridianus* according to Evagrius Ponticus was staring at the sun to the point of blindness. It is significant therefore that Melville's Tommo never goes blind, and even more so that his double and partner in crime, Toby, at one point disappears from the narrative, for this may have something to do with Melville's critique of productivity and its class status.

From the beginning of his story, Tommo does not have a clear identity, and searches for a reflective mirror against whose image he could measure himself and give his identity a coherent shape. He therefore chooses to plot his escape from the ship together with one of his shipmates, Toby, a 'black eyed', 'melancholic' and 'wayward' man whose social status is to Tommo entirely unclear. He is 'like [him]self' in that he 'evidently moves in a different sphere of life', but he is also 'of that class of rovers . . . who never reveal their origin, never allude to home'.[190] Tommo choses this acediac vagabond as a blank screen on to which he will from then on project his own ideas, desires and fantasies, one of the first being the projection of class which he draws from a detailed examination of Toby's comportment:

> Toby, like myself, had evidently moved in a different sphere of life . . . There was much even in the appearance of Toby calculated to draw me towards him, for while the greater part of the crew were as coarse in person as in mind, Toby was endowed with a remarkably prepossessing exterior.[191]

What opens the possibility of identification is that Toby is not vulgar and that there is an 'imperturbable gravity of his tone and manner', which secures the congruity of character Tommo so desperately seeks.[192] What seals it is the 'congeniality of sentiment' established during the weary hours on the ship.[193] One may, of course, following a well-trodden critical vista, read Tommo's attraction to Toby through the lens of queer criticism and emphasise its homoerotic element, but while the erotic in the sense of its bodily component is definitely important here in terms of how *Typee* aestheticises norm transgression, it is equally noteworthy to emphasise that part of this attraction is vectored towards an acediac rover, a Romantic avatar of an Evagrian monk, who inertly floats through life and seems to adhere to no conventional ideas of productivity or purpose.

There is, in other words, a peculiar class blindness in the character of Tommo that contradicts his ability to spot the minutest details of appearance. In Myra Jehlen's essay 'Melville and Class' this is regarded as an inevitable consequence of Melville's fantasies about classlessness and 'divine equality'. While Melville's central issue is 'how to reconcile the romance of individual self-creation with the political narrative of class', he withdraws from pursuing equality via class-identification and imagines it as class extinction.[194] Melville might be an ideological critic of his time, but the idea of constitutive contradiction (class-identification for the purpose of class transgression) is definitely not a part of his project. For Jehlen, while Melville 'does seem to embrace a democracy undivided by rank or prestige', it is 'less an embrace than a quick hug'.[195] Thus when Tommo presents himself and his other as 'unclassed', he 'transcends class altogether which is the highest status of all'.[196]

This seems to be the case in *Typee* on the level of content. When we recall the passages introducing lazy time on the *Dolly*, languorous temporality encompasses everyone on board regardless of rank or origin, including Tommo. It truly is inclusive. But the minute Tommo joins in the languor, the shame imagined as the shark's evil eye exposes his sense of being socially discredited in his unproductive laxness. Thus, Tommo hurries to explain to his readers that he was not entirely unproductive: while he 'could not avoid yielding in a great measure to the general languor', he 'contrived to shake off the spell, and to appreciate the beauty of the scene around me'.[197] In Jehlen's perspective, this is a classic gesture of the democratic ideal turning into an object of sophisticated (ocular) inspection. Indeed, having been corrected into productive looking by the evil eye of the shark, Tommo upgrades his vision to be even more incisive, as is expressed in his growing resentment towards the other sailors. If shame defines the space 'where the question of identity arises most originally and most relationally', then it also transforms Tommo from a rebel to the agent of the colonialist gaze.[198] Thus, on the following night when he observes his companions carousing with the locals, he distances himself from them mentally. Shame turns into disgust – an affective reaction which in Tomkins's terms completes the process of negative identification – and Tommo gives way to the most moralising exclamations about the sailors' 'unholy passions', 'riot and debauchery', 'grossest licentiousness' and 'most shameful inebriety'.[199]

However, while on the level of events the dream of classless utopia is shattered by what Tommo sees during the night, it prevails on the level of form, where the poetic language remains excessive to the point of voiding such grammatical categories as comparatives and superlatives and such poetic devices as hyperbole and litotes of their usual hierarchising function. In a somewhat entropic fashion, Melville makes language, the material body of his text, so overproductive that it becomes entirely unproductive. What Otter calls 'the corporeal excess' of *Typee* should thus not only be understood with reference to the book's content, but with reference to its textual predicament.

In the novel, when the dream of classless utopia returns in Tommo's ambivalent mixture of outbursts of enthusiasm about the Taipi culture and outcries of terror about the cannibal threat, Melville's language is equally as overdone as it was in the revolted descriptions of the sailors' debaucheries. The tension of contradictory feelings is neutered by the linguistic fabric of his expression. The Taipis basically do as the sailors do on the night of the party, but the language is similarly excessive: dubbed the 'booby-minded'[200] cannibals, they host 'cannibal *banquets*' and enjoy the '*boundless* delights' of love. Their life is 'little else than an often interrupted and *luxurious* nap' where everyone enjoys 'freedom from *all* restraint', '*no one* assume[s] arrogant pretensions', '*all* appear to mix together freely, and without *any* reserve' [my emphases].[201] The Taipis are as indulgent in their weaknesses as the colonists, and as hierarchised as Western patriarchies, with women doing all the household chores and men governing; but inasmuch as Tommo recognises the pattern, he insists that the Taipis display complete '*unanimity* of feeling . . . on *every* occasion'.[202] On the level of plot, Melville cannot go beyond himself and criticise the colonialist-orientalist perspective, for every attempt will turn into some kind of moralising. What he can do, however, is challenge the norm of productivity altogether via stylistic mannerism that explodes the didactic value of his text from within, as well as ridiculing the industry of moral interventionism.

Michael Snediker points out that the novel's corporeal and aesthetic excessiveness has to do with 'overreaching' with respect to 'erotic, epistemological, political and affective stability':

> Melville challenges how we normally think about characters and desire . . . Our wish to make interpretive sense of Melville sometimes cozens us into not adequately recognizing the degree to which we share [the] sense that Melville's characters are jerky, that they are too thinly or exorbitantly conceived for us to 'believe them' enough to fall into their story . . . In *Typee*, Melville experiments with the 'more and less' of characters who *nearly* seem like characters . . . Tommo is too much a character to function seamlessly as a narrator, but too much a narrator to seem sufficiently embodied as a character.[203]

The characters are therefore not Melville's main point. The real object of his experiment is the oversignification and stylistic exaggeration, in short that which in twentieth-century terms we would call *camp*. 'To emphasize style is to slight content, or to introduce an attitude which is neutral to content', writes Susan Sontag in her 1964 essay 'Notes on Camp', thus capturing Melville's attempt to make the productivity of his narrative entirely inoperative.[204] The more he expresses delight or disgust with laziness, the more neutered his judgements become in their meaning.

Typee's campiness is not only about exaggeration but about a type of sensibility. Its oscillation between delight and disgust brings to mind Sontag's confession, which could very well be part of Melville's Preface:

> For myself, I plead the goal of self-edification, and the goad of a sharp conflict in my own sensibility. I am strongly drawn to Camp, and almost as strongly offended by it. That is why I want to talk about it, and why I can. For no one who wholeheartedly shares in a given sensibility can analyze it; he can only, whatever his intention, exhibit it. To name a sensibility, to draw its contours and to recount its history, requires a deep sympathy modified by revulsion.[205]

Melville's treatment of the topos of laziness is marked by a similar conflict of sensibility, the tension between being drawn to and disgusted by it, which manifests itself in the tension between the optic and haptic exaggerations throughout the text. It is a treatment driven by deep sympathy interspersed with revulsion. *Typee*'s poetics of textual-corporeal excess built around laziness is campy in the sense that it is too stylised not to be self-conscious, too serious and moralistic not to be half-serious. It is also 'edifying' as it catches the most imposing conflict of conscience: the conflict between desire and repulsion. From this perspective, Melville's excessive oscillation between delight and disgust need not be dismissed as 'formless mess' but rather recognised 'for the edification it provides, or the dignity of the conflict it resolves'. Anticipating Sontag by more than a century, Melville pleads the goal of self-edification in his Preface, declaring that although he knows his narrative may appear 'strange, or perhaps even incomprehensible' to his reader, he nevertheless has the 'anxious desire to speak the unvarnished truth 'about the unbounded liberty of conscience in the Taipi valley. He speaks this 'truth' in a mixture of superfluous admiration for their easygoing nature and overflowing revulsion against their cannibalism, and therefore overwrites the pastoral with camp sensibility. To travesty Sontag again, *Typee* features pastoralism insofar as it is pastoralism in quotation marks.

But Melville does not play with pastoralist convention just for fun. When his poetics of overproductivity and oversignification reaches its critical point and becomes inoperative, he does not disrespect his content as if he were unaware of the politics of his aesthetics. In the context of Melville's campiness Sontag's line 'to emphasize style is to slight content, or to introduce an attitude which is neutral to content' should be understood politically, along the lines of the Barthesian concept of neutrality discussed in Chapter 1.[206] In his lectures on *The Neutral*, Barthes, if we remember, renders the abstract term neutrality in terms of bodily laziness, the empirical, corporeal expression of a neutral, Pyrrhonic ethico-political position. It is not a minimalistic pose but a pose of *heaping*: that is, accumulating or amassing one's body and self. And hence, Barthes's point is that it is a pose that reveals something very important about the modes of resisting social pressure to participate in socio-economic reality, because it represents the retention of a choice between being productive and being unproductive. To be neutral is not to be apolitical, but to stand for the possibility of not taking sides and conserving dissensual power.

Melville's 'heaping' language, and the 'heaping' literary subjectivity it constructs in *Typee* – most literally through the doubled, self-neutralising figures of the protagonist, Tommo, who returns to civilisation, and Toby, who escapes permanently – may well be read as an attempt to approximate such a form of resistance to social pressures. Writing in an epoch obsessed with productivity, from within the aesthetic regime of Romanticism stabilised by the ethics of moral interventionism, compassion and representational norms of pastoral extraction, Melville's *Typee* manages to render literature inoperative with respect to the pedagogical role of instructing and delighting that it has been assigned in the emerging nineteenth-century leisure industry.

From this angle, *Typee* might be rehabilitated from the category of Melville's admirable yet unsuccessful attempt at an ideological critique of colonial exploitation and capitalist values dressed up as an adolescent fantasy to the status of a serious literary intervention that targets the normatisation of productivity and the triumph of industriousness in every sphere of nineteenth-century life. The ideas to be later perfected in 'Bartleby, the Scrivener' seem to find their embryonic form in *Typee*'s aesthetics of inoperativity and the idea of dissensual neutrality, and predate Thoreau's idea of protest by withdrawal from 'Civil Disobedience'. If Melville's 1853 short story about Wall Street is viewed as an elaboration of a project begun in *Typee*, then it is hardly surprising that instead of words, Bartleby chooses to communicate with his readers in the haptic mode and suspend all physiological functions of his body – he doesn't move, sleep or eat, nor eventually, breathe. Melville does not make the pale scrivener say much, but he overcompensates for this reticence by making his character tragically emphatic in terms of his bodily expressiveness, reminiscent of the lost, melancholic rover Toby. Hyperbole aside, however, the point is that the haptic aesthetics is introduced by Melville to mediate the extent of the biopolitical intervention of capitalist norms of productivity into the bodily rhythms of individual society members. What Jonathan Crary's book on sleep in capitalism claims to be a contemporary phenomenon is actually already intuited by Melville in his experiments with creating a character who will communicate with his audience through kinaesthetic and physiological gestures.

Such is then the small but loud part played by the trope of laziness in the discourse of American Romanticism. As my examples of Emerson's philosophical, Whitman's poetic and Melville's fictional uses of the figure demonstrate, Romantic writers resorted to this difficult theme to signal their dissent from the disciplining work of the socio-economic norms of the mid-nineteenth century, and to expose the ambivalent structures of feeling and body regime that such normatisation mobilised. Even though this has been called 'the Golden Age for the idea of work', the moment of the formation of the nineteenth-century paradigm of productivity, some turned to laziness as its unpopular other to search for ways out of its disciplining apparatus.[207] In the rich affective spectrum of the modalities of laziness – inaction, inertia, inoperativity, lassitude, relaxation and indulgence – Emerson, Whitman and Melville saw the possibility of exposing and perhaps detouring the intersection of the biological, the political and the aesthetic regimes that the norm of productivity had as its function to conceal.

Notes

1. John Winthrop, *The Journal of John Winthrop 1630–1649*, ed. Richard Dunn and Laetitia Yeandle (Cambridge, MA: Belknap Press of Harvard University Press, 1996), 4.
2. John Winthrop, 'A Model of Christian Charity', in *The Norton Anthology of American Literature*, ed. Nina Baym (New York: W.W. Norton, 2007), Vol. A, 146.
3. Ibid., 147.
4. Matthew 5:42
5. Winthrop, 'A Model of Christian Charity', 150.
6. See Michelle Burnham, *Folded Selves: Colonial New England Writing in the World System: Reencounters with Colonialism: New Perspectives on the Americas* (Hanover, NH: University Press of New England, 2007).
7. Hugh J. Dawson, '"Christian Charitie" as Colonial Discourse: Rereading Winthrop's Sermon in its English Context', *Early American Literature* 33.2 (1998), 121.

8. John Cotton, *Gods Promise to His Plantation as It Was Delivered in a Sermon, by Iohn Cotton, B.D. and Preacher of Gods Word in Boston* (London: William Iones of Iohn Bellamy, 1630), 2.

9. Ibid., 7.

10. Ibid., 9, 8.

11. Ibid., 10.

12. Ibid., 11.

13. Ibid., 11–12.

14. John Norton, *Memoir of John Cotton: 1606–1663* (New York: Saxton and Miles, 1842).

15. See Stephen Innes, *Work and Labor in Early America* (Chapel Hill, NC: University of North Carolina Press, 1988); Stephen Innes, *Creating the Commonwealth: The Economic Culture of Puritan New England* (New York: W.W. Norton, 1995).

16. Kenneth L. Kusmer, *Down & Out, On the Road: The Homeless in American History* (Oxford: Oxford University Press, 2002), 14.

17. Increase Mather, 'An Earnest Exhortation To the Inhabitants of New-England (Boston, 1676)', in *Electronic Texts in American Studies*, ed. Reiner Smolinski, http://digitalcommons.unl.edu/etas/31 (accessed 25 January 2019).

18. Increase Mather, 'The Day of Trouble Is Near (1673)', in *Evans Early American Imprint Collection* (Cambridge, 1674), http://name.umdl.umich.edu/N00137.0001.001 (accessed 25 January 2019).

19. Perry Miller, *The Puritans*, rev. edn (New York: Harper and Row, 1963), Meditation 11, 565.

20. Ibid., Meditation 17, 566–7.

21. Ibid., Meditation 15, 566.

22. Ibid., Meditation 30, 576.

23. Ibid., 576.

24. Ibid., 579.

25. Ibid., 579.

26. Ibid., 579.

27. Jonathan Edwards, 'The Preciousness of Time and the Importance of Redeeming It' (1734), sec. I, https://archive.org/details/ThePreciousnessOfTimeByJonathanEdwards (accessed 25 January 2019).

28. Ibid., sec. I.

29. Ibid., sec. I.

30. Ibid., sec. V.

31. Ibid., sec. III.

32. Ibid., sec. III.

33. Ibid., sec. III.

34. Jonathan Edwards, *The Works of Jonathan Edwards, A.M.: With an Essay on His Genius and Writings*, ed. Henry Rogers and Sereno Edwards Dwight (New York: W. Ball, 1839), 52.

35. Ibid., 103.

36. Ibid., 179.

37. Ibid., 52, 179; Michel Foucault, *Security, Territory, Population: Lectures at the Collège de France, 1977–78* (New York: Palgrave Macmillan, 2007), 172–3.

38. 'Difficulty of Gaining Their Assent', *Mr. Brainerd's Journal* (1746), in Rogers and Dwight (eds), *The Works of Jonathan Edwards*, 428.
39. Benjamin Franklin, *Selections from Autobiography, Poor Richard's Almanac, Advice to a Young Tradesman, The Whistle, Necessary Hints to Those That Would Be Rich, Motion for Prayers, Selected Letters*, ed. Bliss Perry (New York: Doubleday and McClure, 1898), 153.
40. Albert O. Hirschman, *The Passions and the Interests: Political Arguments for Capitalism before its Triumph* (Princeton: Princeton University Press, 1977), 56.
41. Franklin, *Selections*, 141; Tom Lutz, *Doing Nothing: A History of Loafers, Loungers, Slackers and Bums in America* (New York: Farrar, Straus and Giroux, 2006), 67–8.
42. Franklin, *Selections*, 139.
43. Lauren Berlant, *The Female Complaint: The Unfinished Business of Sentimentality in American Culture* (Durham, NC: Duke University Press, 2008).
44. Sarah Jordan, *The Anxieties of Idleness: Idleness in Eighteenth-Century British Literature and Culture* (New York: Bucknell University Press, 2003), 45.
45. John Barrell, *The Dark Side of the Landscape: The Rural Poor in English Painting, 1730–1840* (Cambridge: Cambridge University Press, 1980), 83.
46. *The Instructive Story of Industry and Sloth. Ornamented with Cuts* (Hartford, CT: J. Babcock, 1796), 20.
47. Ibid., 15–16.
48. Ibid., 17, 19.
49. Ibid., 19.
50. Karen Ann Weyler, *Intricate Relations: Sexual and Economic Desire in American Fiction, 1789–1814* (Iowa City: University of Iowa Press, 2004), 228.
51. See Lesley Ginsberg and Monika M. Elbert, *Romantic Education in Nineteenth-Century American Literature: National and Transatlantic Contexts* (New York: Routledge, 2015).
52. Deborah Weiss, 'Maria Edgeworth's Infant Economics: Capitalist Culture, Good-Will Networks and "Lazy Lawrence"', *Journal for Eighteenth-Century Studies* 37.3 (2014), 395.
53. Ibid., 396, 397.
54. Even in the account of stealing Jem's money, lazy Lawrence is not described as evil, but rather as indecisive, afraid, with 'blood running cold in his veins' and 'horrors of guilt' creeping up upon his soul.
55. Robert Grant White, *Law and Laziness; or, Students at Law of Leisure* (New York: Golden Rule Office, 1846); Andrew Knighton, 'The Bartleby Industry and Bartleby's Idleness', *ESQ: A Journal of the American Renaissance* 1.2 (2007), 186.
56. White, *Law and Laziness*, 26.
57. Ibid., 6–7.
58. Ibid., 9.
59. Ibid., 9.
60. Ibid., 9.
61. Thomas Carlyle, *Critical and Miscellaneous Essays* (Ann Arbor: University of Michigan Press, 2005), 92.

62. Leslie A. Fiedler, *Love and Death in the American Novel*, rev. edn (New York: Stein and Day, 1966), 335; Leo Marx, *The Machine in the Garden: Technology and the Pastoral Ideal in America* (New York: Oxford University Press, 1964), 18.

63. Robert A. Ferguson, 'Rip Van Winkle and the Generational Divide in American Culture', *Early American Literature* 40.3 (2005), 530.

64. Washington Irving, 'Rip Van Winkle', in *The Sketch Book of Geoffrey Crayon, Gent.*, ed. Will Bradley (New York: R.H. Russell, 1897), 10–11.

65. Howard Horwitz, '"Rip Van Winkle" and Legendary National Memory', *Western Humanities Review* 58.2 (2004), 35; Sarah Wyman, 'Washington Irving's Rip Van Winkle: A Dangerous Critique of a New Nation', *ANQ: A Quarterly Journal of Short Articles, Notes, and Reviews* 23.4 (2010), 217.

66. Jennifer S. Banks, 'Washington Irving, the Nineteenth-Century American Bachelor', in *Critical Essays on Washington Irving*, ed. Ralph M. Aderman (Boston: G.K. Hall, 1990), 253–65.

67. Wyman, 'Washington Irving's Rip Van Winkle', 217.

68. Fiedler, *Love and Death in the American Novel*, 348.

69. Donald R. Anderson, 'Freedom's Lullaby: Rip Van Winkle and the Framings of Self-Deception', *ESQ: A Journal of the American Renaissance* 46.4 (2000), 277.

70. Richard Henry Dana (ed.), *The Idle Man* (New York: Wiley and Halsted, 1821), 16–17, 18.

71. Ibid., 29.

72. Ibid., 30.

73. Ibid., 31.

74. See Virginia Krause, *Idle Pursuits: Literature and Oisiveté in the French Renaissance* (Newark, DE: University of Delaware Press, 2003).

75. In *Marxism and Literature* (Oxford: Oxford University Press, 1977), Williams discusses this as a Romantic repression of its initially productive revolutionary impulse tied to the Enlightenment idea of rational and public action.

76. Raymond Williams, *The Country and the City* (New York: Oxford University Press, 1973), 279.

77. Ibid., 281.

78. Ibid., 281.

79. Ibid., 284; Raymond Williams, *Towards 2000* (London: Chatto and Windus, 1983), 86.

80. Williams, *Marxism and Literature*, 250.

81. Lawrence Buell, 'American Pastoral Ideology Reappraised', *American Literary History* 1.1 (1989), 5.

82. Sacvan Bercovitch and Myra Jehlen (eds), *Ideology and Classic American Literature* (New York: Cambridge University Press, 1986); Annette Kolodny, *The Lay of the Land: Metaphor as Experience and History in American Life and Letters* (Chapel Hill, NC: University of North Carolina Press, 1975); Marx, *The Machine in the Garden*; Jane P. Tompkins, *Sensational Designs: The Cultural Work of American Fiction, 1790–1860* (New York: Oxford University Press, 1985).

83. Scott Hess, 'Postmodern Pastoral, Advertising, and the Masque of Technology', *Interdisciplinary Studies in Literature and Environment* 11.1 (2004), 71–100.

84. See Terry Gifford, *Pastoral* (London: Routledge, 1999).

85. Lauren Gail Berlant, *Cruel Optimism* (Durham, NC: Duke University Press, 2011), 2.

86. Roberto Esposito and Zakiya Hanafi, *Living Thought: The Origins and Actuality of Italian Philosophy* (Palo Alto: Stanford University Press, 2012), 211.

87. Hess, 'Postmodern Pastoral', 71–2. Hess's understanding of technology is a bit too straightforward – what he means is electronic gadgets and televisual hyperreality. As the work of Foucault, Agamben and Esposito on biopolitics has demonstrated, mechanical technicity is only part and parcel of larger control apparatuses of power. Therefore, to say that consumer pastoral refracts back at us the illusion of a sensual and temporal idyll in new technologies is also to say that it is a technique of regulating behaviours and feelings, especially with regard to idleness and disengagement.

88. Raymond Williams, *Modern Tragedy* (London: Chatto and Windus, 1966), 256.

89. D. W. Winnicott, 'The Capacity to Be Alone' (1957), *International Journal of Psycho-Analysis* 39 (1958), 416–20.

90. Marx, *The Machine in the Garden*, 87.

91. Andrew Lyndon Knighton, *Idle Threats: Men and the Limits of Productivity in Nineteenth Century America* (New York: New York University Press, 2012), 86.

92. Jacques Rancière, *Aisthesis: Scenes from the Aesthetic Regime of Art* (London: Verso, 2013).

93. Lawrence Buell, *The Environmental Imagination: Thoreau, Nature Writing, and the Formation of American Culture* (Cambridge, MA: Harvard University Press, 1995), 35.

94. Rancière, *Aisthesis*, 56–7.

95. Ibid., 68.

96. Ralph Waldo Emerson, *Emerson's Prose and Poetry: Authoritative Texts, Contexts, Criticism* (New York: W.W. Norton, 2001), 192.

97. Ibid., 192, 194.

98. Ibid., 195.

99. Thomas A. Tweed, *The American Encounter with Buddhism, 1844–1912: Victorian Culture and the Limits of Dissent* (Bloomington: Indiana University Press, 1992).

100. Emerson, *Prose and Poetry*, 198.

101. Ibid., 208.

102. Ibid., 206.

103. Eve Kosofsky Sedgwick, *Touching Feeling: Affect, Pedagogy, Performativity* (Durham, NC: Duke University Press, 2003).

104. Ibid., 174.

105. Rancière, *Aisthesis*, 72.

106. Branka Arsić, *On Leaving: A Reading in Emerson* (Cambridge, MA: Harvard University Press, 2010).

107. Walter Benjamin, *The Writer of Modern Life: Essays on Charles Baudelaire* (Cambridge, MA: Harvard University Press, 2006), 176.

108. Sedgwick, *Touching Feeling*, 157.

109. Emerson, *Prose and Poetry*, 211, 206.

110. Giorgio Agamben, 'The Power of Thought', *Critical Inquiry* 40.2 (2014), 486-7.

111. Emerson, *Prose and Poetry*, 206.

112. Agamben, 'The Power of Thought', 487.

113. Ibid., 487.

114. Kalpana Seshadri, 'Agamben, the Thought of Sterēsis: An Introduction to Two Essays', *Critical Inquiry* 40.2 (2014), 478.

115. Emerson, *Prose and Poetry*, 129.

116. Ibid., 211.

117. Ibid., 202.

118. Ibid., 206.

119. Ibid., 206.

120. As Catherine Malabou observes in her interpretation of Freud's *Beyond the Pleasure Principle*, Freud's definition of elasticity as an 'expression of inertia inherent in organic life' and therefore the quality of the death drive renders it the most commanding mode of energy distribution, one which nothing, not even the plasticity of the life drive, may supersede and overcome. See Catherine Malabou, 'Plasticity and Elasticity in Freud's *Beyond the Pleasure Principle*', *Diacritics* 37.4 (2007), 78-85.

121. Michel Foucault, *The History of Sexuality, Vol. 3: The Care of the Self*, trans. Robert Hurley (New York: Vintage, 1988), 66.

122. Stanley Cavell, *The Senses of Walden: An Expanded Edition* (Chicago: University of Chicago Press, 2013), 134.

123. Emerson, *Prose and Poetry*, 68.

124. Philip Cafaro, 'Thoreau's Virtue Ethics in Walden', *The Concord Saunterer* 8 (2000), 23-47.

125. Walt Whitman, *Walt Whitman's Backward Glances: A Backward Glance o'er Travel'd Roads, and Two Contributory Essays Hitherto Uncollected* (Freeport, NY: Books for Libraries Press, 1968), 17.

126. Ibid., 19, 26, 20.

127. Vincent J. Bertolini, '"Hinting" and "Reminding": The Rhetoric of Performative Embodiment in "Leaves of Grass", *ELH* 69.4 (2002), 1047.

128. Jacques Rancière, *The Emancipated Spectator* (London: Verso, 2011), 72.

129. See Jacques Rancière, *Dissensus: On Politics and Aesthetics* (New York: Continuum, 2010).

130. Walt Whitman, *Leaves of Grass, 1855 Edition* (New York: W. Whitman, 1855) 33.

131. Ibid., 99, 96.

132. Ibid., 97-8.

133. Ibid., 32.

134. Ibid., 18.

135. Nili Wazana, 'A Case of the Evil Eye: Qohelet 4:4-8', *Journal of Biblical Literature* 126.4 (2007), 691.

136. Whitman, *Backward Glances*.
137. Whitman, *Leaves of Grass, 1855 Edition*, 19.
138. Ibid., sec. 33: 6, 39, 30, 51, 49, 52, 70, 71, 74.
139. Ibid., 54.
140. Ibid., 38.
141. Ibid., 25.
142. Michel Foucault, *The Government of Self and Others: Lectures at the Collège de France, 1982–1983* (London: Macmillan, 2011), 346–7.
143. Ibid., 287.
144. Whitman, *Backward Glances*, 31, 30.
145. Jacques Rancière, *Disagreement: Politics and Philosophy* (Minneapolis: University of Minnesota Press, 2004), 35.
146. Ezra Greenspan, *Walt Whitman and the American Reader* (Cambridge: Cambridge University Press, 1990), 54.
147. Walt Whitman, *Leaves of Grass [Microform]*, ed. Canadiana.org (Toronto: Musson, 1900), 333.
148. Martin Puchner, *Poetry of the Revolution: Marx, Manifestos, and the Avant-Gardes* (Princeton: Princeton University Press, 2006), 12.
149. Leslie Derfler, *Paul Lafargue and the Founding of French Marxism, 1842–1882* (Cambridge, MA: Harvard University Press, 1991), 177.
150. Paul Lafargue, *The Right to Be Lazy* (1883) (Chicago: Solidarity Publications, 1969), 23–4.
151. Adam Phillips, 'Against Self-Criticism', *London Review of Books* 37.5 (2015), 13.
152. Milton R. Stern, 'The Publication of Typee: A Chronology', in *Critical Essays on Herman Melville's Typee*, ed. Milton R. Stern (Boston: G.K. Hall, 1982), 18.
153. Herman Melville, *Typee: Complete Text with Introduction, Historical Contexts, Critical Essays* (Boston: Houghton Mifflin, 2004), 166.
154. Ibid., 10.
155. Phillips, 'Against Self-Criticism', 14.
156. Quoted in Stern (ed.), *Critical Essays on Herman Melville's Typee*, 34, 75.
157. Myra Jehlen, 'Introduction', in *Herman Melville: A Collection of Critical Essays*, ed. Myra Jehlen (Englewood Cliffs, NJ: Prentice Hall, 1994), 4.
158. Friedrich Nietzsche, *Daybreak: Thoughts on the Prejudices of Morality*, trans. R. J. Hollingdale (Cambridge: Cambridge University Press, 1997), 101.
159. Lutz, *Doing Nothing*, 119.
160. Ibid., 120.
161. Robert C. Suggs, *The Archeology of Nuku Hiva, Marquesas Islands, French Polynesia*, Anthropological Papers of the American Museum of Natural History, vol. 49, pt. 1 (New York: American Museum of Natural History, 1961); Mary K. Bercaw Edwards, *Cannibal Old Me: Spoken Sources in Melville's Early Works* (Kent, OH: Kent State University Press, 2009); Greg Dening, *Islands and Beaches: Discourse on a Silent Land: Marquesas, 1774–1880* (Honolulu: University Press of Hawaii, 1980), 148.
162. John Bryant, 'Taipi, Tipii, Typee: Place, Memory, and Text. A Response to Robert C. Suggs', *ESQ: A Journal of the American Renaissance* 51.1 (2005), 138.

163. Geoffrey Sanborn, *The Sign of the Cannibal: Melville and the Making of a Postcolonial Reader* (Durham, NC: Duke University Press, 1998), 79.

164. John Bryant, *Melville and Repose: The Rhetoric of Humor in the American Renaissance* (New York: Oxford University Press, 1993), 9.

165. Ibid., 9.

166. Ibid., 131–2.

167. Samuel Otter, *Melville's Anatomies* (Berkeley: University of California Press, 1999), 158.

168. Melville, *Typee*, 27.

169. Ibid., 26.

170. Sanborn, *The Sign of the Cannibal*, 78.

171. Melville, *Typee*, 27.

172. Ibid., 27.

173. Silvan Tomkins, *Affect, Imagery, Consciousness. Vol. 2: The Negative Affects* (New York: Springer, 2008), 384–5.

174. Ibid., 385.

175. Ibid., 385.

176. Ibid., 374.

177. Ibid., 379.

178. Ibid., 386.

179. Ibid., 386.

180. The question of the evil eye in Melville's fiction has been explored in Joseph Adamson's psychoanalytic *Melville, Shame, and the Evil Eye*; however, Adamson does not address gaze dynamics in *Typee*. See Joseph Adamson, *Melville, Shame, and the Evil Eye: A Psychoanalytic Reading* (Albany: State University of New York Press, 1997).

181. To put it differently, the aesthetic expression of shame stemming from his voyeuristic/exhibitionist desire to share the intimacy of laziness with his readers is set to oscillate between projections of what Tommo calls 'animal lust' on to the cannibal islanders, and introjections of their hospitable gestures. However, as long as shame dictates the rhythm of *Typee*'s narrative, and brings Tommo a degree of self-awareness, it also occasions the moments of catching the shaming conscience red-handed, provoking him to develop a desire to escape.

182. Tomkins, *Affect, Imagery, Consciousness*, 387–8.

183. Ibid., 377.

184. See Martin Jay, *Downcast Eyes: The Denigration of Vision in Twentieth-Century French Thought* (Berkeley: University of California Press, 1994).

185. Melville, *Typee*, 68.

186. Mitchell Breitwieser, 'False Sympathy in Melville's Typee', in *Herman Melville: A Collection of Critical Essays*, ed. Myra Jehlen (Englewood Cliffs, NJ: Prentice Hall, 1994), 15.

187. Melville, *Typee*, 44.

188. 'The baths of Tior' are the waters of the western bay of Nuku Hiva, the home of the Taioa (Tior) tribe.

189. Ibid., 44.

190. Ibid., 47.
191. Ibid., 47.
192. Ibid., 47–8.
193. Ibid., 47.
194. Myra Jehlen, 'Melville and Class', in *A Historical Guide to Herman Melville*, ed. Giles B. Gunn (New York: Oxford University Press, 2005), 88.
195. Ibid., 84.
196. Ibid., 89.
197. Melville, *Typee*, 27.
198. Sedgwick, *Touching Feeling*, 37.
199. Melville, *Typee*, 32.
200. Ibid., 116.
201. Ibid., 150, 151, 179.
202. Ibid., 194.
203. Michael D. Snediker, 'Melville and Queerness without Character', in *The New Cambridge Companion to Herman Melville*, ed. Robert S. Levine (Cambridge: Cambridge University Press, 2013), 157.
204. Susan Sontag, 'Notes on Camp', *The Partisan Review* (autumn 1964), 516.
205. Ibid., 515.
206. Ibid., 516.
207. Adriano Tilgher, *Work, What It Has Meant to Men through the Ages*, trans. Dorothy Canfield Fisher (New York: Harcourt, Brace and World, 1930), 90.

The Modernist Moment of Laziness

CHAPTER 3

Cessation and *inaction externe*: Gertrude Stein and Marcel Duchamp

I am trying for a minimum of action.

Marcel Duchamp

Marcel Duchamp's line seems rather atypical of the modernist sensibility. In fact, we usually associate 'trying for a minimum of action' with modernism's successor, postmodernism. As one of the formulations of the postmodern sensibility – John Barth's 'Literature of Exhaustion' –famously put it, postmodernism was distinguished for its attitude of disengagement, 'the felt exhaustion of certain possibilities'. For Barth, exhaustion was a word that best defined the dominant ways of feeling and thinking in the 1960s, and indeed 'Literature of Exhaustion' quickly grew to the status of a postmodernist manifesto. Yet there was something contradictory about the weariness formula. For 'exhaustion' was not to be understood in standard dictionary terms as 'drawing off of strength', or an act of drawing out' with respect to being withdrawn. It had nothing to do with passivity or loss of vigour. On the contrary, it was a 'chic' attitude of febrile recyclism towards the 'used-upness' of certain aesthetic forms.[1]

The career of the exhaustion formula would not be worth reviving were it not for this intriguing combination of the drawing off of strength on the one hand and virility on the other. Given that *The Labour of Laziness* takes an interest in the cultural function of laziness as a concept-metaphor, the postmodern rehabilitation of exhaustion, one of the modalities of laziness, demands a closer scrutiny. The synthesis of exhaustion and weariness with the idea of freshness is clearly paradoxical. A question therefore appears: where does the paradox come from? What is its genealogy? Is the exhausted mode we tend to associate with postmodern sensibility indeed so postmodern, fresh and new?

One answer to the question of just how new the cultural formations that declare themselves to be such actually are is offered by Raymond Williams and his theoretical distinction between the old and new elements of every cultural formation. In the famous section of *Marxism and Literature* devoted to the division, Williams isolates three types of values (by which he means areas of experience or practices of sensibility) that constitute a culture of a given epoch: the *dominant* values, consolidated in the institutions of the time; the *residual* values, which come from the past; and the *emergent* values, which are continually under construction and have not yet consolidated into a clear cultural formation.[2] Of special interest for Williams in the interplay of this triad is the relation between the residual and the emergent values. Despite their name, the residual values are not to be confused with values that are entirely archaic; though 'formed in the past', residual values, very much unlike archaic values, are still 'active in the cultural process, not only as elements of the past, but as effective elements of the present'.[3] Residual practices are therefore always a 'necessary complication' in the processes of an emerging cultural formation.[4] Yet this being said, Williams goes on to add, residual values should also not be confused and thought of as one with the emergent sensibilities:

> What matters, finally, in understanding emergent culture, as distinct from both the dominant and the residual, is that it is never only a matter of immediate practice; indeed it depends crucially on finding new forms and adaptations of form. Again and again what we have to observe is in effect a *pre-emergence*, active and pressing but not yet fully articulated, rather than the evident emergence which could be more confidently named.[5]

The residual and the emergent elements may partake of the same cultural space-time – of the same distribution of the sensible, as Rancière would have it – but the element of the emergent will always be quite distinct. Not as a form of 'silence', 'absence' or 'the unconscious', so idolised by bourgeois culture, but rather as 'a kind of feeling and thinking which is indeed social and material', as something tangible though still 'in an embryonic phase'.[6] It is only in the subsequent phase of cultural development that it becomes fully grown and articulated in discourse.

The emphasis on the pre-emergent, embryonic moment in cultural formation is perhaps that which most distinguishes Williams's theory of structures of feeling from its revitalised version presented by Rancière in the conception of the distribution of the sensible. While for Rancière, certain aesthetic perlocutions such as Ralph Waldo Emerson's *The Poet* (1844) or Dziga Vertov's *Man with a Movie Camera* (1929) cause ruptures in their respective aesthetic regimes, for Williams the process of cultural transformation is much less abrupt.[7] Instead of violent shifts or events, Williams envisions a gradual *pre*-phase, characterised by a set of evolving sensibilities, which are tangibly real and 'material' but at the same time not fully named and conceptualised.

This precisely seems to be the case with exhaustion. In Williams's optics, the 1960s idea of refreshing weariness is not so much a distinctly postmodernist novelty as it is the articulation and conceptualisation of an element of the earlier, modernist sensibility which was available and at work long before the 1960s, albeit only in its embryonic, intangible form. From this perspective, the postmodern idea of being actively withdrawn is a finalised format of the modes of perception, which in the earlier cultural formation of modernism merely lingered under the surface of available discourse in a pre-emergent, undefined state. If the mode of exhaustion could emerge at all as a marker of postmodern sensibility, it is only because it had inhabited the residue of culture for some time already. And hence, in the structure of postmodern sensibility, exhaustion clearly is, despite all proclamations of its freshness, an old, residual value, in the sense that it is active in the cultural process as an effective element of the (postmodern) present, while its origin lies in the modernist past.

But isn't modernism the one cultural trend in which one can hardly trace any signs of the drawing off of strength and vitality? At the first glance, exhaustion is the last thing we would associate with modernist sensibility, with its love of movement and virility. Yet on

a closer look, modernist vitalocentrism does bear traces of engagement with the more withdrawn modes of existence. The French-
American artist Marcel Duchamp, for example, openly embraced
inaction externe, or 'laziness' as he also called it, as his main artistic
strategy – 'please understand, I am trying for a minimum of action',
he would explain in 1929. On a more philosophical note, his contemporary Kazimir Malevich would announce in a short 1921 pamphlet that 'Лень' (laziness) is 'the truth of the human condition' as
well as the ultimate goal of everything we do – the attitude to be
echoed later in John Steinbeck's reflection that 'only in laziness can
one achieve a state of contemplation which is a balancing of values,
a weighing of oneself against the world, and the world against
itself'. Outside of the artistic world, the issue of lassitude was no
less pivotal. Edmund Husserl and Martin Heidegger explored the
existential depths of *Lässigkeit* (lassitude), Bertrand Russell wrote
in praise of 'idleness', and Siegfried Kracauer urged his contemporaries to abandon vulgar excitability and embrace *Langeweilen*, an
unrestrained boredom-time for contemplation.[8]

All of which is to say that the cultural formation we call modernism seems to have had after all as much to say about vitality
as about its cessation, as we saw with the discussion of William
James in Chapter 2. It was this tension within the modernist ways
of feeling that gave birth to the pre-emergent form of the sensibility
of exhaustion. It is therefore worthwhile exploring how exhaustion
was framed in modernism and to what cultural ends. Thus, in the
following pages, I examine metaphorical and conceptual renditions
of exhaustion by early twentieth-century innovators, primarily
Gertrude Stein and Marcel Duchamp, in order to challenge the
qualification of the modernist politics of aesthetics as vitalocentric.
I don't simply want to turn the vitalocentric opposition around
and accord privilege to the previously unacknowledged modes of
'lethargy' and 'listlessness'.[9] Rather, given that the metaphorology
of inactivity in a given epoch is always an expression of its culture's
resistance to normativity, I aim to trace this 'sentiment of *puissance*'
in artistic visions of inaction, cessation, stasis and lassitude in order
to map the possible field of its counter-normative intervention.

Modernist Vitalocentrism

Before we get there, however, let me recap the official story. Modernism, the standard interpretation goes, was an era of unprecedented, almost feverish embracing of the Bergsonian *élan vital*, the galloping, creative life-force, of machinic motion, action and velocity. Technological advancements of the late nineteenth and early twentieth centuries, revolution in urban architecture, the rise of photography and cinema, and the libidinal hermeneutics brought about by the psychoanalytic theories of Sigmund Freud, to name only the most general influences, all furnished a sublimely complex mode of perceptivity that reiterated and amplified the Baudelairean aesthetics of hyperpneic panting. The dominating mode of sensibility in modernism was still the Romantic mode of the restless, shock-driven *flâneur*, who as Walter Benjamin reminds us, has no time for passive contemplation and lives instead in the constant state of 'vigilant consciousness' to an overabundance of stimuli.[10] It is difficult to deny that the sensibility of vibrant stimulation, or as Baudelaire called it, the sense of 'vertigo' to the point of madness, structures the tone as well as the logic of early modernist manifestos.[11]

Unstoppable motion and restless energy clearly dominate the poetics of Filippo Marinetti's 'Manifesto of Futurism' of 1909 and his Tactilist Manifesto of 1921. Describing for the first time the founding of Futurism to the readers of the French newspaper *Le Figaro*, Marinetti pictures this vertiginous atmosphere in a way that symptomatises the vitalocentric aspect of modernist sensibility:

> We had stayed up all night – my friends and I – beneath mosque lamps hanging from the ceiling. Their brass domes were filigreed, starred like our souls; just as, again like our souls, they were illuminated by the imprisoned brilliance of an electric heart. On the opulent oriental rugs, we had crushed our ancestral lethargy, arguing all the way to the final frontiers of logic and blackening reams of paper with delirious writings. Our chests swelled with immense pride, for at that hour we alone were still awake and upright.[12]

And just as there is no room for rest or sleep at the first Futurist meeting, there is no room for stasis in the style of Marinetti's manifesto, abundant with references to violent speed, 'polyphonic tidal waves' of revolutionariness, and the 'nocturnal fervor' of artistic work.[13] 'We have already created velocity which is eternal and omnipresent' and fuels creation, declares Marinetti. To perceive differently and 'admire an old painting is the same as pouring our sensibility into a funerary urn, instead of casting it forward into the distance in violent spurts of creation and action'.[14] The slightest withdrawal of vigour is, in short, equal to death and decay. Rotting in the urn – an imagine reminiscent of Hegel's rendition of laziness as *Faulheit* (rottenness) – is thus a deadly penalty for giving in to inaction.

If Marinetti's language offers a somewhat extreme sample of the modernist fascination with heightened attention, velocity and movement, its less feverish manifestations feature in other literary manifestos of the time, such as Mina Loy's 'Feminist Manifesto', Ezra Pound's 'Retrospect', anticipatory of the poet's later 'McLuhanesque' characterisation of poets as the antennae of the race with its hyperattentive definition of the poetic image, or Willa Cather's vision of the poetics of demolition in 'The Novel Démeublé'.[15]

The Hidden Logic of Vitalocentrism: Gertrude Stein's Philosophy of Inoperativity

Perhaps the most sustained reflection on motion and activity can be found in Gertrude Stein's theoretical essays on art, which bear witness to her fascination with movement and her complex relation to philosophical vitalism. As argued by Juliana Chow in 'Motion Studies: Vitalism in Gertrude Stein's Work', the entire body of Stein's writings on art, creative minds and creative processes can be approached as an extensive inquiry into vitality and animation, as a series of studies in motion.[16] Though focusing only on Stein's 'Portraits and Repetition', and in particular on her reflections on the technological phenomenon of the car engine that is going even when the car is not moving, which the poet likens to the creative energy of the mind, Chow suggests that Stein's interest in vitality of movement is emblematically vitalocentrist.

According to Chow, when Stein writes in her 1935 essay 'Portraits and Repetition': 'As I say a motor goes inside and the car goes on, but my ultimate business as an artist was not with where the car goes as it goes but with the movement inside that is of the essence of its going', her words express in a nutshell the vitalist idea about life as powered by some physical-as-well-as-psychic, materialised yet interiorised animate force.[17] In that sense, progressive as Stein's idea of an engine seems to be, it strongly draws on philosophical vitalism, which is anything but a revolutionary philosophical trend.

> Stein's sense of movement is a vitalism claim of some nonmechanistic essence – let us say, personality – of life that is present in the car and also present in art. At the heart of vitalism, which itself is both a counterpart and reaction to science, is inquiry of the relation of the anima to the physical body made troubling by Carthesian duality and an abiding belief that metaphysics matter. If vitalism sounds old-fashioned and a-modern, that is because it is; and if it resonates in the modernist era, it is because it realizes that we have never been modern.[18]

Chow thus acknowledges that the vitalist strand in Stein's thinking represents a broader modernist tendency: that motion-action is not so much a modernist invention but a residue of a discredited philosophical trend (reaching at least as far back as Aristotle), which for some reason still caters to the early twentieth-century sensibility of Stein's contemporaries. As Omri Moses intimates in *Out of Character*, most prominent modernist theories of creativity which we we think of as innovative in fact bear a strong mark of vitalist influence. The a-modern (in the sense of non-scientific and counter-technological) idea of some energising force that vitalises the mind was central to theories of art for writers from Henry James and T. S. Eliot to Virginia Woolf and Willa Cather, whether or not they were willing to admit it directly.[19]

The focus on vitalism has quite significant consequences for how we historicise modernist sensibility. For what Chow's and Moses' arguments imply is that vitality is not modernism's own kind of value, but something inherited from the past. First, it is residual in the sense that it comes from the 'old-fashioned' past, the past prior to when the Industrial Revolution complicated the Aristotelian distinction between animate humans and inanimate, non-human matter with its inception of animate, non-human machines. Second, it is residual in the sense of pertaining to the present; its a-modern scientific fallaciousness mediates modernist anxiety with the technological sublimity of inanimate, non-human technicity.

Another implication of the vitalist hypothesis is that the privileging of vitality in the discourse of the modernist avant-gardes might explain the latter's preference for announcing what Rancière calls their 'desperate' and 'ambitious claims to a revolution' in the form of manifestos.[20] As scholars of the genre point out, the force of manifestos lies in their perlocutionary potential; they are so to speak performative acts of agency, events of the will that ignites and legitimises itself.[21] In this sense, with manifesto poetics being based on the principles of self-containment and self-animation, we may think of the modernist manifestos as the evidence and the most formalised expression of its galloping 'vitalocentrism'.

And finally, what we can also derive from Chow's and Moses' readings is that the modernist valorisation of virility via an emphasis on perpetual movement and intense activity might have been the constituent element of the affective core of modernist claims to revolutionary innovativeness and modernist demands for the emancipation of art from ordinary life. The belief that art could exist for its own sake seems tenable only insofar as it is supported by the idea that art has its own motor that keeps it going. From this perspective, the seminal document of the modernist sensibility, Stein's 'most important essay' 'What Are Master-Pieces and Why Are There So Few of Them', might be read as an application of vitalist beliefs to the realm of modernist art.[22]

Although Stein forges the idea of the unstoppable creative motion of the human mind without making explicit reference to vitalism, the perspective nevertheless upholds her argument about what a true artistic masterpiece is. Indeed, one might say that Stein virtually translates the vitalist dualism of matter and life into the language of art: there is 'human mind', she reasons, which is always at work; there is 'human nature', which is an insignificant envelope (or 'clothing') for the mind's motions; and finally, there is a 'master-piece', that is, an ineffable, independent entity that makes the human mind spin:

the master-piece has nothing to do with human nature ... it has to do with the human mind and the entity that is with a thing in itself and not in relation. The moment it is in relation it is common knowledge and anybody can feel and know it and it is not a master-piece. At the same time every one in a curious way sooner or later does feel the reality of a master-piece. The thing in itself of which the human nature is only its clothing does hold the attention. I have meditated a great deal about that. Another curious thing about master-pieces is, nobody when it is created there is in the thing that we call the human mind something that makes it hold itself just the same ... they [masterpieces] exist because they came to be as *something that is an end in itself and in that respect it is opposed to the business of living which is relation and necessity.* That is what a master-piece is not although it may easily be what a master-piece talks about. It is another one of the curious difficulties a master-piece has that is to begin and end, because actually a master-piece does not do that it does not begin and end if it did it would be of necessity and in relation and that is just what a master-piece is not [my emphasis].[23]

In the vitalist reading of this passage, the concept of a 'master-piece' is Stein's artistic conceptualisation of the *alpha*-and-*omega* of creation, of that which is the beginning and the end of artworks. The actual works of art are masterly when they are precise incarnations or actualisations of this genius life-force. This happens extremely rarely (if at all), and explains why there are so few masterpieces in the world. Otherwise put, the sense of 'master-piece' as an actual painting or poem is secondary to the primary sense of the word: namely, the sense of a governing master cause of a creative process, 'something that is an end in itself', and for that matter something quite far removed from the everyday business of living. A master-piece is a documented master-spark of vitality in artistic endeavours as well as proof of why art is always already separate from the mundane reality of everyday life, from 'relation' and from 'necessity'. By its vitalist nature, master-art cannot but be for its own sake. It is its own intrinsic value.

Here, we may note briefly, Chow's point about the essentially vitalist prejudice in Stein's teleological project of modernism and its sensibility resonates with Rancière's critique of the modernist slogan 'art for art's sake' in *The Politics of Aesthetics*. Rancière's reading demystifies the slogan, by juxtaposing the 'desperateness' of modernism's attempt to establish art's distinctiveness with the actual unattainability of such projects in the capitalist, fully commercialised and functionalised art market of the early twentieth century.[24] The strength of the modernist desire, Rancière argues, is measured against 'the emptiness of its self-declaration', the emptiness stemming from the fact that true breakthroughs and true revolutions had already had their inaugural moment in the earlier stages of capitalism and technological revolution at the time of the mimetic experimentations of realism.[25] In the first decades of the twentieth century, when the world of art is entirely dominated by commercial laws, claims to art's independence from those laws were no more subversive with regard to the politics of art that the charms of a mesmerist. What links Rancière's argument with the idea that vitalism was a way of legitimising the independence and self-animation of art is the recognition of a notable repressive tendency within modernism to deny any symptoms of inactivity, stagnation and passivity implicated in the phenomena of commercialisation and mechanical reproducibility. At stake in modernism's fascination with movement is a deep-seated distrust towards all signs of what Marinetti called lethargy, a distrust coupled with a special privileging of vitality-as-animation. And it was this valorisation of vibrant vitality over lethargic inactivity that was a necessary fuel for the modernist rebellious claims to uniqueness.

Except that, I would like to argue, the modernist understanding of vitality might not have been as straightforward as readers such as Chow or Rancière would like to think. Think of Agamben's reading of Aristotle's vitalism, which demonstrates that at the core of the original vitalist project in *De Anima* there lies the idea of passive inoperativity, *sterēsis*. In an analogous way, we may therefore look at modernism's ostensible vitalism and ask whether it does not contain within its structure a similar deviation.

Despite their persuasiveness and compatibility with current political interpretations of the early twentieth-century avant-garde, the vitalist readings of modernism unwittingly bring into focus a significant rupture, or a redoubling (to use Derrida's now classic term), in the univocality of modernist vitalocentrism. Once we pursue the question 'of what does the vital, the active, the virile actually consist?', we cannot but see significant cracks in the action-obsessed discourse, cracks through which appear embryonic modes of inoperativity and inanimateness.

So, of what does the vitalist viewpoint actually consist? As Giorgio Agamben reminds us in 'The Power of Thought', his revision of the Aristotelian notions of potentiality, actuality and privation in vitalism is not to be reduced to a simple idea that the power of our faculty is measured by the intensity of our actions: it is not simply about its actualisation. Instead, power is measured against that which does not pass into act: namely, power's capacity to be suspended, *sterēsis*.[26] Think of an architect, Agamben explains, who remains one not only when he designs buildings, but also when he does not actualise his skills. A painter remains a painter also when he does not paint; a writer, also when he does not write.[27] The power of an architect, a painter or a writer would not be a true power were it not founded upon the possibility of that power to not be exerted. One might say, therefore, that if power is at the same time the potentiality to do something and not to do something, then power contains within itself an ambivalence of actuality and privation. The vitality of one's faculty contains within itself and depends upon an 'irreducible inoperativity' of vitality, that is to say, on the arresting of power, a non-vitality.[28]

That such re-readings of the Aristotelian concept of power have gained Agamben the label of a 'linguistic vitalist' makes his term 'irreducible inoperativity' even more pertinent to Gertrude Stein's definition of the mastery and vitality of the human mind, for Stein's vitalism is also very much linguistic.[29] Given this reciprocity, Agamben's concept may bring to the surface a sense of inoperativity in Stein's 'Master-Pieces' essay which standardised readings of modernism usually fail to register, thus failing to register as well the element of passivity and impotentiality at the core of modernist sensibility.

What quickly becomes apparent on this second reading of Stein's essay is that she talks about the poetic art of writing as something that is radically distinct from an actualisation and from a simple, affirmative realisation of the artist's identity. Rather than being an incarnation of the vital creative force of an individual artist, the poetic act is a suspension of that force. In the opening lines of the text Stein says: 'there is something about what has been written having been printed which makes it no longer the property of the one who wrote it . . . one has no identity that is when one is in the act of doing anything'.[30] A creative act is thus opposed to a deliberate action controlled by an identity. Identity is linked to the conscious labour of actualisation in the poetic act; it is a mere putting to work of a faculty that has 'nothing to do' with true creation. Creation is all about identity's withdrawal as well as the withdrawal of labour. Contrary to the common understanding of creative processes, the relation between 'the act of creation' and 'the subject the creator uses to create that thing' is established via suspension of power, as the creator withholds operative control over his piece. Stein quotes Pablo Picasso on capturing this idea when he said he didn't care who or what influenced him in the act as long it was not himself, which for Stein means that creation goes only so far as one is able to suspend one's control over one's skilful hand and arrest one's identity. There is, then, in the artistic act a radical resistance to the self and all of its talents and abilities, which is also a manner of their conservation in the poetic act. And it is precisely in *the act of suspension-while-creating*, the strange gesture of impotence, that Stein locates her notion of a masterpiece.[31]

Arguing for the coexistence of creation and resistance within faculty during the creation of a work of art, Agamben explains that the link between the idea of suspending power to control the act and resistance can be traced to the etymology of the word. From the Latin *sistere* (a root that resistance shares with assistance), 'to resist' means to arrest, to restrain something, as well as to stand still. It is in this very literal sense (a sense reminiscent of Lafargue's Andalusian and the body elastic like a rod of steel in its indomitability), Agamben argues, that resistance is built into the structure of an artistic act. Picasso's *Les Demoiselles d'Avignon* of 1907, from this perspective, represents the suspension, an arresting of a certain way of seeing and a certain kind of brushwork at the same time as it is also the exposition of that vision and gesture.

In the scheme of inoperativity, it is not enough to possess the creative ability to deliver masterpieces, because the question of whether they will be works of mastery or mere products of labour depends on how the artist passes through what Agamben calls 'the field of tensions stretching out between potency and impotency, to can and to cannot, acting and resisting'.[32] Agamben and Stein are thus virtually univocal when it comes the definition of mastery. Only in one case can we talk about mastery and that is when a creator delivers himself, 'fully and helplessly': that is to say, without exercising conscious control, into his own impotentiality. An artist, says Agamben, 'can master his potentiality only through his impotentiality but precisely for that reason there is no such thing as a mastery on potentiality'; mastery is 'not a formal perfection, a talent, an execution of an order or talent that *must* pass into art'. In Stein's words:

> It is awfully difficult, action is direct and effective but after all action is necessary and anything that is necessary has to do with human nature and not with the human mind. Therefore a master-piece *has essentially not to be necessary*, it has to be that is it has to exist but it does not have to be necessary *it is not in response to necessity as action is because the minute it is necessary it has in it no possibility of going on* [my emphasis].[33]

Stein's master-act is not simply action, an actualisation, for that would imply that it originated in the act of rule execution. It would be something one necessarily must do. In contrast, a masterful piece has essentially 'not to be necessary', because necessity would annul and consume the critical power-as-impotentiality (*sterēsis*) that founds the mastery of the masterpiece – 'that makes it', as Stein puts it, 'hold itself just the same'.[34]

In her discussion of Stein's theory of genius, Barbara Will highlights precisely this aspect of the poet's approach: namely, Stein's insistence that the genius participates in the moment of composition without evaporating from the work. By quoting Stein's view that 'nothing would bother me more than the way a thing goes dead when it has been said', Will touches upon the same problem of the amphibological nature of power that Agamben isolates as the key to understanding creative potency.[35] For Stein, just as for Agamben, master works of art

> do not exist by human nature because everybody always knows everything there is to know about human nature, they exist because they came to be

as something that is an end in itself and in that respect it is opposed to the business of living which is relation and necessity. That is what a master-piece is.[36]

That which is the commonly available ability to polish a skill or to enhance one's understanding of life – the business of living as human nature, which is all about identity and knowledge (relation) and rules of craftsmanship (necessity) – does not increase the value of a masterpiece. What is needed instead is a relinquishing of relation and necessity, or resisting them from the depths of the individual mind's idiosyncratic 'ability to not', which suspends all that the mind knows and is able to put into the act and conserves the suspended ability in the act of creation.

Once again, Stein's philosophy strikes a chord with Agamben's. The modernist poet illustrates her point with an example drawn from *Hamlet*, in whose masterful creation Shakespeare captures the ambivalence between potentiality and actuality, because although Prince Hamlet could speak to the ghost of his father in a way that would be familiar to anyone, he is capable of not doing so, and yet to put this 'capacity to not' into words:

It is not the way Hamlet reacts to his father's ghost that makes the master-piece, he might have reacted according to Shakespeare in a dozen other ways and everybody would have been as much impressed by the psychology of it. But there is no psychology in it, that is not probably the way any young man would react to the ghost of his father and there is no particular reason why they should. If it were the way a young man could react to the ghost of his father then that would be something anybody in any village would know they could talk about it talk about it endlessly but that would not make a master-piece and that brings us once more back to the subject of identity.[37]

Adam Phillips writes of Hamlet that he captured Freud's imagination in *The Interpretation of Dreams* (1900) because Hamlet thought and spoke in ways in which no one spoke before, which may well be another way of putting Stein's idea of masterly creativity.[38] And it is perhaps because this idea defines the artistic act as an exertion of the potentiality to not-create that John Ashbery poetically describes Stein's poetic method based on this theory as a 'hymn to possibility'.[39]

Further Away from Vitalocentrism: Marcel Duchamp's Concept of *inaction externe*

Somewhat along these lines, Marjorie Perloff traces an affinity between Stein's unconventional view of what makes a work creative and masterful and the artistic tactics of Marcel Duchamp. Both Duchamp and Stein, Perloff intimates, were equally interested in the suspension of faculty's engagement and the idea of the withdrawal of the senses. In order to show this affinity, in 'Of Objects and Readymades: Gertrude Stein and Marcel Duchamp' Perloff claims that both Stein and Duchamp are similarly 'indifferent' to modes of 'retinal representation'.[40] Instead of representing by means of actualising, they use objects (Duchamp) and words (Stein) as parts of 'systems of pointing' that break the representational contract.[41] In this sense, Stein and Duchamp have much more in common than, say, Stein and Picasso or Stein and the Futurists, whose experiments still involve paint and manual skills to represent objects of the real world such as bottles or plates. As Perloff puts it: 'neither the Futurists nor the Cubists broke the tradition visual contract with the viewer, a contract whereby the images presented, however distorted, fragmented, or abstracted they may appear, are to be understood as retinal representations'.[42] In contrast, Stein and Duchamp insist on signifying beyond the rules of this contract; what they put into the act is both the ability to write/paint *and* the ability to not write/paint.

Duchamp's sculptures *Fountain* (1917) and *Prelude to a Broken Arm* (1915) embody this inherent tension and manage to capture inoperativity in operation. The making and the reception of readymades or *objets trouvés* is 'based on a reaction of visual indifference with total absence of good or bad taste', for it is not an object that is created but an in-sensibility.[43] For Perloff, the inoperativity of 'retinal' in-sensibility is that which makes all the difference as to the absolutely 'central issue' in experimental art, the issue that critics usually sweep under the carpet with diagnoses such as 'X is deconstructing Y' or 'X is playing with Y': namely, 'when is free play, nonsense, non-referentiality effective and when we consider it mere gibberish'.[44] Deconstructing and playing with are still ways of operating within the contract of the senses; mastery in Duchamp's sense is suspending the contract altogether. It is with reference to these characteristics that Perloff detects a theoretical resemblance between Duchamp and Stein. Stein too believed that pieces of art should *not* resemble any things (or mark a presence of a good or bad identity), but should instead be based on a suspension of agency and of any visual or linguistic difference this agency could bring. In 'A Cessation of Resemblance' Perloff reaffirms this reciprocity, emphasising not only the formal aspect of their rejection of the retinal contract but also its philosophical implications.[45] There may be no *textes trouvés* in Stein's work in the way that Duchamp has his found objects, but the principal rule of artistic creation – to make a rule of inoperativity and put inoperativity into an act – is shared by the two artists to a striking, though rarely acknowledged degree.

If Stein's philosophy of art is strikingly similar to Duchamp's in its emphasis on inoperative power, there is nevertheless a difference in how the two artists present their philosophical positions. Stein, as argued above, dwells in the vocabularies of vitalism, even though the meaning of this vitalism is in the end very Agambenian, or Aristotelian proper, because it frames the essence of vital power as *sterēsis* or as power-under-privation. Duchamp, on the other hand, deploys the categories of work and laziness.

Is this a deliberate reference to the tradition of the French Anti-work Movement? There is no evidence of Duchamp's direct allusion to the movement's key texts, Paul Lafargue's *Le Droit à la paresse* or Eugene Marsan's *Éloge de la paresse*, in the formulation of his 'ethic of laziness'; however, possible analogies to politico-economic theories of unproductivity can certainly be drawn.[46] In 'Where's Duchamp? Out Queering the Field', Robert Harvey acknowledges these links and dubs Duchamp's artistic tactic 'active laziness', an approach that suspends the dialectical tension between work and unproductivity.[47] By using the tactic and producing readymades, Duchamp 'embodied affable passivity, a woefully deficient disregard for the virility tacitly required of vanguard artists', while at the same time he did create art that was most avant-garde. Duchamp's own name for active laziness was *inaction externe* ('outward inaction'), a term that resonates with Stein's/Agamben's concept of the apparent but productive stasis that takes place in the non-virile mode of laziness.[48] The way Duchamp explained *inaction externe* was that, while on the surface of things in the outward sphere of productive actions nothing seems to be happening, another kind of creative power conserves itself in the act. Think of it, Harvey prompts, as 'putting waste to wasteful "uses"'.[49] In Duchamp's words this would be 'harnessing the energy of the infra-slim', an energy that emerges out of the tension when the actualised power/potentiality meets its non-actualised other: to take an example from Duchamp, when one's movement produces the squeaking music of corduroy trousers.[50]

In 'The Power of Thought' Giorgio Agamben says that the amphi-bological character of human power exposes its link to the idea of power-of-freedom in its political sense. And this linkage can also be traced in Duchamp's aesthetics of *inaction externe* in that its logic suspends the capitalist productivity/unproductivity binary. In 'Work Avoidance: The Everyday Life of Marcel Duchamp's Readymades', Helen Molesworth points out how aware Duchamp was of the subversive potential of his artistic tactic *vis-à-vis* the norm of productivity:

> In 1913 Duchamp jotted a note to himself: 'Can one make works which are not works of "art"?' Can one make something that has no function, that performs no work, that is not beholden to a purpose, even that of art? Something not beholden to leisure either? In such a formulation, art and play exist in an analogously tenuous realm of (im)possibility.[51]

Duchamp's note highlights the counter-systemic intervention of the artist's method but also the axiological implications of its sub-versiveness. Isn't the value of art for art's sake an untenable dream rather than a real possibility? Is independence gained at the cost of the loss of artistic identity? Molesworth's answer to these question is quite optimistic:

> Duchamp's readymades are an attempt to think outside the logic of work, a logic in which 'the goal of labor is the full reality of human existence.' Not to work – to be lazy – is then to deny the full reality of human

existence, to deny the category of 'I', at least the form familiar to bourgeois capitalism.[52]

Duchamp's *inaction externe* is as philosophically original as it is politically radical in the sense that it is a practical method of performing acts of protest against the economic servitude accepted by modernist art groups, for example the Surrealists, and implied in the virility of their programme statements. While 'Surrealism, prematurely announcing the revolution, ultimately played into capitalism's propensity to commodify everything, Duchamp parodied the commodification of art' without succumbing to its trappings: 'loafing produces readymades. The solution to man's enslavement to labor is being resolved.'[53]

There is then a small but significant difference between Duchamp's and Stein's expositions of the tactics of inoperativity which are otherwise so alike, and this difference can be reduced to the presence (in Duchamp) and absence (in Stein) of the notion of laziness. This is not because Stein condemned the idea – 'It takes a lot of time to be a genius, you have to sit around so much doing nothing, really doing nothing', she once said – but because the notion of laziness is indivisible from the issues of the bodily, and Stein was considerably less interested in the role of the body in the creative dynamics than was Duchamp. While Duchamp's approach of *inaction externe* mobilises the entire spectrum of physiological experiences – lying down, breathing slowly, tripping over waste, listening to the sound of his corduroys – Stein's philosophy of inoperativity tends to dwell in abstraction.[54]

This disparity on the body issue illuminates the problem of modernist engagement with the modalities of inaction that are buried in the ideology and rhetoric of vitalocentrism: 'drawing off of strength', lethargy, immobility, indolence and their relation to the idea of productivity. From this angle, modernism does not seem as 'desperate' or 'naïve' about its claims to art's independence as Rancière would like to see it. Rather, it turns out to be secretly contemplative about the radical modes of breaking the social and the representational contract, thus nurturing the sensibility of exhaustion which writers and artists of the next epoch would claim as their very own.

Notes

1. John Barth, *The Literature of Exhaustion and the Literature of Replenishment* (Northridge, CA: Lord John Press, 1982), 64.

2. Raymond Williams, *Marxism and Literature* (Oxford: Oxford University Press, 1977), 122.

3. Ibid., 122.

4. Ibid., 126.

5. Ibid., 126.

6. Ibid., 122.

7. Jacques Rancière, *Aisthesis: Scenes from the Aesthetic Regime of Art* (London: Verso, 2013).

8. See Bertrand Russell, *In Praise of Idleness and Other Essays* (New York: Routledge, 2004) and Siegfried Kracauer and Thomas Y. Levin, *The Mass Ornament: Weimar Essays* (Cambridge, MA: Harvard University Press, 1995).

9. F. T. Marinetti, 'Tactilism (1921)', in *Futurism: An Anthology*, ed. Lawrence Rainey, Christine Poggi and Laura Wittman (New Haven, CT: Yale University Press, 2009), 265.

10. Walter Benjamin, *The Writer of Modern Life: Essays on Charles Baudelaire* (Cambridge, MA: Harvard University Press, 2006), 176.

11. Charles Baudelaire, 'On the Essence of Laughter and, in General, on the Comic in the Plastic Arts' (1846), in *The Painter of Modern Life and Other Essays*, trans. Jonathan Mayne (London: Phaidon, 1965).

12. F. T. Marinetti, 'The Founding and Manifesto of Futurism (1909)', in Rainey et al. (eds), *Futurism: An Anthology*, 49.

13. Ibid., 52.

14. Ibid., 51.

15. Mina Loy, 'Feminist Manifesto', in *Postmodern American Fiction: A Norton Anthology*, ed. Paula Geyh, Fred G. Leebron and Andrew Levy (New York: W.W. Norton, 1998), 1502–5; Ezra Pound, 'A Retrospect' (1914), in Geyh et al. (eds), *Postmodern American Fiction: A Norton Anthology*, 1506–7; Nina Colosi, 'The Antennae of the Race', *Leonardo* 35.5 (2002), 579; Willa Cather, 'The Novel Démeublé', in *Not Under Forty* (New York: Knopf, 1922), 43–51.

16. Juliana Chow, 'Motion Studies: Vitalism in Gertrude Stein's Work', *Arizona Quarterly: A Journal of American Literature, Culture, and Theory* 69.4 (2013), 77–109.

17. Ibid., 78.

18. Ibid., 78–9. Chow references here Bruno Latour's problematisation of animateness and inanimateness in nature and technology in *We Have Never Been Modern*, trans. Catherine Porter (Cambridge, MA: Harvard University Press, 1993), but another useful reference, because related to the history of technological revolution and its violation of the Aristotelian concept of anima distribution, could be Bernard Stiegler's *Technics and Time: The Fault of Epimetheus*, trans. George Collins and Richard Beardsworth (Stanford: Stanford University Press, 1998), which I discuss in the context of modernist fascination with technology in Zuzanna Ladyga, 'Technophobia and Technophilia in American

Postmodern Criticism', *Anglica. An International Journal of English Studies* 24.1 (2015), 161–75.

19. See Omri Moses, *Out of Character: Modernism, Vitalism, Psychic Life* (Stanford: Stanford University Press, 2014).

20. Jacques Rancière, *The Politics of Aesthetics*, trans. Gabriel Rockhill (London: Continuum, 2010), 28.

21. Martin Puchner, *Poetry of the Revolution: Marx, Manifestos, and the Avant-Gardes* (Princeton: Princeton University Press, 2006).

22. Gertrude Stein, 'What Are Master-Pieces and Why Are There So Few of Them' (1940), in *The Best American Essays of the Century*, ed. Joyce Carol Oates and Robert Atwan (Boston: Houghton Mifflin, 2001), 131–8. For this claim, see John Whittier-Ferguson, 'The Liberation of Gertrude Stein: War and Writing', *Modernism/Modernity* 8.3 (2001), 426; Barbara Will, *Gertrude Stein, Modernism, and the Problem of 'Genius'* (Edinburgh: Edinburgh University Press, 2000).

23. Stein, 'What Are Master-Pieces', 134.

24. Rancière, *The Politics of Aesthetics*, 28.

25. Ibid., 24.

26. Giorgio Agamben, 'The Power of Thought', *Critical Inquiry* 40.2 (2014), 480–91.

27. Ibid., 483.

28. Giorgio Agamben, 'Resistance in Art,' 2014, https://www.youtube.com/watch?v=one7mE-8y9c (accessed 28 January 2019).

29. Lorenzo Chiesa and Frank Ruda, 'The Event of Language as Force of Life: Agamben's Linguistic Vitalism', *Angelaki* 16.3 (2011), 163–80; Jenny Doussan, 'Time and Presence in Agamben's Critique of Deconstruction', *Cosmos and History: The Journal of Natural and Social Philosophy* 9.1 (2013), 200.

30. Stein, 'What Are Master-Pieces', 131.

31. In 'Resistance in Art', Agamben provides his illustration of this ambivalence using Kafka's early story 'The Great Swimmer', which features an Olympic record holder who admits that she doesn't know how she won the race because she is unable to swim. She does not use any skill, and yet by force of some strange, uncontrolled, mannered motion she manages the swimming race and wins the title. Allegorically speaking, then, a masterpiece is produced by the swimmer though without the control of any identity and without conscious application of the skill, in an act of impotence.

32. Agamben, 'Resistance in Art'.

33. Stein, 'What Are Master-Pieces', 133.

34. Ibid., 134.

35. Will, *Gertrude Stein, Modernism, and the Problem of 'Genius'*, 83.

36. Stein, 'What Are Master-Pieces', 134.

37. Ibid., 132.

38. Adam Phillips, 'Against Self-Criticism', *London Review of Books* 37.5 (2015), 13–16.

39. John Ashbery, 'The Impossible: Gertrude Stein', in *Selected Prose*, ed. Eugene Richie (Ann Arbor: University of Michigan Press, 2004), 11–15.

40. Marjorie Perloff, 'Of Objects and Readymades: Gertrude Stein and Marcel Duchamp', *Forum for Modern Language Studies* 32.2 (1996), 139.

41. Ibid., 140.
42. Ibid., 139.
43. Hans Richter, *DADA: Art and Anti-Art* (New York: Oxford University Press, 1978), 89.
44. Perloff, 'Of Objects and Readymades', 153.
45. Marjorie Perloff, 'A Cessation of Resemblance', *Battersea Review* 1.1 (2012), http://thebatterseareview.com/back-issue-content/75-marjorie-perloff (accessed 28 January 2019).
46. Robert Harvey, 'Where's Duchamp? Out Queering the Field', *Yale French Studies* 10.9 (2006), 90, 95.
47. Ibid., 91.
48. Ibid., 89, 91.
49. Ibid., 93.
50. Ibid., 93.
51. Helen Molesworth, 'Work Avoidance: The Everyday Life of Marcel Duchamp's Readymades', *Art Journal* 57.4 (1998), 57.
52. Ibid., 61.
53. Harvey, 'Where's Duchamp?', 93, 84.
54. Molesworth, 'Work Avoidance', 58. It is interesting to note that a similar body bias informs both Agamben's 'Resistance in Art' and Stein's 'Master-pieces'. At the end of the lecture, Agamben mistranslates the title of Malevich's pamphlet 'Laziness as the Truth of Mankind' as 'Inoperativity as the Truth of Mankind', clearly avoiding the signifier 'lazy', as if even the slightest intimation that the sublime Aristotelian concept of *sterēsis* be compared to something so vulgar as 'Лень' could ruin his argumentation.

CHAPTER 4

Laziness and Tactility in Ernest Hemingway's *The Garden of Eden*

To be an artist is to be delivered fully and helplessly into one's own impotentiality.

Giorgio Agamben

When, in 'Resistance in Art', Agamben says that an artistic performance is 'a field of tensions stretching between potency and impotency, between *the ability to do* and *the ability to not do*, resisting', he stresses the particular character of impotency which is neither simply 'not doing anything' nor 'putting something into practice'. As I argued in Chapter 3, the same philosophical logic underlies Gertrude Stein's essay 'What Are Master-Pieces and Why Are There So Few of Them', even though the language of her essay overtly privileges the active, potent aspect of creative power; it also underlies Marcel Duchamp's concept of *inaction externe*, which additionally brings forth an economic dimension. I have also suggested that Duchamp's emphasis on the body complements Stein's abstract theory of inoperativity. In this chapter, I would like to turn to literature and its figurative modes of mediating the sensibility of inaction in its embryonic form. To this end, I would like to focus on Ernest Hemingway's *The Garden of Eden*, which brings together the abstract and bodily strands of their theories of inaction. Hemingway might have been an uneven student of Stein's teaching, and certainly was not a great admirer of Duchamp's art, but his last, unfinished novel stands at the threshold of modern and postmodern aesthetic regimes and is therefore an appropriate place to start an investigation of how modernist inoperativity has been wrestled from its embryonic state and given a literary form.

Hemingway started *The Garden of Eden* in 1946 and it was written over many years, but it was not published until 1986, posthumously. The novel captures the tension between creative potency and impotency by dramatising it as a conflict of two characters, Catherine and David Bourne, each haunted by their individual, internal conflict between creative vigour and creative resistance. The tension sustains *The Garden of Eden*'s narrative and dictates its pace. Occasionally, however, there occur in the story languorous moments of slowing down and the drawing off of vigour, when the interpersonal and internal conflicts cease, while the text itself approximates a self-reflexive commentary on its own power dynamics. Self-referential as these fragments are, however, they are also exercises in haptic aesthetics in that their insight into the essence of creativity incorporates, via the theme of laziness, the bodily, sensuous dimension of all creative endeavours.

What I wish to argue in the following pages is that Hemingway's manipulation of the theme is a radical attempt at articulating by literary means the sensibility of exhaustion that underlies the modernist love of action. In *The Garden of Eden*, the poetics of laziness serves a double function. First, it works to express from within the conventions of modernist stylistics the idea of the privative origin of creative power and the desire to maintain a position of neutrality within the field of tension between creation and resistance. This is achieved by Hemingway's engagement with the poetics of touch and ipseity. Second, it functions to produce an ideological commentary on the issues of the axiological nature of productivity and the economic valorisation of literary creation in the early to mid-twentieth-century capitalist colonisation of the realm of art. As a story centred around the question of what it means to create, a story whose author could not bring himself to finish it, *The Garden of Eden* provides a unique sample of a modernist text struggling to give shape to an inexpressible, pre-emergent sensibility of exhaustion. Read metafictionally, *The Garden of Eden* is a story about what stylistic measures it takes to spell out by literary means of the vitalocentric norm that element of inoperativity that defines the poetic act, and therefore inevitably counters that norm. On another level, as a book about a successful writer who regularly produces pages of manuscript, *The Garden of Eden* is also an attempt to comment on the loss of artistic freedom that the twentieth-century capitalist biopower has taken away from writers by forcing them to accept the norms of the book market.

In the blissful, edenic setting of the French and the Spanish Riviera, a young American writer David Bourne enjoys a 'happy and lazy' honeymoon with his wife Catherine.[1] Most of the time they swim, sunbathe, make love, indulge in food and drink, and pretty much do nothing, except for David's short periods of work on his new book. The chronotope of honeymoon – this 'silly' and 'sticky' idea, as David's friend, the Colonel calls it, thus anticipating the nightmare into which the Bournes' bliss eventually turns – frames the temporal organisation of *The Garden of Eden*, with the rhythm of lazy siestas intertwining with the vertiginous madness of events that Catherine plans for every day.[2] Hemingway's choice of a honeymoon frame is not simply autobiographical, even though his biographers' contextualised readings of the novel against the events of Hemingway's life make a point of anchoring it to his trips with Hadley Richardson and Pauline Pfeiffer. Outside of this frame, and more theoretically, honeymoons are not simply a type of holiday time, which may or may not go wrong. As Michel Foucault observes in 'Of Other Spaces', a honeymoon is also a form of tangible experience in the sense that it is a whole new spatio-temporal milieu in which certain things happen. It is a 'heterotopia of crisis', a 'nowhere' place for the experience of 'sexual virility':[3]

> the first manifestations of sexual virility were in fact supposed to take place elsewhere than at home. For girls, there was, until the middle of the twentieth century, a tradition called the 'honeymoon trip' which was an ancestral theme. The young woman's deflowering could take place 'nowhere' and, at the moment of its occurrence the train or honeymoon hotel was indeed the place of this nowhere, this heterotopia without geographical markers.[4]

Hemingway's decadent honeymooners are, of course, not part of this tradition; moreover, unlike in the case of Foucault's 'nowheres', their trip has very specific geographical coordinates. Nevertheless,

the space-time of their holiday does lay down the heterotopic conditions for Catherine's sexual virility to enter the phase of erotic
experiments and decisions that will eventually bring her marriage
to an end. If, in Foucault's typology, honeymoon is a heterotopia
of crisis, it is worth stressing that in *The Garden of Eden* this crisis
is both sexual and artistic. What is more, it is not critical in the
sense that it is a moment of norm induction as in the classic honeymoon scenario, but is rather an event of norm destabilisation.
Instead of accepting the social role of a wife, Catherine undermines it. She cuts her hair short, dresses like a man, drinks absinth,
experiments in bed, does not want to have children, and invites
another woman to join her relationship with David. David in turn,
instead of accepting the modern, economically regulated social role
of an artist, struggles in a similar fashion with his identity as a
writer. While he passively assents to Catherine's transgressions of
the patriarchal norm and participates in her body-change project,
David is immersed in his own crisis of creativity, where the idea of
subverting the normativised role of an artist-as-producer threatens
his identity. He is able to mechanically produce pages of writing,
but he suffers from an inability to make those pages 'come alive'.[5]
Not that David is suffering from a classically Romantic version of
writer's block; he is quite aware that it is not the lack of heavenly
inspiration that paralyses his prose. The inability to make the pages
come alive has more to do with David's inner resistance to the
changing parameters of literary self-expression. Thus, on the most
basic level of teleological organisation of the novel, we witness the
tension between virile potency and its cessation, with Catherine
initially representing the active element, and David embodying the
withdrawal of vital powers. As the narrative of *The Garden of Eden*
unravels, however, this distribution of roles turns out to be much
more unclear.

Ever since the publication of *The Garden of Eden* in 1986, the
opposition between David and Catherine has appeared central
to Hemingway scholars, whether they worked with the edited
Scribner's version or with the original manuscript, which features
three sets of sexually tense relationships like the one between David
and Catherine,[6] and whether they were interested in teasing out
the biographical facts of Hemingway's problematic marriages to

Richardson and Pfeiffer and the resemblances between Catherine and the author's sister, his mother, Zelda Fitzgerald and so on.[7] In the vast body of scholarship devoted to this dichotomy, two approaches are particularly relevant for my discussion of Hemingway's haptic poetics of inoperativity and the productive tension between creation and non-creation in his last novel.

The first, feminist critical approach stresses the creative and emancipatory side of Catherine's virility, whereas the second approach contextualises the opposition between Catherine and David, treating the two characters as contrasting aspects of Hemingway's self-portrait as an artist.[8] In this reading, the conflict between Catherine and David parallels the artist's own ambivalence about his style and method and its place in the modernist politics of aesthetics, an ambivalence of which the unfinished manuscript of *The Garden of Eden* and its eventual publication in edited form are undeniable indicators. In other words, one approach focuses on the bodies of Hemingway's characters and the other on the corporeality of the text, but in each case, 'the body' remains a symbolic construct rather than a somaesthetic threshold. This is why it seems worthwhile to review those critical insights through the metaphorical lens of laziness, which links the symbolic with the haptic, in order to tease out from *The Garden of Eden* modernism's pre-emergent structures of feeling.

Let us first look at the interpretations that emphasise Catherine's creative power. Through the feminist lens, Catherine is sometimes 'transgender', sometimes she 'eroticizes race' for anti-patriarchal purposes, and sometimes she simply 'writes with her body'.[9] But whatever she is or does, Catherine always represents what Rose Marie Burwell has called the 'creative struggle' of women under patriarchy.[10] An exchange between Catherine and David is often quoted:

> 'I have these flashes of intuition,' he said. 'I'm the inventive type.'
> 'I'm the destructive type,' she said. 'And I'm going to destroy you.'[11]

Hemingway's critics emphasise that, contrary to what the fragment says, Catherine isn't simply destructive, but rather rebellious and insatiable in her appetite for creation. The relationship within the

opposition between Catherine and David is far from uncompli-
cated, despite the editorial intervention by Tom Jenks at Scribner's,
which forces this 'simple dichotomy of creation and destruction';
in fact, the manuscript of *The Garden of Eden* has David nickname
Catherine none other than 'the inventor'.[12] And yet one does not
have to reach for the manuscript to argue for Catherine's creative
power. Even in the above exchange from the Scribner's edition,
she follows her famous declaration of destructiveness with an
announcement that she is 'going to wake up in the night and do
something you've never heard of or imagined', thus informing
David as well as the reader of her febrile creativity, her willingness
to stay attuned and reactive even in the lax hours of sleep.[13] Here,
however, we encounter the first complication in Catherine's representation of virility, for most of her creative power originates in
acts of doing nothing whatsoever.

If Catherine is a creative artist, then it is definitely not of a traditional kind. Upon their arrival in Spain, she admits to her husband:
'The whole way here I saw wonderful things to paint and I can't
paint at all and never could. But I know wonderful things to write
and I can't even write a letter that isn't stupid.'[14] In other words,
Catherine's penchant for attunement by way of the senses is responsible for her inability to represent this attunement mimetically. She
is a performance artist, whose acts consist of not being able to paint
or write. She performs by changing locations, drinks and hairstyles,
planning erotic scenarios, and reorganising her marriage into a
love triangle with Marita. But because her efforts do not follow
the representational contract, her creative role does not receive full
recognition. In spite of what might seem like a 'Bovarist' excitement
that confuses life for art, Catherine is ultimately as legitimate a
designer of the narrative of the novel as is her writer husband.[15]
That she realises this is one proof of Hemingway's recognition of
her creative potency. The world of the novel is a world 'I made up;
we made up I mean', she says to David.[16]

In 'Who is "the Destructive Type"?', Carl Eby describes Catherine's
special mode of storytelling in the following way:

> she does script the honeymoon narrative that David commits to words
> on the page ... she creates in the register of the imaginary; David in

the symbolic. Her imagination is driven by identification; David's by representation. She stresses the signified; David the signifier . . . Catherine and David's creativities work very differently.[17]

Eby thereby intimates that Catherine creates in a mirror-stage fashion, with her main tool being her body identity. However, Catherine does not seem to strive for a complete self-image, as the psychoanalytic logic of the mirror-stage would imply, inasmuch as she aims at its unattainable other: a potential ideal, a heterogeneous masterpiece that is devoid of any traits of individual identity. She wants to be a boy and a girl, but she does not want the bisexual identity either. 'I don't go in for girls', she explains to Marita, uneasy about the fact that she could have been so easily categorised.[18] Similarly, she wants David and herself to look identical and talks him into tonsorial experiments, but at the same time wishes for them to stay unchanged. In short, she wants her identity to stay suspended between its multiple potentialities, but also to transfer this ideal multiplicity into the narrative. As I discuss below, this is achieved by the mobilisation of the haptic mode.

Hemingway's Haptic Aesthetics

In her performance art, Catherine seems to be doing really little – she is just a 'lazy naked wife' – and at the same time doing a tremendous lot.[19] The way she achieves this effect and builds her power position as a co-creator of *The Garden of Eden* is to engage into her performances her haptic sense. She uses her skin, her hair and even the surroundings that she smells and tastes as 'found' transitional objects in Donald Winnicott's sense: that is, as tools of creative self-expression that do not represent mimetically but communicate the potentiality of an ideal self and a desire for this potentiality to be conserved in the creative act while not being represented. Catherine's performances are, as Winnicott put it when analysing his patients' lazy squiggles, 'potentially . . . a masterpiece'; her literary presence, on the other hand, is like a blank 'dream screen' against which the narrative of a dream fantasy might be dreamed.[20] Winnicott, let us remember, linked the longing for masterly perfection with states of laziness and other forms of somatic misrepresentations of the self. His 'Squiggle Game' and 'Psycho-Somatic Illness' describe the putatively impedimental somaesthetic habits and mannerisms usually linked to conversion disorder or depression as positive signals of an unceasing desire within a self towards psychosomatic rebooting and reintegration.[21] Lazy and inert experiential phenomena, Winnicott thought, might be our way of loading the potentiality of psychical equilibrium via creative uses of the body's kinaesthetic and proprioceptive faculty. Such is precisely the logic behind Catherine's numerous haptic performances of lassitude in Hemingway's novel. Crucial to those performances is a lax pose that Catherine so frequently adopts in the novel.[22] Lying motionless, 'arms by her sides', 'breathing carefully', 'feeling' (and asking David to feel) her skin and hair, registering the forces and the gravity, she regains her psychological orientation and thus the power to perpetuate the narrative.[23]

To vector critical attention to Hemingway's haptic references is to gain a fresh perspective on what critics usually term the novel's trouble with androgyny, mediated through its characters' experiments with the body.[24] For from the angle of the haptic, the body in Hemingway's novel appears to be less an object of the mind's experiments and more a perfectly self-sustained agency of proprioceptive recalibration. The reason why tactile experiments, in which Hemingway's characters in *The Garden of Eden* so frequently indulge, are so important to creativity is because the haptic sense is autotelic and thus fundamental to artistic self-expression. From a philosophical perspective, tactile experiments are essentially exercises in ipseity, for when we touch we mostly feel our own skin and its receptive faculty rather than anything outside of its haptic envelope. All touching is virtually about self-touching – it is an auto-affection – as Jean-Luc Nancy famously professed.[25] And as Karen Barad has pointedly added, it is a *self*-touching only in the sense that it is 'an encounter with the infinite alterity of the self as matter' and not a mode of identity-affirmation.[26] In this light, Catherine Bourne's mode of communicating through touch – 'something that I have to do' – is her way of preserving her potency as a literary character, without assuming any identity, but via building her (and the narrative's) creative potential on the haptic experience of herself as a *sujet trouvé*.[27]

If the lazy bodies of Catherine and David are invoked over and over again in Hemingway's novel, thus joining the list of his stylistic mannerisms, it is because the repetition of the languorous bed scenes helps Hemingway to capture the idea that the essence of creative power is inextricably linked to haptic passivity, and thus undermine one of the pillars of modernist aesthetics: the belief in the absolute value and creative force of movement and activity that has to be transposed into the literary act.

Haptic Aesthetics and the Anti-Haptic Bias

Catherine is a legitimate creator of *The Garden of Eden*'s narrative who writes with her inability to write. How to explain, then, her eventual relegation from the narrative? If we agree with the critics that this is Hemingway's self-portrait as a modernist artist, then Catherine's and David's creative approaches represent the two creative modes that Hemingway as a writer personally struggled between. In this metafictional reading, Catherine stands for a refusal to accept the representational contract and give in to the norm of the literary market, while David embodies the expenditure of creative energy that confuses real art with productive work. For *The Garden of Eden* to enter the publishing circuit, therefore, Catherine must be disposed of, which is why she 'murders' her character, to use the Lacanian phrasing, and joins *The Garden of Eden*'s symbolic register as its creative reservoir. To that end, the disposal of her character is anticipated much earlier in the story, when she apologises to David: 'I was impossible, like a painter, and I was my own picture. It was awful,' thus simultaneously confirming that she is a co-creator of the narrative she partakes in, as well as signalling that full transposition of identity into art is 'impossible' in that it would be 'awful'.[28]

All in all, Catherine Bourne is an ambivalent construct. She is Hemingway's own voice inasmuch as she is also that which he would perhaps desire to eliminate from his writerly practice because he *ought to* condemn it as normatively unproductive. This unwitting rejection is dramatised in the novel through references to her artistic inferiority. The condemnatory tone features with particular force in chapter 7 when Catherine talks to the Colonel about her visit to the Museo del Prado. It is significant that it is not David but the Colonel who is Catherine's interlocutor here, because the Colonel, the character who condemned the sticky idea of a honeymoon, functions in *The Garden of Eden* as a voice of conscience.

> 'I saw you in the Prado looking at the Grecos,' the Colonel said.
> 'I saw you too,' she said. 'Do you always look at pictures as though you owned them and were deciding how to have them re-hung properly?'
> 'Probably,' the Colonel said. 'Do you always look at them as though you were the young chief of a warrior tribe who had gotten loose from his counsellors and was looking at that marble of Leda and the Swan?'[29]

The modernist verdict communicated in the Colonel's insult pinpoints everything that is 'wrong' with Catherine's creative method, while it also recognises its subversive strength. She is compared to a rebellious warrior with energy so unstructured that it might cause damage when 'gotten loose'. Her method lacks refinement. Like a barbarian, she is stunned by *Leda and the Swan*, as if unable to distinguish which is more awe-inspiring; the violent rape it represents, its mythological secret, or the gentleness of the sculptor's carving. But criticised as Catherine's artistic sensibility is, it is also her biggest asset, because were it not for the power sealed off in her way of living there would be no narrative at all. In other words, Hemingway needs Catherine in his story since she embodies the forbidden artistic option of writing for oneself, in a mode of self-ownership that ignores fashions and modernist directives and says 'no' to the norm.

Feminist interpreters of *The Garden of Eden* would agree on this point. From the feminist perspective, the conversation between Catherine and the Colonel reads as an assertion of agency on the part of the female character, as her act of protest against the patriarchal tradition represented by the Colonel, which thinks it 'owns' feminine identity and may 'rehang' it any way it wants. In that sense, the conversation mimics Catherine's earlier exchange with David when, upon her frustration with not being able to paint or write, he explains to her that 'nobody wanted to buy pictures of Castilla the way you saw it'.[30] In other words, she is not part of the Western, masculine artistic tradition. However, as Ryan Hediger pointedly remarks, the feminist lens is in this case quite reductive. 'Not only gender conventions are at stake here', the critic writes, 'but more broadly, what counts as meaningful in human life – products or relationships, art or lived reality, text or embodiment? . . . *The Garden of Eden* can only elaborate these dilemmas, failing to resolve them.'[31] Indeed, the stakes in Hemingway's project are high, if we agree that *The Garden of Eden* is a dispute with the modernist regime of the sensible, a dispute so ideologically fundamental and at same time so personal that, as some commentators speculate, Hemingway refrained from publishing the novel because he was intimidated by his own conclusions.[32]

Catherine's haptic creativity type would not have been approved of by Gertrude Stein, and certainly is not approved of by the masculine conscience of *The Garden of Eden*, but Hemingway still seems to find it compelling. And that is because, with all her apparent 'barbaric' sensibility, Catherine allegorises the element of impotentiality and channels into the narrative act the potentiality not to, the irreducible element of resistance on which a true act of creativity depends. Another way of saying this is that Catherine represents a more elemental resistance than the one captured by feminist readers of *The Garden of Eden*. She may not know how to write or how to paint, but it is precisely because of this inability that she can produce effects that no writer or painter would be capable of achieving. In the dictionary of Hemingway's characters, Catherine thus signifies the resistance that has to do with sealing potency and impotency off in the creative act. In *The Garden of Eden*, she figures as a poetic reminder that potentiality (to create a work of art) is defined, essentially, by its possibility of not being exerted, in the form of privation. Her fascination with the sleeping Leda is one of Hemingway's ways of communicating this privative side of his self-portrait.

One of the episodes in *The Garden of Eden* where this sealing off – or the conservation of potency and impotency – is foregrounded most clearly is the description of a siesta after the lunch with the Colonel. For it is at this point that David understands the privative power of Catherine's haptic method:

'Let's first lie very quiet in the dark,' David said and lowered the latticed shade and they lay side by side on the bed in the big room in The Palace in

Madrid where Catherine had walked in the Museo del Prado in the light
of day as a boy and now she would show the dark things in the light and
there would, it seemed to him, be no end to the change.[33]

In this dreamy vision, reality cannot be discerned from fiction.
David imagines Catherine and himself as a work of art, a painting
or a sculpture. They are their real selves as well as the aesthetic
ingredients of a tableau in some painter's imagination, perhaps
already captured on canvas. From such an oneiric perspective,
Catherine's 'dark magic of change', her play with gender and racial
identity, is, to David, less of a Tactilist experiment than a metaphor
of an ideal art object in which reality and fiction endlessly interfere
and transform into one another without consuming the artists.[34]
David's phrase, 'there would seem to be no end to the change',
suggests that he recognises the power potential of an interference
between his and Catherine's creative approaches. To mix her
'sculpting in reality' with his 'sculpting in language' would promise
endless vitality to a work of art they could co-create. In other words,
while at other times in *The Garden of Eden* David may distance his
creative sensibility from that of Catherine – at the beginning of
the novel, for example, he makes it clear that their place is 'like
the painting of Van Gogh's room at Arles *except* there [is] a double
bed and *two* big windows'– in the siesta scene he undeniably puts
an equals sign between what each of them stands for in terms of
creative approach.[35]

Finally, it is not at all accidental that this recognition comes to
David from under half-closed eyelids during a languorous nap. Given
the importance Hemingway ascribed to his settings, the shaded
room, their lying quiet and dozing off is precisely the circumstance
in which such balancing of worldviews and sensibilities can take
place. As the space of the room merges with the Palace and the
Museo halls, reality reciprocates artistic vision to the point of complete synthesis. In that way, Hemingway's theme of repose, which
rhythmically punctuates the plot of the novel, brings the haptic
mode into the literary, and furthermore, designates the narrative
space for his characters' exploration of the possibility of artistic
neutrality: that is, an independence from the modernist dictum of
incessant animateness which represses the haptic.

The Haptic, the Symbolic and Norm Exposure in
The Garden of Eden

Through Catherine's sensuousness and through the teleological rhythm of siestas, the figure of a languorous nap in *The Garden of Eden* signifies Hemingway's distrust of the modernist fascination with vitality and the anti-haptic bias on which this fascination is founded. Whether that distrust is deliberate or only intuited is not the main point. What is essential about Hemingway's choice of the metaphor of laziness is that it puts into question the social injunction to live actively as well as the aesthetic injunction to translate this virility into artistic productivity. In this sense, the metaphor of laziness targets and exposes the intersection of the discipline of biological life and the discipline of symbolic life which tags the twentieth-century norm of active life. In short, the trope both exposes and challenges the apparent naturalness of social and aesthetic vitalocentrism.

If *The Garden of Eden* is framed as a literary act of resistance, it seems necessary to set it *vis-à-vis* the typically Western, colonial dichotomy of idleness and productivity, which, as David Murad points out, usually informs his work. After all, Hemingway's plots, such as that of *For Whom the Bell Tolls* (1940), privilege work as a social and cultural category that measures the value of an individual against his productivity.[36] But while that might be the case with some of Hemingway's earlier fiction or his correspondence, in *The Garden of Eden* the idea of productivity does not receive such generous treatment.

Of course, at first glance David is the laborious type, and Catherine the decadent type who loafs around and gets bored easily. But a second glance at Hemingway's last novel reveals that David's productivity does not really increase his vital powers, bringing him instead dissatisfaction, stupor and indifference. David forces himself to work mainly because he receives advances from his publisher, but despite all his self-disciplining effort to convince himself that work under such conditions makes him happy, that he must 'remember to do the work . . . to better fork up with the work',[37] David ceases to feel anything. He becomes an abuliac to whom nothing matters any more and who feels void of life.[38] He writes mechanically and re-reads with no feeling or sense of involvement, as if the putting of his ability and talent into practice was draining him of creative strength. Outside of work, he also grows increasingly indecisive and inert, allowing Catherine to dye his hair and staying indifferent to her Marita project.

After David begins to work on his elephant story, his numbness reaches such proportions that it gives way to a sense of tiredness and exhaustion, which soon informs the tone of his story. A pattern emerges therefore that when David finishes writing for the day, he is 'empty and hollow-feeling from having driven himself long past the point where he should have stopped'.[39] Like his characters who exhaust themselves chasing an elephant, David goes on 'working and [feels] as tired as if he had spent the night crossing the broken volcanic desert'.[40] All in all, the description of how the elephant story is created thematises the way David feels about his writing in general. As a result, we get an 'awful' kind of a short story, as well as 'a bad Hemingway', to use E. L. Doctorow's words, on the level of the main narrative of *The Garden of Eden*:[41]

> Tiredness brought the beginning of understanding. The understanding was beginning and he was realizing it as he wrote. But the dreadful true understanding was all to come and he must not show it by arbitrary statements of rhetoric but by remembering the actual things that had brought it. Tomorrow he would get the things right and then go on.[42]

What dawns on David at this point is that no figurative and rhetorical means will ever fully capture and transfer into the creative act his true African memories or the way those memories coincide with his present relationship situation with Catherine. The only way to access those states would be to stop working. Continuing the work only proves what he had learned earlier, lying side by side on the bed with Catherine: that dramatising his private memories into publicly approvable modernist aesthetics is not a mode of self-expression but a mode of self-transvaluation.

Of the two women in his life, Catherine is the one who understands that his approach, albeit productive, is counter-creative and therefore conformist with regard to contemporary aesthetic standards;

whereas Marita, who loves David-the-critically-acclaimed-Author, does not differentiate between productivity and creativeness. It is only logical from this perspective that Catherine would burn David's notebooks, which she does not out of jealousy, but out of a political insubordination to the demands of the publishing market. It is also inevitable that Catherine's departure makes David resume writing, which with Marita's support goes more smoothly than ever. For after Catherine's relegation from the novel – after the elimination from the creative act of the subversive sensibility – the writing of 'the bad Hemingway' can go on smoothly and productively. In this sense, *The Garden of Eden* might be considered a proto-postmodern text, whose ending expresses its author's – or rather, its Scribner editor's – assent to the rules of the culture industry. From this perspective, it is difficult to agree with Burwell that *The Garden of Eden*'s closure protects Hemingway's masculine text. If anything, it reduces it. The optimistic ending of *The Garden of Eden*, in which David writes happily and 'unceasingly' ever after – an ending explicitly selected by his editor – ironically comments on the unspoken rule of modernist aesthetics which, under the guise of slogans about innovativeness and vitality, puts an equals sign between creativity and productivity.[43]

The other, non-normative creativity, a creativity that evades the measures of the market, is captured in the novel in its rhythm of naps, swims and siestas, which are perhaps Hemingway's mannered reworking of Mark Twain's motif of 'lazying' on the raft on the Mississippi in *Huckleberry Finn* (1884) that provided Huck and Jim with the heterotopic experience of growing aware of their desire for freedom. However, while for Twain's characters this desire was directly concerned with political independence from biopower, Hemingway's honeymooners in *The Garden of Eden* seek liberation from the norm that we might term artistic. Both Catherine and David want freedom from the necessity to *produce* works of art and therefore manufacture their creative identities. In moments of loafing, they seem to protest, even if the only way of doing so is via passivity, against the authorisation of this necessity by the modernist pedagogies of vitalocentrism. The following conversation between Catherine and David well captures the dynamics of this desire:

'Don't make plans, Devil. Tomorrow I'll get up very early and work and
you sleep as late as you can.'

'Then write for me too,' she said. 'No matter if it's where I've been bad put
in how much I love you.'

'I'm nearly up to now.'

'Can you publish it or would it be bad to?'

'I've only tried to write it.'

'Can I ever read it?'

'If I ever get it right.'

'I'm so proud of it already and we won't have any copies for sale and none
for reviewers and then there'll never be clippings and you'll never be self
conscious and we'll always have it just for us.'[44]

Catherine's dream, as expressed at the end of the exchange, is to
be part of a narrative that would never see the publishing market,
a narrative independent of reviews, indifferent towards critical
reception and entirely irreproducible. She encourages David not
to follow the rules – 'no matter if it's where I've been bad put in
how much I love you' – which is another way of saying that no
matter how bad, mannered or idiosyncratic the writing might
turn out, it will produce a masterpiece to be proud of, precisely
because it will not be commercially appealing. Evidently then,
while Hemingway might have made Catherine epitomise a sensibility that he as a canonised modernist was publicly expected
to find vulgar, this sensibility also carried for him a promise of
subversiveness against mechanical reproducibility and the commercialisation of art, as well as all other forms of artistic and
intellectual dependence.

In a recent discussion of affect in Hemingway's writing, David
Wyatt considers *The Garden of Eden* and the Catherine–David creative dichotomy in terms of remorse.[45] Reiterating the views of
Hemingway's most eminent scholars, Wyatt emphasises that *The
Garden of Eden* was written 'the longest' and 'the hardest' among the
author's four unfinished self-portraits, even though it was written
with discipline, perhaps because 'the discoveries that Hemingway
made about himself while writing . . . made him unable to finish
it'.[46] While such claims can never be fully verified, it is tempting
to think that one of those discoveries was that he was not such a

whole-hearted modernist after all, that there was something about the modernist sensibility that he could not fully accept.

In *Politics of Aesthetics*, Jacques Rancière says that it took postmodernism to openly express the truth of art's commercialisation that had already taken place in modernism. Hemingway's *The Garden of Eden*, however, proves that attempts at such demystification were also made from within the modernist stronghold, and that they were not unsuccessful. The exhaustion of certain possibilities is certainly an idea that dictates the structure of Hemingway's last novel and is its main theme. It finds its allegorical representation in the rhythmical repetition of languorous scenes. It transpires from Catherine's resistance to writing and painting as well as her devotion to haptic performativity. It underlies David's first-hopeful-then-tragic inertia. And finally, it is dramatised in the final chapters when one character exits the creative stage while the other turns into a chattering typewriter. In short, Hemingway's final novel stands as a document of a modernist effort to go against the current of vitalocentrism. By giving poetic form to inoperativity, *The Garden of Eden* also gives shape to the embryonic structure of feeling that dominates postmodern sensibility – the mode of exhaustion.

Notes

1. Ernest Hemingway, *The Garden of Eden*, ed. Charles Scribner (New York: Scribner, 2003), 11.
2. Ibid., 61.
3. Michel Foucault, 'Of Other Spaces', *Diacritics* 16.1 (1986), 22.
4. Ibid., 22.
5. Hemingway, *The Garden of Eden*, 166.
6. Robert E. Fleming, 'The Endings of Hemingway's Garden of Eden', *American Literature: A Journal of Literary History, Criticism, and Bibliography* 61.2 (1989), 261–70.
7. Rose Marie Burwell, 'Hemingway's Garden of Eden: Resistance of Things Past and Protecting the Masculine Text', *Texas Studies in Literature and Language* 35.2 (1993), 198–225; Rose Marie Burwell, *Hemingway: The Postwar Years and the Posthumous Novels* (Cambridge: Cambridge University Press, 1996); Suzanne del Gizzo and Frederic J. Svoboda (eds), *Hemingway's The Garden of Eden: Twenty-Five Years of Criticism* (Kent, OH: Kent State University Press, 2012).
8. Mark Spilka, *Hemingway's Quarrel with Androgyny* (Lincoln: University of Nebraska Press, 1990); Burwell, *Hemingway*; Carl P. Eby, 'Teaching Modernist

Temporality with *The Garden of Eden*', *Hemingway Review* 30.1 (2010), 116–21; Linda Patterson Miller, '"In the Stream of Life": Teaching "The Garden of Eden" Contextually', *Hemingway Review* 30.1 (2010), 107–15.

9. For these readings, see Valerie Rohy, 'Hemingway, Literalism, and Transgender Reading', *Twentieth Century Literature* 57.2 (2011), 148–79; Samantha Long, 'Catherine as Transgender: Dreaming Identity in *The Garden of Eden*', *Hemingway Review* 32.2 (2013), 42–57; Carl Eby, '"Come Back to the Beach Ag'in, David Honey!": Hemingway's Fetishization of Race in *The Garden of Eden* Manuscripts', *The Hemingway Review* 14.2 (1995), 98–117; and Kathy Willingham, 'Hemingway's *The Garden of Eden*: Writing with the Body', *The Hemingway Review* 12.2 (1993), 46–61.

10. Burwell, *Hemingway*, 113.

11. Hemingway, *The Garden of Eden*, 5.

12. Carl P. Eby, 'Who Is "the Destructive Type"? Re-Reading Literary Jealousy and Destruction in *The Garden of Eden*', *Hemingway Review* 33.2 (2014), 100.

13. Hemingway, *The Garden of Eden*, 5.

14. Ibid., 53.

15. Catherine's practical mode of creativity might be compared to Gustave Flaubert's character Emma Bovary's fervour for making her life resemble the novels she reads, which Jacques Rancière interprets in 'Why Emma Bovary Had to Be Killed' as Flaubert's critique of the un-artistic, vulgar type of creativity that confuses art with life and true creation with kitschy excitability. In this reading, Flaubert makes Emma die at the end of his novel to punish the creative impulse that she represents. Noting the analogy between Catherine and Emma, we could read Catherine's sculptures in real life along the lines of Rancière's interpretation – she is also relegated from the novel at its very end – but it is equally legitimate to argue instead that, unlike Emma, Catherine does influence the literary (properly artistic) narrative of her author, especially since she does make her exit from the book in writing (in a letter to David), and her suicide is rendered only as a faint possibility.

16. Hemingway, *The Garden of Eden*, 54.

17. Eby, 'Who Is "the Destructive Type"?', 100.

18. Hemingway, *The Garden of Eden*, 105.

19. Ibid., 43.

20. D. W. Winnicott, *Collected Papers, through Paediatrics to Psycho-Analysis* (London: Tavistock, 1958), 302.

21. Donald W. Winnicott, 'Psycho-Somatic Illness and its Positive and Negative Aspects', *International Journal of Psychoanalysis* 47 (1966), 510–16; Donald W. Winnicott, 'The Squiggle Game' (1964–68), in *Psycho-Analytic Explorations*, ed. Clare Winnicott, Ray Shepherd and Madeleine Davis (Cambridge, MA: Harvard University Press, 1989).

22. Hemingway, *The Garden of Eden*, 11, 18, 54, 56, 67, 113, 115, 151, 161.

23. Ibid., 47.

24. Spilka, *Hemingway's Quarrel with Androgyny*, 117.

25. See Jacques Derrida, *On Touching, Jean-Luc Nancy* (Palo Alto: Stanford University Press, 2005).

26. Karen Barad, 'On Touching – The Inhuman That Therefore I Am', *Differences* 23.3 (2012), 213.
27. Hemingway, *The Garden of Eden*, 114.
28. Ibid., 54.
29. Ibid., 62.
30. Ibid., 52.
31. Ryan Hediger, 'The Elephant in the Writing Room: Sympathy and Weakness in Hemingway's "Masculine Text", *The Garden of Eden*', *Hemingway Review* 31.1 (2011), 83.
32. Ibid., 79–80.
33. Hemingway, *The Garden of Eden*, 67.
34. Ibid., 20.
35. Ibid., 4 [my emphasis].
36. David Murad, 'The Conflict of "Being Gypsy" in *For Whom the Bell Tolls*', *The Hemingway Review* 28.2 (2009), 92.
37. Hemingway, *The Garden of Eden*, 127.
38. John Smith, 'Abulia: Sexuality and Diseases of the Will in the Late Nineteenth Century', *Genders* 6 (1989), 102–24.
39. Hemingway, *The Garden of Eden*, 164.
40. Ibid., 128.
41. E. L. Doctorow, 'Ernest Hemingway R. I. P.', in *Hemingway's The Garden of Eden: Twenty-Five Years of Criticism*, ed. Suzanne del Gizzo and Frederic J. Svoboda (Kent, OH: Kent State University Press, 2012), 20.
42. Hemingway, *The Garden of Eden*, 182.
43. Ibid., 247.
44. Ibid., 77–8.
45. David Wyatt, *Hemingway, Style, and the Art of Emotion* (Cambridge: Cambridge University Press, 2015), 197–211.
46. Ibid., 198.

PART III

The Postmodern Moment
of Laziness

CHAPTER 5

Exhaustion of Possibilities: Harold Rosenberg, John Barth and Susan Sontag

Hence, the worker feels himself only when he is not working; when he is working, he does not feel himself. He is at home when he is not working, and not at home when he is working.

Karl Marx

In Chapters 3 and 4, I argued that the mode of exhaustion claimed by postmodernism as its own had in fact emerged earlier, within the modernist sensibility, to serve a subversive function against the dominant ideology of vitalocentrism. The question for this chapter is therefore what happened to the mode of exhaustion after its normatisation as the dominant value at the cultural moment we call postmodernism. When, at that moment, exhaustion becomes co-opted as part of the new ethos of artistic productivity, reconciling all tensions of the pre-emergent mode in 'the postmodern habit of thought', does there also emerge an as-yet-unspecified way to counteract it?[1] And if there does, what non-habitual forms of feeling, thinking and writing does it involve?

Let us return to the most apparent contradiction within the postmodern mode of exhaustion signalled in Chapters 3 and 4. The mode had nothing to with, say, Levinas's idea of *paresse*, that is, with a sense of fatigue as a position of refusal towards existence, with indolence or decreased potency. To quote the famous phrase from John Barth's seminal essay 'The Literature of Exhaustion', postmodern weariness was 'by no means a cause of despair' but a fresh, vibrantly active sensibility.[2] In fact, its name should have been, as Barth corrected himself years later, the mode of 'replenishment'.

The pluralism and hybridisation of arts implied in the postmodern sensibility of exhaustion is usually credited with destroying modernism's theoretical edifice, but it could not but construct its own inherently contradictory discourse. While exposing the 'desperate' denialism of modernist claims about art's separation from the economic sphere, veiled in the vocabularies of radical avant-gardism, the postmodern sensibility of exhaustion generated its own denial strategies in relation to the idea of literary productivity and literary value.[3] In other words, postmodernism's recognition of the economic parameters of the relation between literary value and productivity was never articulated explicitly; the parameters, such as management of resources and efficiency, did not necessarily take the form of overt references to commerce and capitalism. In turn, they were translated and expressed in the language of technical prowess and freedom politics.

Postmodern theoreticians, writers and artists quite freely explored the residual, modernist notion of technical up-to-dateness, with its valorisation of motion and animateness over stasis, and free associated it with the notion of democratic liberty. Given the historical context of postmodern aesthetics, namely the political protests of the Civil Rights movement, the cultural revolution and anti-war demonstrations, the postmodern take on the concept of mobility seems at first glance to be perfectly in tune with the democratic impetus of liberation politics. In fact, the majority of critics agree that the democratic differential is the only distinguishing criterion between the aesthetic modes of modernism and postmodernism, especially in the case of the classical postmodernism of the 1960s and 1970s. But the ideas of movement on the aesthetic plane and of movement on the political plane are actually far from harmonious. This discord transpires in the language of postmodern manifestos.

Aesthetics of Action and Inaction

One of the first expressions of the postmodern habit of thought comes in Harold Rosenberg's 1959 *Tradition of the New*. In this famous tribute to Action Painting, Rosenberg writes:

At a certain moment the canvas began to appear to one American painter after another as an arena in which to *act* – rather than a space in which to reproduce, re-design, analyze or 'express' and object, actual or imagined. What was to go on the canvas was not a picture but an event.

The painter no longer approached his easel with an image in his mind; he went up to it with material in his hand to *do* something to that other piece of material in front of him. The image would be the result of this encounter [my emphasis].[4]

The arena of acting and doing things is the canvas itself. An artwork such as Jackson Pollock's drip painting texturises action understood very narrowly as the activity of his hand and thus also the activity of his mind in the process of painting. The painter, Rosenberg writes, 'lives through the instrumentality of his materials', thus creating a new mode of representation without mediation, a mode of abolishing the classical distinction between art and life.[5] Thus, as Jerome Klinkowitz understands it, 'what is created is the artist's self, and the emphasis on action above order means the self can be remade at will'.[6] To Friedrich Nietzsche this constant mode of making and remaking would probably appear as a nightmarish reification of the incessant drive towards productivity and self-commodification. Filippo Marinetti, in turn, would love the idea as a proof of art's distinctiveness. For Rosenberg, the mode of active self-creation is not simply reinvigorating; it is the synonym of democratic freedom: 'What could be more immediate and more democratic?' he asks rhetorically. Yet the freedom achieved in this 'democratic' process is a strangely impotent one:

Many of the painters . . . had been trying to paint Society. Others had been trying to paint Art . . . The big moment came when it was decided to paint . . . just *to paint*. The gesture on the canvas was a gesture of liberation, from Value – political, aesthetic, moral . . . It was movement to leave behind the self that wished to choose its future.[7]

What seems banal from the contemporary perspective of Instagram and blog culture is the cruelly optimistic – to use Lauren Berlant's term – nature of Rosenberg's recipe for self-fashioning, which rests on the abandonment of agency that could choose its future and the renunciation of the capacity for political, aesthetic or moral freedom. Somewhat unwittingly perhaps, Rosenberg himself at one point renders the parity of democratic freedom and self-commercialisation explicit: 'whoever undertakes to create soon finds himself engaged in creating itself' as in the 'revolutionary' gesture of 'a single stroke that makes the painter exists as a Somebody . . . the man who started to remake himself has made himself into a commodity with a trademark'.[8] In other words, the optimistic promise of freedom of self-creation and the fantasy of sovereignty it perpetuates rests on adopting 'the promise of exchange value' as one's affective pattern.[9] If we agree with Rancière that the idea of democracy rests on the possibility of dissensus, a strengthening of agency rather than its abandonment, the claims to democratic freedom in Rosenberg's argument clash with his premises. What Rosenberg celebrates is not democracy but the affective event of freedom's removal from the sphere of thinking about oneself as an active agent. In the wake of the event, the artist becomes 'an actor', in the sense that while the movement and gestures are his, the lines definitely are not.[10]

Lauren Berlant speculates that the way to circumvent this affective pattern is to embrace the moments of impasse in the dynamics of self-creation. Echoing Thomas Pynchon on 'pockets of resistance', she encourages the pursuit of 'small self-interruptions as the heterotopias of sovereignty'.[11] The question remains, however, what such acts of self-interruption could look like. Having been co-opted in the postmodern paradigm, passivity, for example, is no longer the answer. Rosenberg's *Tradition of the New* is in this respect an accurate record of this co-option.

For exactly at a point where *Tradition* introduces the idea that the only active agent in action painting is the artist – his mind, his gestures, his image – and that the spectator or critic can do what they like, Rosenberg reminds his readers that the spectator (as well as the critic) must also change. He 'must recognize' the assumption inherent in the new mode of creation, think and react 'in a vocabulary of action'.[12] Participation thus must take on the form of 'concentration, relaxation of the will, passivity', all of which are the gestures of 'alert waiting'.[13] It is thus also a form of self-fashioning, where the tension of the viewer's body, the duration of pensive contemplation and the direction of the gaze are normativised by 'the new' regime of engagement.

If one amplifies the historical context in which Rosenberg's idea originates, that of the 1960s reality and the Vietnam War, one may find his definition of action as 'an inspired act of doing nothing, nothing other than the self-affirmation of the artist', as well as his notion of spectatorship as intense passivity, quite self-defeating. But Rosenberg was not the only one partaking in the discourse that presents hyper-engaged passivity as the affect of liberty. Another canonical example of postmodern sensibility informed by this logic is Susan Sontag's 1966 essay 'Against Interpretation'.

In this protest against critical and spectatorial interpretations that privilege content over the form of the works of art, Sontag, similarly to Rosenberg, invokes the opposition between movement and stasis, activity and passivity. Interpretations are 'rudimentary, uninspired and stagnant' to the point of offending 'real art', which tries to 'liberate' itself from their constraints:

> The most celebrated and influential modern doctrines, those of Marx and Freud, actually amount to elaborate systems of hermeneutics, aggressive and impious theories of interpretation . . . Interpretation is reactionary, impertinent, cowardly, and stifling. It makes art manageable, conformable.[14]

Translation: interpreting is totally bourgeois because it is not a sufficiently active interaction with the artistic medium and is thus imprisoning. If we pursue codified interpretative schemas, Sontag says, we prove that we are just cogs in a complex hermeneutic machine rather than free-feeling agents. And real agency is 'to *see* more, to *hear* more, to *feel* more' – to hyper-activate one's sensorium and thus uncover 'art's liberating value'.[15] On the surface, this sounds very much in tune with Walt Whitman's embrace of loafing – the interpretative mode is stifling; the sensory mode is liberating. But what in Whitman (or Emerson for that matter) was available through looseness and silencing of the sensorium is here achieved through intensity and sensory vehemence. Indeed, Sontag's post-Romantic vision frames the postmodern mode of receptivity in terms of Friedrich Schiller's play-drive (*Spieltrieb*), as an impulsion that desires to overcome stagnation (*Formtrieb*) with restlessness (*Sinnentrieb*).[16] In existentialist language, one could add that the postmodern mode as presented by Sontag is not the attunement through mind-body laxation (*Lässigkeit*), but through the vigorous mobilisation of attention. But what could possibly be liberating about Sontag's approach if it entails a vision of the haptic self as a productive machine? What or who is being liberated by such an 'erotics' of art?

Let us not forget that Schiller's concept of drives was created in the service of a greater ideological project of the aesthetic education of man, as the title of his memorable work has it. The project's aim was to normativise not to liberate, and diversify ways of feeling, thinking, writing and reading. Therefore, if Rosenberg's and Sontag's attempts to reinvent inattentive passivity as a higher form of vigorousness are updates or variations on the Romantic concept of leisure, the implication would be that they are similarly prescriptive in their message and similarly rigid in their visions of freedom.

The problem with those visions is, of course, as I argue throughout *The Labour of Laziness*, that real freedom – that is, the non-normative freedom of small self-interruptions – cannot be taught and prescribed. It also cannot be learned through the disciplining of one's attention. And yet, curiously, in the postmodern era where freedom was the number one buzzword, the emotional states that generate it – passivity, inattention, unproductivity– are employed as new modes of productive labour. Both *The Tradition of the New* and 'Against Interpretation' document a discernible tendency in postmodernism to wrestle passivity and the mode of exhaustion from the repositories of inaction and unproductivity. Not only do these texts reclaim the passive mode, but they also redefine it in terms of sensory expenditure, in movement or tensity. Considering, as Roland Barthes points out in *The Neutral*, that the *sentiment de puissance* in the stillness of passivity is all about 'derailment', 'bifurcation' and 'rerouting', not about being vigilant, on one's toes, the postmodern habit of thought does not really allow this sentiment to develop.[17]

And this habit is not limited to Rosenberg and Sontag. Indeed, in other postmodern manifestos, the activation of passivity takes the metaphorical form of textual *perpetuum mobile*. In 'The Literature of Exhaustion', John Barth embraces J. L. Borges precisely for the capacity of his metafictions to self-generate *ad infinitum*. Barth's Borges is not only a 'technically up-to-date artist', whom mastery of the apparatus of literary creation endows with creative potency, he is a victorious inventor who 'rediscovers' the artifices of language, literature, grammar, punctuation and even plot.[18] Borges's 'artistic victory', Barth writes, is that 'he confronts an intellectual dead end and employs it against itself to accomplish new human work'.[19] Nothing is left unused in this form of productiveness, which employs even dead ends against itself. The new human work, the product of the artist's victory, is thus *making use* of art's dissensual potential, *making it work* in the service of the literary industry. If all that remained to be conquered and revitalised by this industry are literature's dead ends – its heterotopias of freedom – then who are the real victors? Individual artists or the capitalist market? Barth's flirtation with the language of technical productivity, when he says that Borges constructs narrative *perpetuum mobiles* and generates 'dual' *regressus* and 'dizzying' character multiplications, reveals the dynamics of the co-optation of the formerly dissensual tropological field of the word exhaustion into the mainstream, residual norm of literary value.[20]

Similar gestures appear in the manifestos of other postmodern-ists. Consider, for instance, William Gass's style in his 1970 essay 'The Medium of Fiction':

> in the hollow of a jaw, the ear, upon the page, concepts now begin to move: they appear, accelerate, they race, they hesitate a moment, slow, turn, break, join, modify. Truly (that is to say technically), narration is that part of the art of fiction concerned with the coming on and passing of words – not the familiar arrangement of words in dry strings like so many shriveled worms, but their formal direction and rapidity.[21]

Gass sounds almost like Marinetti in the 'Manifesto of Futurism', except that it is not the artists but their creative product that is intensely 'awake and upright'; postmodern fiction thus literally embodies permanent movement – a strange thing to say at the time of television, video installations and elaborate cybernetic systems. In their context, the book seems to be the only medium where movement is really not the point. The print just sits there on the page, and the reader might do with it virtually anything he or she pleases. But in the postmodern regime of sensibility, this liberty is for some reason no longer available. Just as the postmodern writer has to be the Rosenbergian action artist who transforms his self into a product, the postmodern reader has to become the Rosenbergian spectator who merges with this product. He or she must read poised and alert, because literature is not 'dry strings of words' but an animate, 'fluid and changing' object.[22] If the artist has had to triple his efforts to become a 'Somebody' congealed in his product, so must the audience refashion its patterns of readership, from free play to revered admiration for the victorious product. Thus, in Marxist terms, an ideal postmodern work seems to be one that congeals productiveness in its fabric by obliterating traces of the individual hands and minds involved in its creation and reception.

At a crucial moment in 'The Literature of Exhaustion', Barth puts it best himself, although unwittingly: 'the accomplishment [of an up-to-date artist] is of such imaginative power that, once conceived, it begins to *obtrude* itself into, and eventually to *supplant* our prior reality [my emphasis]'.[23] A technically up-to-date artist achieves his victory '*paradoxically*, because by doing so he transcends what had appeared to be his refutation . . . like a mystic'.[24] It is formulations like this that throw out with the bathwater the promise of coun-ter-normative resistance that literature may provide. Indeed, it is a paradox of a kind that a postmodern writer, a writer who claims to have shunned the modernist ambition to be the antenna of the race, to use Ezra Pound's phrase, would at the same time be com-pared to a mystic with insight into mysteries that surpass ordinary human knowledge. Yet this paradoxical formulation allows Barth to endow the postmodern writer with special capacity to overcome the dead ends of literary production; more importantly, it allows him to intimate that this capacity is achieved through exceeding the writer's individual privacy. In the logic of what Marx would call the concealment of human labour, Barth's dead ends of literature and exhaustion of possibilities undergo an unusual transformation into other forms of writing and living that turn exhaustion into self-generating productiveness and the consequent proliferation of possibilities for enjoyment. However, while such a transformation reifies the value of those literary dead ends on the publishing market, it also diminishes, if not annuls entirely, their subversive potential. Thus, 'becoming a Somebody' in the era of postmodernism, to invoke Rosenberg's phrase again, is an oxymoron. For this 'Somebody' is not so much an artist-as-agency but a marketable version thereof. His newly discovered, almost mystical alertness is only a cover story for how disciplined his attention and creative capacities have become by the literary industry.

The main differential of this new affective event, and the new approach to fiction that it breeds, is, of course, economic. Marx's words from his 1844 *Manuscripts* quoted in the epigraph to this chapter capture it very succinctly: 'hence, the worker feels himself only when he is not working; when he is working, he does not feel himself. He is at home when he is not working, and not at home when he is working.' This is precisely the problem with the postmodern ideology of artistic work. Where the artist's self is a product, where writing and reading is intense production, there is no place for the artist or the reader to feel oneself and be at home with oneself. Using more contemporary terms, introduced by Luc Boltanski and Eve Chiapello in *The New Spirit of Capitalism*, one may describe the postmodern 'activation of inactivity' as a symptom of capitalism's last stage, which began in the second half of the twentieth century and lasts until today: namely, the phase of total effacement of the separation between private life and professional life, whose effect is the demise of the idea of 'self-ownership'. The conceptual erasure of the difference between activity and inactivity featured in postmodern visions of the artist, the work and the audience reflects how this effacement has permeated the sphere of artistic creation. For just as in the social sphere the distinction has disappeared between private dinners with friends and business lunches, between affective bonds and useful relationships, between private leisure and professional labour, so have the ideas of private self-ownership and professional self-ownership and the structures of feeling that used to uphold that division. In the literary world, the erasure was sealed with the creation and expansion of academic creative writing programmes, which, as Mark McGurl persuasively argues in *The Program Era*, have come to be the key determinant in the formation of post-60s aesthetics and its affective modalities.[25]

But with the economic circumstances of this formation being clear, the question remains: what emergent values and styles of thinking can be traced on the fringes of the cultural world presided over by the dominant virtue of exhaustion? If the affective mode of exhaustion, redefined as a new form of productiveness, is the residual value of postmodernism, where are the emerging and subversive modalities? What form do they take? To begin answering these questions, let me return to Raymond Williams and specifically his remark about emergent values:

> What has really to be said, as a way of defining important elements of both the residual and the emergent values, and as a way of understanding the character of the dominant, is that *no mode of production and therefore no dominant social order and therefore no dominant culture ever in reality includes or exhausts all human practice, human energy, and human intention.* This is not merely a negative proposition allowing us to account for significant things which happen outside or against the dominant mode. On the contrary it is a fact about the modes of domination that they select and consequently exclude the full range of human practice. What they exclude may often be seen as the personal and the private, or as the natural, or even the metaphysical. Indeed it is usually in one or other of these terms that the excluded area is expressed ... What matters, finally, in understanding the emergent culture, as distinct from both the residual and the dominant, is that it is never a matter of immediate practice ... Again and again what we have to observe is in effect a *pre-emergence*, active and pressing, but not yet fully articulated, rather than the evident emergence which could be more confidently named.[26]

Read in the context of my argument about postmodernism's usurpation of exhaustion and passivity as its own invention, Williams's passage from *Marxism and Literature* urges us to look beyond the immediate praxis of the postmodern habit of thought to find its pre-emergent aspects; that is to say, those not yet nameable areas of experience which – primarily because they are 'ignored' and 'dispensed with' by the cultural norm – accommodate the potential of counter-normative resistance.[27]

Pre-emergence, let us remember, is a term that paves the way in *Marxism and Literature* for Williams's canonical concept of structures of feeling, defined as 'characteristic elements of impulse, restraint, and tone; specifically affective elements of consciousness and relationships, not feeling against thought, but thought as felt and feeling as thought'.[28] It is therefore those elements of impulse, restraint and tone, elements that register differently than Rosenberg's alert waiting or Barth's exhaustion-as-replenishment, which would be the pre-emergent affective elements in postmodernism and their tone. And it is to those elements that we should now turn our attention.

Unconscious Scanning and Attention Vacancy

The problems with valorising attention and its productive capacities are usefully illuminated by Adam Phillips in his 2017 talk 'On Vacancies of Attention', which frames the annulment of subversive potential as a suppression of privately personal, creative inattention. Presenting what seems to be his own definition of cruel optimism, Phillips discusses Samuel Johnson's *The History of Rasselas, The Prince of Abyssinia*, a 1759 story about an idyllic kingdom where people seek relief from their seclusion in the happy valley, boredom and time weighing down on them. To alleviate boredom, 'to fill up the vacancies of attention and lessen the tediousness of time', they invent various modes of procrastination and leisure activities.[29] This, however, does not work and boredom does not go away. According to Phillips, what Johnson's moral tale alerts us to are

> the dangers of living an apparently satisfied life in an over-organized environment ... the terrors of some version of social engineering in which we are entombed in our supposed preferences and ideals ... What is absent in the happy valley is the freedom to think about what is missing and what might be missed ... Enjoyment can be used to preempt desire.[30]

John Barth's 'The Literature of Exhaustion,' which later became 'The Literature of Replenishment', as Barth rewrote his essay in 1984, is precisely the postmodern version of the happy valley. Enjoyment of possibilities pre-empts the desire for what is not or might not be there. Enjoyment fills up the vacancies of attention, and takes away the freedom to think about what is missing. What Barth does not seem to notice is that which Johnson's *Rasselas* points to: namely, the tension of attention and inattention. Here's Phillips on Johnson again:

> So much depends on where our attention is. If acculturation is among other things the organizing of attention, or the organizing of desire as the organizing of attention, then there is a tension, Johnson intimates, between what we are supposed to attend to and what we find ourselves wanting to attend to . . . Johnson [in his dictionary] defines 'vacant' as 'void, empty' but also 'free, unencumbered' 'thoughtless', 'empty of thought', 'at leisure'.[31]

Johnson's emperor eventually leaves the happy idyll because he desires the unknown, some other kind of knowledge that is missing in the valley. Instead of attention to the replenishment of exhausted-but-still-vital possibilities, he chooses inattention. His freedom results from a 'shift in attention', because vacancies of attention are the 'precondition' of change and freedom in that they allow for curiosity as well as other fresh, uncontrolled and un-normativised modes of cognition. If there is anything to be 'alert' to, it is

> the ways in which systems, or regimes, or vocabularies try to preempt our vacancies of attention, and to what kind of attention they tend to insight . . . vacancies of attention is a phrase worth attending to, because 'at leisure', 'unencumbered' we are in a different kind of elsewhere. In such vacancies significant realizations may occur. Gaps in knowledge may be revelatory, or inspiring, or confounding. Other desires may float into view . . . What happens to attention and desire when there is nothing to organize it?[32]

Revelatory gaps in knowledge are also, let us not forget, Adorno's point in *Minima Moralia*, when he talks about the benefits of an unencumbered, lazy morning in bed. By missing the mathematics class, Adorno's 'boy' opens himself to a possibility to think as he never had before. For no legitimate insight is possible without 'gaps and omissions', Adorno says. An original 'thought waits to be woken one day by the memory of what has been missed'.[33] Original fictions, that is, fictions that exceed and subvert the industry of replenishment, are also born in such a different kind of elsewhere – in vacancies of attention.

Phillips's 'Vacancies of Attention' is by no means a random reference here, for his way of thinking goes back to the psychoanalytic tradition of the 1960s, especially the work of Donald Winnicott and Anton Ehrenzweig, whose theories of creativity influenced postmodern writers on both sides of the Atlantic. For Ehrenzweig and Winnicott alike, artistic creation was based in the capacity for inattention and the relaxation of conscious thought. Ehrenzweig's 1967 *The Hidden Order of Art* links creativity to the processes of what he called 'unconscious scanning', by which he means the uncontrolled wandering of ideas and associations. This kind of mental state, Ehrenzweig posits, is the only one which is *per se* creative, because it is not controlled by any conventional or already existing mode of expression. One might call this mode unconscious, but Ehrenzweig's language on the matter was never the language of classical psychoanalysis; instead, he preferred the word 'syncretic', to emphasise that creation happens not when the mind is disciplined or when it waits alertly for ideas to come forth, but rather when it wanders elsewhere and is completely uninterested in itself or those ideas. The artist 'needs the more dispersed (undifferentiated) structure of low-level vision in order to project the missing order into reality' he wrote in the opening pages of *The Hidden Order of Art*, since 'the undifferentiated vision is altogether more acute in scanning complex structures' than the differentiated one.[34]

> We do not know yet the full extent and structure of our (unconscious) scanning powers, but somehow we must search for undifferentiated low-level sensibilities not unlike syncretism for an explanation ... Undifferentiated unconscious scanning extracts from the many variable details a common denominator or fulcrum which serves as the 'cue'.[35]

What Ehrenzweig seems to intimate is the opposite of Rosenberg's alert artist who focuses to transpose his mind on to the canvas, Sontag's reader who should feel and see more intensely, and Barth's writer who employs dead ends of literature against themselves. Ehrenzweig says that creation is born in an unfocused, inert and inactive state of the mind.

> The complexity of any work of art, however simple, far outstrips the powers of conscious attention, which, with its pinpoint focus, can attend to only one thing at a time. Only the extreme undifferentiation of unconscious vision can scan these complexities. It can hold them in a single unfocused glance . . . Because of its wider sweep low-level vision can serve as the precision instrument for scanning far-flung structures offering a great number of choices.[36]

Translated into the language of philosophy, Ehrenzweig's unconscious scanning partakes in the metaphorological field of the concept-metaphor of laziness. Let us recall, for instance, Levinas's concept of *paresse*, as a position of 'poise' and 'inhibition' where the mind is capable of recalibrating its sensorium. *Paresse*, Levinas writes, 'concerns beginning, as though existence were not there right off, but preexisted the beginning in an inhibition. There is more here than a span of duration, flowing imperceptibly between two moments.'[37] There is more going on than just time passing, because the withholding of action and attention occasioned in laziness functions as a threshold phenomenon which is prerequisite to all future sensory and thought experience. Just as Levinas considers this state to be the vantage point of all legitimate philosophical reflection, Ehrenzweig claims that the withdrawal of conscious attention is the fulcrum of artistic creation. Holding everything in an unfocused glance – a precision instrument of scanning far-flung structures – shares with *paresse* the features of it being a preparatory instance of attention-scaling, whose purpose is to calibrate channels of more complex interactions with the world on the level of sensibility and reflection. Perhaps, therefore, on a broader cultural level, the mode of extreme inattention capable of holding everything in an unfocused glance is what Raymond Williams called a form of pre-emergence – its impulse, restraint and tone.

The analogies between unconscious scanning and the concept-metaphor of laziness do not end with Levinas's *paresse*. In the following passage from *The Hidden Order of Art*, Ehrenzweig comes remarkably close to Martin Heidegger's notion of fundamental boredom or *Lässigkeit* in *Fundamental Concepts of Metaphysics*:

> How often have we not observed how an artist suddenly stops in his tracks without apparent reason, steps back from his canvas and looks at it with a curiously vacant stare? What happens is that the conscious gestalt is prevented from crystallizing. Nothing seems to come into his mind. Perhaps one or another detail lights up for a moment only to sink back into the emptiness. During this absence of mind an unconscious scanning seems to go on. Suddenly as from nowhere some offending detail hitherto ignored will come into view. It had somehow upset the balance of the picture, but had gone undetected. With relief the painter will end his apparent inactivity. He returns to his canvas and carries out the necessary retouching. This 'full' emptiness of unconscious scanning occurs in many other examples of creative work. Paul Klee's scattered attention that can attend to figure and ground on both sides of a line is of this kind. As far as consciousness is concerned, it is empty.[38]

Emptiness of the mind in unconscious scanning, described here by Ehrenzweig, resembles Heidegger's sense of profound emptiness encountered in states of being absolutely unencumbered. Let us recall again the passage about a relaxed party:

> Can we say that in contrast to being left empty, the casualness of joining in is a being satisfied, because we let ourselves be swept along? Or must we say that this casualness [*Lässigkeit*] is a being left empty that is *becoming more profound*? To what extent? Because as this term [*Lässigkeit*] is meant to indicate – in this casualness we abandon ourselves to our being there along and part of things . . . our seeking nothing more . . . is what is decisive about our comportment. With this 'seeking nothing more' something is *obstructed* in us. In this chatting along . . . we have . . . left our proper self behind in a certain way . . . we slip from ourselves.[39]

In the emptiness of *Lässigkeit* we discover the full sense of what we are, and may contain all complexities of what we are in one, unfocused glance. For Heidegger, just as for Ehrenzweig, the mind is left behind and replaced by a precision instrument of full emptiness which scans far-flung structures.

'Empty of thought' was also, let us remember, Samuel Johnson's synonym for radical freedom of thought. And Ehrenzweig's concept of unconscious scanning also registers the connection. The process of unconscious scanning happens, as he puts it, in 'gaps' of consciousness.[40] Gaps or vacancies of attention are revelatory but also always already missed if one tries to capture them. And that is because the scope of vision accessed in de-differentiation is too wide and the possibilities too abundant. Here is how Ehrenzweig describes this potential:

> What is common to all examples of dedifferentiation is their freedom from having to make a choice. Undifferentiated perception can grasp in a single undivided act of comprehension data that to conscious perception would be incompatible. I have elsewhere called these mutually exclusive constellations the '. . . or–or . . .' structure of the primary process . . . Such structures recur regularly in any creative search . . . What matters in our context is the fact that the undifferentiated structure of unconscious (subliminal) vision is far from being weakly structured or chaotic as first impressions suggest, but displays the scanning powers that are superior to conscious vision.[41]

Again, if we view Ehrenzweig's argument from a philosophical perspective, the constellation of phrases such as 'freedom from having to make a choice', 'the ". . . or–or . . ." structure' and 'powers superior to conscious vision' have a lot in common with Agamben's power to not act in *sterēsis*, as well as Barthes's idea of the neutral and *paresse*.

First, just as Agamben's *sterēsis*, which is the power to suspend faculty and the true essence of potency, is stronger than the power to employ faculty in action, Ehrenzweig's unconscious scanning is about the suspension of possibilities, which is superior – and primary – to what the conscious mind performs when the artist puts a brush to canvas or types the words of a story. As he puts it, 'consciously we would not be able to grasp all the future usages of a word, but unconscious scanning can'.[42] And since it can do so, its power is that of *sterēsis*. The 'or–or' structure of unconscious scanning in artistic creation is the philosophically and culturally neglected state of suspension that Agamben associates with *sterēsis*. The position of 'hovering between affirmation and negation, acceptance and rejection, giving and taking' is, for Agamben, almost entirely extinct, lost somewhere on the margins of philosophy, but it finds its incarnation in the Sceptics' notion of 'Suspension' or *ou mallon*, that is 'or–or'.[43] If so, Ehrenzweig's *Hidden Order* may be seen as a contribution to philosophical tradition which re-establishes the concept of 'or–or' by locating it at the centre of every artistic endeavour.

Ehrenzweig's remark quoted earlier that 'the complexity of any work of art, however simple, far outstrips the powers of conscious attention' is not only in tune with Agamben's concepts from *Potentialities* and 'The Power of Thought', but also with his idea of mastery in art. Mastery, says Agamben, 'is not a formal perfection but rather it is the ability to conserve impotency and potency in the act, the retention of imperfection in the perfect form. Imperfection is like an exit for the artist.'[44] It is this exact word – imperfection – that Ehrenzweig employs in the service of his theory in *The Hidden Order of Art*.

Students of art, he says, are trained to eliminate imperfections, but it is precisely the opposite that art has to 'retain' in its fabric – be it a musical piece, a story or a painting. It should retain the 'trust in the unconscious logic of spontaneity' rather than struggle for perfection of closure.[45]

> Gestalt perception tends to close gaps and smooth away imperfections that mar otherwise coherent and simple material. For instance, it is difficult to detect among a row of perfect identical circles that one imperfect circle which shows a small gap in its circumference. The 'law of closure' postulated by the gestalt theory will always tend to round off and simplify the images and concepts of conscious thought. It makes it difficult, if not impossible, for rational thought to handle 'open' material without rounding it off prematurely . . . Low-level visualization, by comparison, would be better equipped for dealing with open forms and so avoiding the pitfalls prepared by the 'law of closure' . . .
>
> Little gaps and imperfections in an otherwise perfect gestalt are filled in or smoothed away. This is why analytic gestalt vision tends to be generalized and ignores syncretistic individuality.[46]

The point of a masterful work is not to ignore the imperfections, because they are the frozen instances of the suspension achieved in unconscious scanning. They are instances of resistance to the form congealed in its fabric.

> Beckett uses to convey his own malaise about the emptiness of human relations, the imperfection or the danger of all attempts at communication, perhaps the imperfection also of precise words and images in shaping the fullness of creative vision.[47]

While Ehrenzweig praises the use of creative potency in Beckett, he has much less admiration for Rosenberg's devotion to the art of Jackson Pollock. Abstract expressionism works with accident in a manner that quickly becomes 'incorporated into the artist's planning' and there is less creative tension in it than in a watercolour.[48] Techniques such as Pollock's dripping and splashing paint, while designed to transpose the mind of the artist on to the canvas, are not 'capable of shifting the control of the working process to lower levels of the ego and stimulating unconscious scanning', and so they lose 'all meaning'.[49] However radical, Ehrenzweig's criticism offers an interesting counterpoint to the postmodern theories of Rosenberg, Sontag and Barth. It invites us to look for postmodernism's sources of resistance elsewhere.

Evidently, Ehrenzweig shares with Agamben the vision of how creative power needs to be distributed and dealt with in the artist's process of putting creative ideas into the act. Given that the theory of unconscious scanning also intersects with the concepts of *paresse* and *Lässigkeit*, it illuminates how the issues of inattention and imperfection partake of the metaphorological field of laziness. Travestying Marx's statement from the epigraph, Ehrenzweig seems to be saying that the writer feels himself only when he is not writing; when he is writing he does not feel himself, meaning that it is in the not-writing that the secret of creativity is hidden. Therefore, although the main texts of postmodernism by Rosenberg, Sontag and Barth highlight the opposite approach to this concept of creativity, it seems worthwhile to search within postmodernism itself for signals of a more Ehrenzweigesque sensibility. If Raymond Williams is right about pre-emergence as barely traceable signals of impulse, restraint and tone that resist the discursive formations of a certain trend or epoch, one should look beyond Rosenberg,

Sontag and Barth for instances where that pre-emergence is more indomitably asserted.

Most American literature scholars will exclaim at this point: of course, there's Thomas Pynchon! If postmodernism, as framed by the vocabularies of Rosenberg, Sontag, Barth and others, is a new regime of organising and controlling attention and desire, then who else but Pynchon could represent Rasselas's sensibility of resistance to this regime? And yes, no doubt Pynchon's Oedipa Mass in *The Crying of Lot 49* (1965), Tyrone Slothrop in *Gravity's Rainbow* (1973) or Dock Sportello in *Inherent Vice* (2009) all set off from emptiness of thought at leisure, while the subversion of systems of control is Pynchon's *ur*-theme. However, considering my general argument about laziness as a unique concept-metaphor that reaches the core of normativity, a much more fitting, if unlikely, example is another canonical postmodernist, Donald Barthelme. I say more fitting, because while Pynchon's literary explorations of doing and thinking nothing have been exhaustively covered by critics to the point of having already become a part of the postmodern norm, hence somewhat stalling their subversive potential in the starting blocks, Barthelme's experiments resists such co-optation. And if we agree that radical resistance to a norm is the marker of Adorno's great idea, Barthelme's use of the laziness metaphor seems to cut deepest. This is perhaps because, like no other writer of his generation, he took Ehrenzweig's ideas seriously and emphasised their radically dissensual dimension. As he put it once, unconscious scanning 'is the only thing I know of that makes sense of creativity to me'.[50]

Notes

1. Jerome Klinkowitz, *Rosenberg, Barthes, Hassan: The Postmodern Habit of Thought* (Athens: University of Georgia Press, 1988).

2. John Barth, *The Literature of Exhaustion and the Literature of Replenishment* (Northridge, CA: Lord John Press, 1982), 64.

3. Jacques Rancière, *The Politics of Aesthetics*, trans. Gabriel Rockhill (London: Continuum, 2010), 28.

4. Harold Rosenberg, *The Tradition of the New* (New York: Thames and Hudson, 1962 [1959]), 25.

5. Harold Rosenberg, *The Anxious Object* (Chicago: University of Chicago Press, 1982 [1964]), 19.

6. Klinkowitz, *Rosenberg, Barthes, Hassan*, 7.

7. Rosenberg, *The Tradition of the New*, 30.
8. Ibid., 12, 35.
9. Lauren Gail Berlant, *Cruel Optimism* (Durham, NC: Duke University Press, 2011), 36.
10. Rosenberg, *The Tradition of the New*, 29.
11. Berlant, *Cruel Optimism*, 49.
12. Rosenberg, *The Tradition of the New*, 29.
13. Ibid., 29.
14. Susan Sontag, 'Against Interpretation', in *Against Interpretation* (New York: Farrar, Straus and Giroux, 1966), 10–11.
15. Ibid., 11.
16. See Friedrich Schiller, *Letters upon the Aesthetic Education of Man* (Cambridge, MA: Harvard University Press, 1990).
17. Roland Barthes, *The Neutral: Lecture Course at the Collège de France (1977–1978)*, ed. Thomas Clerc and Éric Marty, trans. Rosalind E. Krauss and Dennis Hollier (New York: Columbia University Press, 2005), 112.
18. Barth, *The Literature of Exhaustion*, 68.
19. Ibid., 69.
20. Ibid., 74.
21. William Gass, 'The Medium of Fiction', in *Postmodern American Fiction: A Norton Anthology*, ed. Paula Geyh, Fred G. Leebron and Andrew Levy (New York: W.W. Norton, 1998), 2490.
22. Ronald Sukenick, 'Innovative Fiction/Innovative Criteria', in Geyh et al. (eds), *Postmodern American Fiction: A Norton Anthology*, 2488.
23. Barth, *The Literature of Exhaustion*, 70.
24. Ibid., 71.
25. Mark McGurl, *The Program Era* (Cambridge, MA: Harvard University Press, 2009).
26. Raymond Williams, *Marxism and Literature* (Oxford: Oxford University Press, 1977), 125–6.
27. Ibid., 125.
28. Ibid., 132.
29. Adam Phillips, 'On Vacancies of Attention', paper given at the 'Provoking Attention' conference, Brown University, Providence, RI, 2017, https://www.youtube.com/watch?v=v4bYbbrs5gI (accessed 28 January 2019).
30. Ibid.
31. Ibid.
32. Ibid.
33. Theodor Adorno, *Minima Moralia: Reflections from Damaged Life*, trans. E. F. N. Jephcott (New York: Verso, 2006), 81.
34. Anton Ehrenzweig, *The Hidden Order of Art: A Study in the Psychology of Artistic Imagination* (Berkeley: University of California Press, 1967), 5, 8.
35. Ibid., 17.
36. Ibid., 21–2, 32.
37. Emmanuel Levinas, *Existence and Existents* (The Hague: Nijhoff, 1978), 26.
38. Ehrenzweig, *The Hidden Order of Art*, 24–5.

39. Martin Heidegger, *The Fundamental Concepts of Metaphysics: World, Finitude, Solitude* (Bloomington: Indiana University Press, 1995), 117–19.
40. Ehrenzweig, *The Hidden Order of Art*, 27.
41. Ibid., 32–3.
42. Ibid., 42.
43. Giorgio Agamben and Daniel Heller-Roazen, *Potentialities: Collected Essays in Philosophy* (Palo Alto: Stanford University Press, 1999), 256.
44. Giorgio Agamben, 'Resistance in Art', 2014, https://www.youtube.com/watch?v=one7mE-8y9c (accessed 28 January 2019).
45. Ehrenzweig, *The Hidden Order of Art*, 193.
46. Ibid., 39, 11.
47. Ibid., 253.
48. Ibid., 61.
49. Ibid., 62.
50. Helen Moore Barthelme, *Donald Barthelme: The Genesis of a Cool Sound* (College Station, TX: A&M University Press, 2001), 104.

CHAPTER 6

Inertia and Not-Knowing in the Fiction of Donald Barthelme

I argued that acedia was a manifestation of fear and I think that's true. Here it would be a fear of the need to submit, of joining the culture, of losing that much of the self to the culture.

Donald Barthelme

The words in the epigraph are spoken by a character in Donald Barthelme's last published story 'January' (1987). In the story, a scholar of religion, Thomas Brecker, is being interviewed about his greatest scholarly achievement, which is a book about the history of *acedia*. Brecker, who is particularly proud of this work – 'a respectable piece of work if not brilliant' – says that he was interested in *acedia* because

> acedia is a turning toward something rather than, as it's commonly conceived of, a turning away from something. I argued that acedia is a positive reaction to an extraordinary demand, for example, the demand that one embraces the *good news* . . . Acedia is often conceived of as a kind of sullenness in the face of existence; I tried to locate its positive features. For example, it precludes certain kind of madness, crowd mania; it precludes a certain kind of error.[1]

Troubled by Brecker's phrase 'the need to submit', the interviewer insists that the writer explain more about the fear of submission. The questions are very scholarly – 'Can you accept a disinterested objectivity as finally normative?' – in reaction to which Brecker's answers become more and more elusive. 'I don't know' and 'it doesn't matter now' are his standard replies. At a crucial moment in the interview Brecker says: 'the "good news" is always an announcement of a reconciliation of a particular into a universal. I have a life-long tendency not to want to be absorbed in the universal, which amounts to saying a lifelong resistance to the forms of religion.'[2] The comment is about religion, but it can also be read, more broadly, as a statement of his resistance to any already available forms, norms and regimes of sensibility. This at least is suggested by how the story unfolds. Following Brecker's reply, the interviewer disappears from the narrative, his last words being 'On the question of—', and Brecker is left alone, free to converse with himself outside of the format of the interview.[3] True acediac that he is, Brecker is thus allowed by Barthelme to express his fears and desire for resistance, and not to lose himself to culture as represented by the interviewer.

'January' was Barthelme's last story, and can therefore be read as a commentary on his life-long and critically overlooked interest in resistance to the good news of postmodernism. Never confrontational or cynically programmatic, this resistance seems to be the affective undercurrent of Barthelme's literary experiments with other ways of knowing and writing. From his literary debut, a poem 'Inertia', written when he was still a student, through his short stories and novels, to 'January' in 1987, the themes of attention and inattention, suspension of capacity to act, passivity, inertia and laziness perform – however graciously and respectfully – an important critical labour with respect to the aesthetic norm of mid-twentieth-century aesthetics.[4] This chapter is therefore an attempt to recover the abandoned thread of Barthelme's work, and present him as a voice of pre-emergent structures of feeling, or as he preferred to call it, of the 'pre new'.[5]

Ironically, Barthelme is never read in this way. Postmodern criticism has always viewed his work as a classic example of the productivity-oriented postmodern mode of vigilant attention. In critics' eyes, Barthelme is all about enjoyment of language and its possibilities, and he is occasionally also a satirist of political reality. Yet read through the prism of the laziness-metaphor, Barthelme's experiments register in a very different way. If we add here the fact that nowadays Barthelme's writing suffers from critical neglect and is virtually absent from the postmodern canon, the intuition that his work reveals the unknown side of the postmodern sensibility is even more certain.

Why has Barthelme almost entirely disappeared from anthologies of American literature and reading lists? The selections in *The Norton Anthology of Postmodernism*, an entire volume devoted to the postmodern tradition, feature only two of the shortest stories by Barthelme, 'See the Moon?' (1966) and 'Sentence' (1970), neither of which represents the full scope of his conceptual intervention into the postmodern experimental scene. In the fifth edition of *The Heath Anthology of American Literature*, Barthelme's story 'At the End of the Mechanical Age' (1981) features with Tim O'Brien, Yusef Komunyakaa, Toni Cade Bambara and John Updike in a cluster on political fiction entitled 'A Sheaf of Vietnam Conflict Poetry and Prose'. In the most recent, seventh edition of *The Heath Anthology*, the same story is moved into the cluster 'Aesthetics and Politics of the 1960s and 1970s – Black, Brown, Yellow, Red' to stand among Pedro Pietri, Alice Walker and Maxine Hong Kingston. The company is honourable, but such placement renders Barthelme obscure with respect to his preoccupation with what Foucault calls 'the weight of experiences constantly eluding themselves, the whole silent horizon of what is posited in the sandy stretches of non-thought . . . the *not-known*'.[6] Forcing Barthelme into such clusters does not do justice to a much more ideologically subtle commentary about freedom, control, attention and desire that his work offers. Finally, although Barthelme remains a writers' writer, admired as one of a kind by such authors as Thomas Pynchon, Salman Rushdie or David Foster Wallace, he is a rather uncomfortable subject for today's scholars. It seems to me that their uneasiness has less to do with his work's irrelevance for contemporary structures of feeling – quite the contrary – but rather with his X-ray insight into their normative core.

One of the reasons why Barthelme is never read as a voice of resistance to the aesthetics of his time is probably the fact that his professional career as a writer was active and avant-garde, which must have had an impact on how his fiction was read. Influenced by the legacy of his father's modernist views about art as a way of re-energising the sensorium – Donald Barthelme Sr was a famous architect working in the style of Le Corbusier and Mies van der Rohe – Barthelme was a promoter and admirer of other experimenters of his generation such as John Barth or Thomas Pynchon. Whether as the director of the Houston Museum of Modern Art in his early days, or as the collaborator of Harold Rosenberg and Kenneth Koch with whom he ran an interdisciplinary art magazine, *Location*, in the early 1960s, Barthelme was perceived as one of the most productive voices of his generation. His most famous remark, that collage is the main principle of literature, indeed of the whole twentieth century, at first sight seems to fit perfectly Barth's formula of exhaustion as replenishment. However, the coherent image of a vigorous artist actually diverts our attention from Barthelme's deeper artistic concern with what he called the new modes of cognition, which he located on the fringes of one's faculty, in the vacancies of attention of what Anton Ehrenzweig called unconscious scanning.

The Essays: 'After Joyce' and 'Not Knowing'

Barthelme's first mention of Ehrenzweig's unconscious scanning appears in his story 'The Glass Mountain' (1968), whose note 56 says: '"A weakening of the libidinous interest in reality has recently come to a close." (Anton Ehrenzweig).' Certainly, Barthelme enjoyed the poetic style of Ehrenzweig's phrase, but he was also perfectly aware of its entire context – *The Hidden Order of Art* was published in 1967, and Barthelme had known the book before writing his short story. The full passage from Ehrenzweig reads as follows:

> I venture to suggest that a cyclical movement towards abstraction, dedifferentiation, a weakening of the libidinous interest in reality has recently come to a close and that a new trend in the opposite direction moving towards a new syncretism and object love may now be in the making. What I am trying to express is only the frustration and confusion in the air, the tired response to further self-destructive twists of our conscious sensibilities, the weariness of the overworked themes of aggression and death, the failure of abstract art to produce more than flat ornaments

and the repeated loss of a dynamic pictorial space. All I want to do is to voice a growing hunger for a form of art not yet existing, a longing that is made only harder to bear when it is mocked by the empty posturing of an academic abstract art.[7]

Hence, while Barthelme's insertion of Ehrenzweig in 'The Glass Mountain' sounds as though he is making fun of the psychoanalytic register, it also directs the reader to Ehrenzweig's message about the hunger for forms of art not yet existing. And that is because Ehrenzweig's point of view corresponds closely to his own vision of the pre-new, which Barthelme put forth in his first theoretical essay 'After Joyce', written for the first issue of *Location* in 1964.

The way 'After Joyce' frames it is that literary art is never about abstraction. Literary objects are 'real' in the sense that one 'bumps' into them just as one stumbles upon a rock or a refrigerator. For that reason, literary objects are always journeys into the unknown. They affect us literally, and most importantly, they do so by surprise. We never know when and how the bumping into might take place. A writer's effort, Barthelme writes in the essay, 'always and everywhere, is to attain a fresh mode of cognition' to those haphazard events.[8] That is because a writer proceeds like 'a man weaving a blanket of what might be found in a hardware store', and while he is weaving 'the fabric falls apart certainly, but when it hangs together we witness worlds made new'.[9] We (that is, the readers) have thus to reconstitute the work by 'active participation, by approaching the object, tapping it, shaking it, holding it to his ear to hear the roaring within'.[10]

Tapping and shaking are verbs of rapid action, so it may almost go unnoticed that in Barthelme's use they actually emphasise the resistance of a literary text to giving clear meanings rather than a willingness to participate in their replenishment. In Barthelme's optics, neither the writer nor the reader know what they will bump into, tap and shake, because the meaning will always in the end be preserved in the state of not being articulated. In the terms of Ehrenzweig's *The Hidden Order of Art*, which Barthelme anticipates in his 1964 essay, the experience of writing and the experience of reading are artistically legitimate and fresh when they engage in the suspension of possibilities, when they celebrate syncretistic individuality, in short, when they perform form as much as the 'or–or' sensibility of unconscious scanning.[11] We might paraphrase this by saying that what the artist has to say is most interesting when he is not trying to communicate his ideas to others but when he speaks to himself, very much like the *acedia* scholar in 'January'.

Ehrenzweig says in *The Hidden Order of Art*: 'consciously we would not be able to grasp all the future usages of a word, but unconscious scanning can', and in 'After Joyce' Barthelme seems to build his own theory about the possibility of doing art that preserves the structure of unconscious scanning.[12] In Agamben's terms we would say that such art performs the *sterēsis* or the power of not-saying. Barthelme's own word for what art should capture – his all-time favourite word – was 'ineffable', from the Latin *effari* (utter), meaning 'unutterable'. In his second theoretical essay, written towards the end of his life, he simply calls this artistic method 'the not-knowing'.

The opening lines of the 1985 essay 'Not-Knowing' faithfully echo Ehrenzweig's idea of unconscious scanning as the essence of artistic creation. Barthelme writes:

> Let us suppose that someone is writing a story. From the world of conventional signs he takes an azalea bush, plants it in a pleasant part. He takes a gold pocket watch from the world of conventional signs and places it under the azalea bush. He takes from the same rich source a handsome thief and a chastity belt, places the thief in a chastity belt and lays him tenderly under the azalea, not neglecting to wind the gold pocket watch so that its ticking, will, at length, awaken the now sleeping thief. From the Sarah Lawrence campus he borrows a pair of seniors, Jacqueline and Jemima, and sets them walking in the vicinity of the azalea bush and the handsome, chaste thief. Jacqueline and Jemima have just failed the Graduate Record Examination and are cursing God in colorful Sarah Lawrence language. What happens next?
>
> Of course, I don't know.
>
> It's appropriate to pause and say that the writer is one, who, embarking upon a task, does not know what to do ... The not-knowing is crucial to art, is what permits art to be made. Without the scanning process engendered by not-knowing, without the possibility of having the mind move in unanticipated directions, there would be no invention.[13]

'Not-Knowing' thus offers such a clear vision of what Barthelme aims at in his experiments that there is no need of a paraphrase. Not-knowing is the one principle that defines creation, as there would be no art without the experience of letting the mind move in all possible directions. Barthelme's words resonate with Ehrenzweig's 'any creative search involves holding before the inner eye a multitude of possible choices that totally defeat conscious comprehension'.[14] Like Ehrenzweig, Barthelme believes in the power of inattention.

'At a certain point', Ehrenzweig writes, 'which has to do with the awakening of creativity', the artist 'has to abandon precise visualization'.[15] At this point, the attention of the artist is 'blank and blurred', while unconscious scanning goes on 'in deeper levels of his mind'.[16] Barthelme abandons the psychological language of the passage, but the whole idea of unconscious processes is very much preserved.

If Barthelme's essay adds something to Ehrenzweig's argument, it is perhaps the emphasis on what he calls problems and prohibitions that the mind encounters in not-knowing: 'the anxiety attached to this situation is not inconsiderable . . . the not-knowing is not simple, because it's hedged about with prohibitions, roads that may not be taken'.[17] Hence, creative inattention, in Barthelme's rendition, is not a blissful dwelling in possibility, but also a process marked by fear. In not-knowing, as the writer is looking for 'the as-yet unspeakable, the as-yet unspoken', he stumbles upon norms and calls for submission to one sign or convention or another, and resists them by not responding to their demand.[18]

Crucially then, Barthelme's philosophy of art includes a deeper ideological reflection, which might be understood in Foucault's terms as a reflection on the problems of individual and private self and its submission to the power apparatus of subjectivation. In *The Order of Things* Foucault writes that 'man' or the Self-as-Subject is an 'empirico-transcendental doublet' where 'the weight of empirical experiences' and submission to structures of power/knowledge intersects with 'the whole silent horizon of what is posited in the sandy stretches of non-thought'.[19] In other words, the Self-as-Subject is not necessarily a hopeless position – though much of Foucault's argument presents it as such – it is also 'positive', because to be always already subjected to power/knowledge does not annul the power potential (*puissance*) to reach outside biopolitical norms.[20] One way of reading Barthelme's essay 'Not-Knowing' politically is therefore perhaps to read it as an attempt to redeem this potential in art. Being less fatalistic than Foucault's proposition, which situates the Self-as-Subject as always already 'tied to the back of the tiger' of power/knowledge, Barthelme sees art as capable of confronting norms and prohibitions through the practice of not-knowing.[21]

Although Barthelme's vision of not-knowing finally crystallises in 'Not Knowing', the idea was already there two decades earlier in 'After Joyce' and his early stories. In 'After Joyce', Barthelme distinguishes between two literary tactics that target the not-known. One is 'the mode of aggression' typical of William Burroughs. Burroughs's cut-up method, Barthelme says, is like a ticking bomb in the reader's hands which can explode at any moment, and thus keeps the reader alert, on the edge of his chair. This makes Burroughs impossible to read for too long at one sitting, and consequently drains the work and the reader of a desire to interact.

Instead of the mode of aggression, Barthelme prefers to be inspired by the privative style of Samuel Beckett's late modernist plays, which he calls in the essay 'the mode of play':

> Beckett painstakingly and with the utmost scholarly rigor retraces the rationales of simple operations, achieving comic shocks along the way by allowing the language to tell him what it knows. His art is reductionary in that . . . he throws ideas away. The things he throws away are . . . character, plot, social fact, gossip. What is retained as the irreducible minimum is the intent of the artist, in Beckett's case a search for the meaning to be gleaned from all the possible combination of all words in all languages.[22]

Barthelme admires Beckett's mode of play over the mode of aggression, or the experiments of the 'painfully slow' French New Wave for that matter, because Beckett 'throws ideas away'.[23] Of course, Barthelme's vision of throwing away aims to be altogether different from Beckett's. As he put it in one interview, 'Beckett's test was to do something that was not-Joyce, and my test, which is not on the same level of course, is to do not-Beckett.' Thus, Barthelme's throwing away is about 'throwing things on the floor to see what shapes they make' – it is not to make them disappear.[24]

Let us not mistake this for a revival of Willa Cather's claims in 'The Novel Démeublé' (1922), discussed above in the chapter on modernist manifestos, which professed the artistic merits of throwing traditional ideas and devices out of the window. Cather's 'demeubling' bore the mark of the avant-garde ambition to do away with the ancestry of realist tradition. Think of it in the manner of the Freudian *fort–da* game, where the throwing away of the spool is a child's way of testing its independence from the absent parent, and a mastery of the fact of being on one's own. Like the child from Freud's 'Beyond the Pleasure Principle', Cather's artist is empowered by the throwing of the ancestral tradition *fort*, out of the window. Not entirely dissimilar, Beckett's throwing ideas away is a development of this thinking, although void of any patricidal impulses towards tradition. In contrast to both Cather and Beckett, Barthelme's throwing away is creation via resistance to their disappearance. Crucially, the resistance to knowing, final meanings, closed forms and the extraordinary demand to submit frequently takes the shape of what I call in this book the trope of laziness.

Short Stories: Rhathymia in 'Paraguay', 'The Balloon' and 'The Falling Dog'

Rhathymia, that is, the psychological term for being 'at ease', 'carefree' but also 'indifferent', is the operating affect of Barthelme's two best-known, early stories, 'The Balloon' and 'Paraguay'. Originally published in *The New Yorker* in 1969, 'Paraguay' is on the surface a mock travel narrative, which mimics the language of old explorer diaries and the scientific discourse of post Lévi-Straussian ethnography and anthropology. For historiographers, it is also an insightful political commentary about South American regimes, most notably the Uruguayan nationalist dictatorship forming under Juan María Bordaberry Arocena.[25] But while formal and historical elements are Barthelme's objects 'found in a hardware store' of writers' resources, it pays to explore how those objects actually 'hang together' as the story intertwines political commentary with the trope of unproductivity.

First of all, the Paraguay in the story 'is not the Paraguay that exists on our maps. It is not to be found on the continent of South America . . . This Paraguay exists elsewhere.'[26] Registering the allegorical character of this passage, many of Barthelme's critics read it as a pure instance of metafiction. But what this Paraguay unfolds to be complicates this reading, because Barthelme's defamiliarised views of the place clearly have political references. Upon entering he sees 'flights of white meat'; the white snow turns red as a result of an error, 'a government error resulting in the death of a statistically insignificant portion of the population'.[27] The department stores across Paraguay, we are told, 'sell silence in paper sacks like cement'.[28] As a doublet of an ignorant tourist and a colonial explorer, Barthelme's narrator is blind to the acuteness of what clearly seems like acts of violence and censorship, and never abandons his surreal vision of things. For example, with great attention and precision, akin to that of the lawyer in Melville's 'Bartleby, the Scrivener', who records the activity of his workers according to the clock, the narrator of 'Paraguay' gives precise measurements and observes the movements and mating rituals of the locals in accordance with temperature:

> Temperature controls activity to a remarkable degree. By and large, adults here raise their walking speed and show more spontaneous movement as the temperature rises . . . the temperature dependent pattern of activity is complex. For instance, the males move twice as fast at 60 degrees as they do at 35 degrees, but above 60 degrees speed decreases.[29]

As one reads through other similarly defamiliarised, quasi-scientific descriptions of Paraguayan habits, one connects the surreal images to the ideological commentary, thus getting the map of Barthelme's way in which bits of reality are put together to offer a 'world made new', where no clear, closed form delimits the multiple possibilities of interpretation. There are simply too many contradictory elements for the reader to pursue any one interpretation. Once the reader hangs on to one way of making sense of the story, it turns its back on him or her. The narrator, to use Barthelme's words from another of his early stories, is free associating, brilliantly, brilliantly, to put you into the problem.

Amid these inconsistent, fragmentary bits and pieces, there are two, however, which by accident also offer a commentary on the field of postmodern artistry. The first is titled 'Rationalization' and reads:

> The problems of art. New artists have been obtained. These do not object to, and indeed argue enthusiastically for, the rationalization process. Production is up. Quality-control devices have been installed at those points where the interests of artists and audience intersect. Shipping and distribution have been improved beyond recognition. (It is in this area, they say in Paraguay, that traditional practices were most blameworthy.) The rationalized art is dispatched from central art dumps to regional art dumps, and from there into the life streams of cities. Each citizen is given as much art as his system can tolerate ... each artist is encouraged to maintain, in his software, highly personal, even idiosyncratic, standards (the so-called 'hand of the artist' concept).[30]

While interpretable as an allegory of politicised art, as well as a commentary on what Ehrenzweig called the programme of Abstract Expressionism, the fragment also offers a more general critique of the usurpation of the postmodern artist by the publishing market. Floating under the level of the metafictional and political meanings is Barthelme's hyperbolic resistance to being part of the vibrantly fertile and privacy-consuming art economy of his time, of which Rosenberg and Barth were so fond. Rationalisation is after all Max Weber's term for a process of proletarianisation of thinking which produces programmatic intelligence, that is, an intelligence that is subjugated to serve the economic apparatus, so-called 'cognitive capitalism'.[31] In *The Dialectic of Enlightenment* (1944), Horkheimer and Adorno explain how such use of reason leads to what they call reification, a commercialisation of thought and art accompanied by the gradual erasure of individual agency. In this context, Barthelme's description in 'Paraguay' of art flowing from central to regional centres and each citizen receiving 'as much art as his system can tolerate' doesn't fall far from the argument in *The Dialectic* that 'while individuals as such are vanishing before the apparatus they serve, they are provided for by that apparatus better than ever before'.[32] This is because the product of individual intellect 'must perish when it is solidified into a cultural asset and handed out for consumption purposes' – or, in Barthelme's parlance, 'each artist's product is translated into a statement of symbolic logic'.[33]

The responses of the Paraguayans to this state of affairs would certainly be of interest to Barthelme's Thomas Brecker, the scholar of *acedia*, for the Paraguayans react to the new mode by none other than acediac withdrawal. In response to the rationalisation of art, they shed their skins, buy silence in 'response to the proliferation of surfaces and stimuli', and their 'preferred mode of presentation of the self is rhathymia'.[34] They are at leisure. All of these gestures of quiet dissent by not-doing are explained in the story by the narrator's hostess in Paraguay, Jean Mueller, in the section aptly entitled 'Terror':

> Such is the smoothness of surfaces in Paraguay that anything not smooth is valuable. She explains to me that in demanding (and receiving) explanations you are once more brought to a stop. You have got, really, no farther than you were before. 'Therefore we try to keep everything open, go forward avoiding the final explanation' . . . Creation of new categories of anxiety which must be bandaged or 'patched' . . . There are hot and cold patches, and specialists in the application of each.[35]

Viewed in the light of Barthelme's theory of art, the passage reads like a statement of his method of dealing with the anxieties of not-knowing, with echoes of Ehrenzweig and his insistence on not rounding up artistic creativity in smooth, closed forms. It is essential, as Barthelme's character puts it, to look for anything that is not smooth, for anything that is not prompted by the system of which the Paraguayans are part.

Furthermore, the shedding of skin by the Paraguayans – another surreal element that resists interpretation as a simple metaphor – indicates their desire to get under the surface layer of their subjugating reality. This is what Agamben would call a not-metaphor, that is, a metaphor that imperfectly represents what it resists saying, namely, that by shedding their skin the Paraguayans express their desire to get under the surface layer of all-encompassing rationalisation.

Otherwise put, while in its historical dimension 'Paraguay' contemplates the error of dictatorship and the Western world's blindness to this state of affairs – the narrator is, after all, an incorrigibly ignorant tourist-explorer – in its philosophical and ideological dimension, it also raises the question of freedom from artistic productiveness, which in postmodernism is productiveness for its own sake. In resistance to what happens in Paraguay, to the rationalisation of art, the rhathymic Paraguayans 'wander' in 'empty spaces . . . trying to touch something'.[36] The Paraguayans thus seem to be vivid incarnations of Barthelme's artist and reader from 'After Joyce' and 'Not-Knowing', who wander around the metaphorical hardware store of the not-known and bump into strange objects. That they do so in the state of rhathymia – another form of laziness – is only logical, because rhathymia is the one state that allows for free, unencumbered thought to be born. Vagabond thoughts wandering around the mind in 'lazy recumbency' may be a problem from the point of rationalised art and other regimes of thought, but in Barthelme's perspective they are precisely the ones one should try to reach.[37]

Readers unfamiliar with Donald Barthelme's biography might find it curious that the writer in fact used the rhathymia mode as his own writing method. Helen Moore Barthelme, his first wife and biographer, recalls in her *Genesis of the Cool Sound* that when in the mornings Barthelme settled down to work in their top floor Houston apartment, overlooking a busy street, he would write down bits and pieces of the conversations of the passers-by that he eavesdropped on from the window.[38] Many of Barthelme's early stories originated in this way, the street being his hardware store of objects as well as the space of unconscious scanning.

To understand the scanning process on a more detailed level, it pays to turn to one of Ehrenzweig's more renowned colleagues in the middle group of British psychoanalysis, who figures as one of the theoretical pillars of *The Labour of Laziness*: Donald Winnicott. What Ehrenzweig calls unconscious scanning in Winnicott's terms is the process of a transitional experience.[39] In Chapter 1, I wrote about his concept of playing as a form of dwelling in nothingness out of which something arises. For Winnicott, when a child plays, it accidentally finds an object in its surroundings, and then neither masters it by endowing it with his meaning nor lets it be for what it is, say, a rock or a blanket. Instead, in a slow process that takes place in the intermediary, transitional space between the child and the object, there emerges a third, new entity, which both retains the material qualities of an object but also becomes inflected with the first glimmers of individual intent and creativity of the child. At this point, the child doesn't even know it is being creative – it does not have a coherent sense of self – but in the process, this sense, awakened by a capacity to be creative, becomes solidified together with the first intuitions of identity. In other words, Winnicott presents a reverse version of the *fort–da* game, because while *fort–da* starts with the already established subject who masters the objects in play, transitional playing starts with the not-knowing pre-self who interacts with the external object until something-like-a-self slowly emerges in the process. Finally, and most importantly, the pattern of creativity invented by the child in early life establishes the basis for a manner, or a mannerism rather, in which adult artists will pursue creative acts.

It is precisely this mode of playing that Barthelme describes in 'Not-Knowing'. Barthelme puts words against one another and then abandons them, letting their resistance to meaning or exact reference and the privation thereof empower the creative act. I use 'privation' in Giorgio Agamben's sense from the lecture 'Resistance in Art', which defines the poetic act as a 'field of tensions between potency and impotency'.[40] In a poetic act 'there is something that resists creation and counters expression', and this resistance is prerequisite to creation in that it is the power source for the expenditure of creative capacity that brings an actual art object into the world. In other words, the poetic act is essentially not about putting potentiality into actuality. The real power of the poetic act stems from the artist's resistance to manufacturing meanings or expressing ideas. For only if his power to actualise and to produce is withheld and conserved, when his creative impulse is retained in impotentiality, can we talk about pure creativity: 'the transition to the act might take place only by transferring into the act the potentiality to not do, resistance'. The central principle of creativity is the ability to conserve the capacity to not create in the act itself, to ingrain the 'to not do' in the artistic fabric.

One of Barthelme's first published stories, 'The Balloon' from 1966, makes the passing of not-doing and not-meaning into the act its central theme. When, in the story, a gigantic balloon suddenly appears in the city, everyone is obsessed with its meaning. The balloon, however, stubbornly resists revealing its purpose.

> But it is wrong to speak of 'situations,' implying sets of circumstances leading to some resolution, some escape of tension; there were no situations, simply the balloon hanging there – muted heavy grays and browns for the most part, contrasting with the walnut and soft yellows. A deliberate lack of finish, enhanced by skillful installation, gave the surface a rough, forgotten quality; sliding weights on the inside, carefully adjusted, anchored the great, vari-shaped mass at a number of points. Now we have had a flood of original ideas in all media, works of singular beauty as well as significant milestones in the history of inflation, but at that moment, there was only *this balloon*, concrete particular, hanging there.
>
> There were reactions. Some people found the balloon 'interesting.' As a response, this seemed inadequate to the immensity of the balloon, the suddenness of its appearance over the city . . . There was a certain amount of initial argumentation about the 'meaning' of the balloon; this subsided . . . It was agreed that since the meaning of the balloon could never be known absolutely, extended discussion was pointless.[41]

As an act of literature, Barthelme's story congeals the capacity/ resistance to produce singular meanings in the object of the undecipherable balloon, which floats above the entire city, oppressing it with its capacity to not signify. The privative power of Barthelme's literary tactic here is in direct proportion to the attention and inquisitiveness on the part of the reader, which produces tension between creative potentiality and privative impotentiality. Throughout the story, that is to say, the narrator does nothing. He refrains from revealing what the balloon is all about, and fills the space of this withdrawal, this suspension of knowledge, with a random, imperfect (Ehrenzweig's word) clutter of what Agamben calls mannerisms – ill-fitted guesses by the people in the city.

The tension between creative potentiality and privative impotentiality is abruptly released in the last paragraph of the story, when the narrator melancholically 'discloses' that he created the balloon out of longing for his absent lover:

> The balloon, I said, is a spontaneous autobiographical disclosure, having to do with the unease I felt at your absence . . . but now that your visit to Bergen has been terminated, it is no longer necessary or appropriate. Removal of the balloon was easy.[42]

With this 'spontaneous disclosure' Barthelme dramatises the moment of difference between the potent creative poetic act which the balloon performed through the story by not-meaning, and the venting of this potency when a meaning is finally revealed. It is the moment in the story where its creative potency is evaporated. The balloon is deflated. This, one might say, is Barthelme's correction to the principles of Abstract Expressionism. Art is not about putting the artist's mind in the act; it is about putting into the act this mind's resistance to be actualised. Barthelme's describes this in 'After Joyce': a literary object 'does not declare itself all at once, in a rush of pleasant naïveté . . . It is a lifetime project . . . the book remains always there.' Its meaning always resists total exposure.[43]

Last but not least, by setting the tension between meaning production and meaning withdrawal, 'The Balloon' also delivers a commentary about the writing industry and literary productiveness. As long as 'The Balloon' is an attraction that offers itself for interpretation, the people in the city enjoy it, but the spontaneous disclosure of the narrator, whether honest or not (which we will never know), intervenes into the fictional convention. It is a private insertion that interests no one. If we take the story as a spoof, it renders our earlier interpretative efforts pointless and unproductive. If we take it seriously, the story loses its attractiveness and we are no longer interested in the balloon. Either way, the story stops producing meanings and leaves the readers suspended in not knowing what to think. And this seems to be precisely what Barthelme wanted to do, or rather to not do, in 'The Balloon'.

Another of Barthelme's stories that dramatises this process – call it unconscious scanning, transitional play or the work of *sterēsis* – is the 1968 story 'The Falling Dog'. At the beginning of the story, the narrator, a Welsh sculptor, is walking down the street when, suddenly, a dog falls out of a high window and knocks him down. The man gets up and then he and the dog just stand looking at one another for the rest of story. First, there is merely wonder:

> Neither of us spoke. I wondered what he was like (dog's life). It was as if you were looking for a house, answering ads, and after you inspected each house, you turned to the real estate man and asked (waving the hand to indicate the neighborhood), 'What are the people like?' And of course he can't say, because he doesn't know. But he says something anyhow. 'What are the people like?' 'Very friendly.' 'What are the people like?' 'They are nice people.' 'What are the people like?' 'They play croquet' . . . I was curious about the dog. Then I understood why I was curious.

> wrapped or bandaged. vulnerability.
> but also
> aluminum
> plexiglass
> anti-hairy materials
> vaudeville (the slide for life)[44]

In the not-knowing of the initial shock, the narrator, who is lying on the ground looking at the dog which looks back at him, starts thinking in a disorganised fashion about sculpting materials, aluminium and so on, and poses for a sculpture. As the story's action remains frozen in that tableau of the man and the dog staring at each other, the narrator's fantasies go back and forth from thoughts about whom the dog belongs to (and possible encounters with more or less attractive owners) to thoughts about possible art pieces he could do featuring the dog:

> who else has done dogs
> Baskin, Bacon, Landseer, Hogarth
> Hals

> with leashes trailing as they fall
> with dog impedimenta following:
> bowl, bone, collar, license. Gro-pup . . .

group of tiny hummingbird-sized falling dogs
Massed in upper corners of a room
with high ceilings 14–17 foot
in rows, in ranks, on their back . . .

styrofoam?[45]

We do not learn what sculpture will emerge out of those ideas, because at the end of the story, the sculptor just grabs the dog and races to his studio. What we do know, however, is that as he is staring at the dog and free associating, he is also reading a letter from an enthusiastic art historian who wants to include pictures of his already existing work – 'The Yawning Man' series – in his book about the best American sculptors. Even though the narrator knows that a great, at least ten-year-long, career lies ahead of 'The Yawning Man' he cannot stop imagining sculptures of the dog.

One way to read Barthelme's piece is as another exercise in arresting the potentiality to create in its nascent form and thus capturing the tension between potency and impotency in the narrative form of a fragmented story. Another way of saying this is that 'The Falling Dog' arrests the state of mind of the artist before he commits to one concrete vision or the other – plexiglas or styrofoam; a collage or an installation. All visions are there and the choice is never made, at least not in the story. 'The Falling Dog' may therefore be read as an allegory of suspension in 'either–or'. At the same time, however, if we consider the narrator's negative reaction to the letter from the historian, 'The Falling Dog' also performs resistance to the demands of the art market and the critics. The sculptor says:

> I was right in not wanting to read this letter. It was kind of this man to be interested in something I was no longer interested in. How was he to know that I was in the unhappiest of states, between images? But now something new had happened to me
>
> dogs as a luxury (what do we need them for?)
> hounds of heaven
> fallen in the sense of fallen angels . . .[46]

Crucially, the something new is a single idea that occurred to the narrator between images. It is the unhappiest of states, because as

Roland Barthes reminds us in 'Osons être paresseux', the position of in-between-ness is as joyful as it is painful. It is a form of *jouissance*. Barthelme thus wants his narrator to dwell in that state for as long as the narrative continues, lying there on the ground with his chin burning from the fall, his mind floating in unknown directions.

The Novels: Inertia in *Snow White* and *The Dead Father*

Donald Barthelme's novels are a different territory than his short fictions. None of them particularly fits the genre of the novel, as they are by and large collections of fragments – anti-forms, to use Ihab Hassan's famous term – put together in book form. But if read through the prism of the laziness concept-metaphor, Barthelme's experiments with the novelistic genre offer themselves as exercises in *paresse* and *sterēsis*.

I have myself written extensively in my book *Rethinking Postmodern Subjectivity* about the trope of fatigue and indolence which runs through all of Barthelme's novels: *Snow White* (1967), *The Dead Father* (1975), *Paradise* (1986) and *The King* (2002). I employed Emmanuel Levinas's concepts to argue for Barthelme's concern with an ethics of referentiality.[47] Fatigue and indolence, I argued, are the starting positions for Barthelme's literary subjectivities to emerge. At the point of writing that book, I did not yet have the concept-metaphor of laziness, nor what I would call today the intellectual courage to even notice the depths of inertia and recumbence that Snow White, her dwarves, the Dead Father, or the protagonist of *Paradise* are so deeply immersed in. And neither did I think about the political implications – ideological labour, if you will – that those themes carried and performed. But I nevertheless think it was in that zone of not-noticing the obvious that my idea of laziness as a norm-resistance trope must have had a start. My Barthelme, just like others critics' Barthelme, was an exemplary postmodernist. I wouldn't change a word in that book today, but in what I have to say below I add that Barthelme also managed to explode the norm that he was part of precisely from within this exemplariness.

On the most general level, Barthelme's novels resist the post-modern norm by imploding the novelistic convention. As mentioned above, *Snow White*, *The Dead Father*, *Paradise* and *The King* are not novels *per se*. They are books comprised of short stories and fragments that do not stand on their own. As compilations of what Ehrenzweig calls 'imperfections' and Agamben calls 'mannerisms', they are all statements of the writer's capacity to not write a novel – performances of *sterēsis*. Moreover, the capacity to not do is also the organising theme of each novel. This being said, I will concentrate in what follows mostly on *Snow White* and *The Dead Father*, rather than *Paradise* and *The King*, because their interventionist use of the theme of doing nothing has been more overlooked than in the case of Barthelme's late fictions. Not only have *Paradise* and *The King* been recognised as critiques of the state of art and the artist in postmodernism, but also, due to their more conventional narrative styles – *Paradise* practically lacks experimentation; *The King* is an mock Arthurian legend – their critical message is more transparent, thus requiring less detailed analysis.[48]

Take *Paradise*, the story of an ageing architect, Simon, on a sabbatical, who 'marinades', as Roland Barthes would call it, in his New York apartment shared with three young women, enjoying his freedom but also suffering from anxiety attacks as he contemplates his past and future designs. If we treat the motif of architecture as a hyperbolic representation of art that has become a form of organised and quantifiable engineering, Barthelme's critique of the art industry is not hard to spot. Similarly, the fact that the protagonist feels trapped in his world, in terms of privacy as well as career, and feels anxious about it, captures what Alan Wilde has called 'the morphology of feeling'[49] that is characteristic of postmodern sensibility. The theme of doing nothing is there throughout the novel, but, very much as in Thomas Pynchon's fiction, it is not so much a disruptive device as a code. And as Fredric Jameson frequently point outs, when themes become codes their ideological power is somewhat diluted. Barthelme's early novels *Snow White* and *The Dead Father* are in that sense much less transparent and much more interventionist. Instead of telling stories about the normativisation of the postmodern style of thinking, they perform a protest towards its distribution of the sensible.

The critic Jeffrey Nealon once wrote that while the existing readings of *Snow White* tend to focus on Barthelme's strategy of distorted reproduction of traditional aesthetic ideas, *Snow White*'s actual sub-versiveness comes, to use Blanchot's phrase, from its performance of 'an aesthetic disaster'.[50] Indeed, disasters and failures are the *modus operandi* of Barthelme's first novel. The eponymous Snow White has the ambition to write a long poem, but try as she might she can only lament, 'I wish there were some words in the world that are not the words I always hear.' When she begins writing she gets stuck on the phrase 'bandaged and wounded' – a cliché bad Hemingway phrase with unimaginatively reversed causal logic. Similarly, when Snow White tries to revolutionise her 'uninteresting' life by playing Rapunzel and letting her hair down from the window for the prince to find her, she is too withdrawn from the role to fully engage in it.[51] Her inertia is shared by other characters in the story, who recognise in Snow White's performance a 'powerful statement of [their] essential mutuality, which can never be sundered or torn, or broken apart, dissipated, diluted, corrupted, or finally severed, not even by art in its manifold and dreadful guises'.[52]

The dwarves, who are tired of menial work at the vat factory, inertly dwell from day to day, and are indifferent to Snow White's artistic or political efforts to assert herself. The prince figure, Paul – a parodic mix of Jean-Paul Sartre and Jackson Pollock – spends his days in a tub 'taking long baffs' and contemplating art which never materialises. Even the sexual activity on the set of *Snow White* is reduced to voyeurism. Despite their desires, the dwarves only peep at Snow White or watch pornography. In short, virtually no one in *Snow White* manages to put their visions and desires into action.

Last but not least, *Snow White* features a reader questionnaire, familiar to all students of postmodern classics, which poses questions to the reader and leaves blanks to be filled, but apart from mimicking the form of a real questionnaire, it does not actually perform its task. The reader might answer, is indeed interpellated or tempted to answer, questions such as 'Do you like the novel so far?' or 'Would you like more emotion?', but of course to no avail, because *Snow White* is an already written text and no one is waiting for answers. All the reader might do is ponder what it would be like if his or her opinion were taken into considera-tion. Importantly, Barthelme's questions in the questionnaire are not just any questions. They are a literary editor's check points for what makes an attractive, widely read book. There are thus questions about the level of experimentation matching the level of readability. There is the ranking question. There are questions about the book reflecting the existential and political climate of the time, such as the question about war, metaphysics and sufficient individualism of the characters. Finally, there are questions which seem to be less editorial and more creativity oriented, such as the question about the Authors Guild and human shoulders, both of which tend to address the problem of originality of thought and its limitations. Just as nothing can be done about the number of shoulders humans have, nothing can be done about the issue of copyright, which is sanctioned by the power apparatus rather than patented by individual artists.

In *Snow White*, the first of such artists is Snow White herself, who fails and withdraws from her creative projects. As she pursues her initiative to hang 'her ebony black hair from the window' she initially voices the hope of creative potency: 'This motif, the long hair streaming from the high window, is a very ancient one I believe, found in many cultures, in various forms. Now I recapitulate it, for the astonishment of the vulgar and the refreshment of my venereal life.'[53] Then, however, Snow White realises that her act brings no refreshment, as she doesn't know if the prince who appears is real or if she has 'projected him in the shape of [her] longing, boredom, ennui, and pain'.[54] She therefore undertakes another project, which never fully materialises: the 'dirty great poem'.[55] The opening lines, as she explains to Bill, would be 'bandaged and wounded . . . Run together' to stand as 'a metaphor of the self armoring itself against the gaze of the Other'.[56] The uninventiveness of Snow White's effort, its programmatic poetics, which anticipates 'the poet' in Barthelme's third novel *Paradise* who overexploits the images of 'burning barns' and 'dust', testify to her effort to fit into the avant-garde convention. If only Snow White wasn't trying so hard. Her 'ontological despair', as one critic calls it, comes from the fact that she does not want to think outside the experimental convention of avant-garde poetry.[57] But what in the protagonist's case is failure and despair is not the case with the creator of the story she inhabits. Snow White's lazy metaphors are Barthelme's way of disabling the emerging convention of the postmodern experimental novel. While Snow White's subversive 'dirty great poem' never materialises, *Snow White* the anti-novel does. What she felt as 'insufficient' is now turned into a work of literature. Using Agamben's language, one might say that Snow White's not-writing a great poem is put by Barthelme into the act of *Snow White*, the book. Barthelme's monotonous, almost 'mechanical' manner of poetic randomisation and fragmentation of her appearances, and the 'implosive impasses' those appearances cause, mirror the character's writing method.[58] What transpires in Barthelme's implosions is, as Jeffrey Nealon puts it, the 'wonder of the desire to know' reminiscent of infantile, timeless curiosity, a wonder that cannot be reduced to cognition.[59] The ontological moment of wonder, so cherished by Ehrenzweig and Winnicott, which is a prerequisite of artistic freedom, is thus what Barthelme tries to recreate in protest against programmatic experimentation.

Snow White is not the only character who fails and suffers from acediac resignation. The dwarves' leader Bill, whose main trait is weariness, also resigns from aiming at 'greatness'.[60] 'Bill is tired of Snow White' and everything else, and refuses to be touched.[61] Faced with such a condition in their leader, the dwarves resort to philosophical speculations as to whether Bill's rejection of physical contact is a symptom of withdrawal understood in a Heideggerian manner as 'a mode of dealing with anxiety', or a sign of withdrawal understood in the vein of Maurice Merleau-Ponty's idea of 'a physical manifestation of a metaphysical condition that is not anxiety'.[62] Or perhaps, they also think, it is 'a sign of a lost mind'.[63] But although everyone is in the dark about Bill's fatigue, he himself knows perfectly what it is all about: answering Snow White's cry to hear words she has not heard before, Bill passionately exclaims: 'Injunctions!'[64] The normative orders about what can or cannot be done is exactly what bothers him and what he wants Snow White's poem to address. Bill's refusal to follow any injunction is so profound that he finds no artistic form for it. However, he stages his protest on every occasion. Like his literary prototype, the scrivener Bartleby, Bill refuses everything. He 'refuses to take off his pajamas'[65] like everyone else, to enjoy communal life, to sing chants while 'washing the buildings' and 'tending the vats'.[66] He refuses to be touched. Eventually, he grows so stubbornly unproductive that the dwarves decide to take his leadership away.

The dynamics of Snow White's and Bill's relation is crucial for how Barthelme intertwines the idea of impotency with the idea of resistance. Snow White's desire to be productive and creative is in tension with Bill's desire for the opposite and his embrace of dissent to norms and rules. By setting them against one another, Barthelme creates a stage for a critique, or a protest against, normativised artistic productivity. This protest is captured in the theme of Bill's *paresse*. However, as I have just said, in the pages of *Snow White* he himself never gives his sentiment an artistic form.

At one point in the story, Bill says 'give me the odd linguistic trip, stutter and fall, and I will be content. Actually, when you get right down to it, I should be the monk, and Paul the leader here.'[67] Indeed it takes Paul, Bill's lethargic double, to invent an artistic practice that will capture the tension between productivity and unproductivity. What Paul does is write palinodes whose key poetic strategy of 'retraction' might be capable, he dreams, of swallowing up the entire world around him.[68] Retraction, he says, 'has a special allure for me. I would wish to retract everything, if I could, so that the whole written world would be . . .'[69] The mode of retraction is also the way Paul functions, spending his days on aimless and unproductive meditations 'in his baff'.[70] He perceives himself as suspended between being 'more experimental than he [his father] was' and at the same time being 'more withdrawn'.[71] As he would retract the whole world, 'retract that long black hair hanging from that window', he finally retracts himself from the plot, by drinking the poisonous vodka destined for Snow White and dying.[72]

Thus, Paul, the unproductive though technically up-to-date none-artist, to recall John Barth's epithet for an anti-postmodernist, becomes a doubly significant character in Barthelme's *Snow White*. For it seems that his artistic method of retractions and withdrawals, so radical as to include the deletion of himself, reflects Barthelme's artistic strategy. It mirrors Barthelme's mode of suspension between two creative approaches. On the one hand, we might interpret Paul's disappearance as Barthelme's dismissal of an inert, unproductive character who prevents the novel from productive closure. On the other hand, we might just as well treat it as a performance of Barthelme's withdrawal of his artistic tools and refusal to give his creations a technically up-to-date, artful finish. The dismissal of the artist figure in *Snow White*, in other words, is Barthelme's dismissal of the role of the artist as imposed by the postmodern industry. In this way, it is also an act of reclaiming his artistic vision of 'either–or' in all its vulnerability, blocking the possibility of this vision being co-opted by the postmodern literary norm.

The doubly signifying suicide of Paul is carried into Barthelme's second novel *The Dead Father*, which features, indeed is dominated by, the gigantic figure of the Dead Father, who is 'dead but still with us, still with us but dead',[73] hauled across the landscape to his burial site by a host of randomly convened characters, one of whom is his son. The Dead Father's in-between status is so plainly stated in the opening lines of the novel that the reader is forced to abandon all impulse to pursue allegorical interpretations. The Dead Father is not dead, as in 'representing dead modernist tradition'; he's not in limbo, as in 'representing the limits of the known'; he is not alive or capable of action in the sense that literary characters are. Indeed, this status alone has caused critics a lot of headache. Some praised the book's stylistic acrobatics and proclaimed Barthelme as the 'disturbing' voice of his era.[74] But others repudiated *The Dead Father*'s 'extreme distance from and mechanistic, counter-productive avant-gardism'. J. D. O'Hara wrote that *The Dead Father* does not remove the doubt aroused by *Snow White* as to whether Barthelme's style is suitable for the novel formula; the writer's 1975 quest tale is all a 'drag, literally and figuratively', which has not been thoroughly designed.[75] In a 1975 radio interview with Barthelme on Pacifica Radio, Judith Sherman confessed that after the first two chapters of the book she was completely puzzled, feeling 'like every time I'm about to put my foot down, because I know it's going to happen, the ground moves', and thus immediately trying 'to grab onto allegory'.[76] This confession triggered quite a startling reaction from Barthelme, who insisted that *The Dead Father* is an 'extremely accessible' and 'plain' book, one which does not so much contain allegory as welcome the allegory being 'brought in' by the reader.[77] Barthelme gave the same evasive response to Charles Ruas in the same interview, when Ruas inquired about *The Dead Father*'s intertexts, to J. D. O'Hara who asked about religious symbolism, and to Jo Brans in the 1981 interview at the Seventh Annual Literary Festival in Dallas, in which

Barthelme consistently dodged all questions concerning the auto-biographical elements in his second novel, comparing his writing method to the experiments of Gertrude Stein.[78] All Barthelme was willing to tell his interlocutors was that the book is 'pure dream material' and that it is a book about being a father and having one, which they sort of already knew.

If we take the cue from Barthelme's comment about Stein, who as I argued in the chapter on modernist aesthetics aimed at sus-pending the representational contract altogether, then reading *The Dead Father* figuratively makes absolutely no sense. In the words of Barthelme's Thomas Brecker from 'January', 'there is so little content that there is almost nothing to talk about'.[79] Indeed, the book is a drag. It is a drag literally, because it has no features of the novel genre, and figuratively, because the plot and in-your-face father-symbolism stubbornly refuse to be interpreted. One grabs for an allegory and discovers it is preposterously conventional and boring. How then does *The Dead Father* generate such an inexhaust-ible capacity 'to not be' a novel and 'to not tell' a story?

A prompt on how to address this question is offered by one of Barthelme's critics, Lois Gordon, who writes that this 'montage of shifting textures' whose sole subject is language lacks any realist dimension and is so deficient in the 'cultural detritus that formerly characterised his figures' social and mental worlds' that it cannot be approached otherwise than as a massive critique of the general functioning of all belief systems.[80] What Gordon seems to be saying is that *The Dead Father* launches an attack on the very nature of any regime of the sensible, at the core of which lies acceptance of and subjugation to its power. This is not to say that it is Barthelme's didactic position; rather, it is his text itself that performs this critique through the transposition of not-knowing the result of writing (and reading) into *The Dead Father*'s literary fabric.

One of the ways in which this is achieved is by the suspension of the ontological status of his protagonist. The Dead Father is at the same time a passive carcass hauled by a cable as well as a vigorous dominator who says 'I am the Father. All lines are my lines', and who produces a religiously prescriptive manual for sons that fills half of the book. This suspension between passivity and submis-siveness on the one hand, and the assertion of powerful agency on the other, renders the Dead Father the fulcrum of what Giorgio Agamben calls the 'tension between potency and impotency' in a creative act.[81] If we agree with Agamben that the essence of a creative act lies in the suspension of power to produce meanings and ideas, *sterēsis*, then the Dead Father transfers this retention of power into the text of Barthelme's novel. He is a metaphor, we might say therefore, of *sterēsis*, the power to-not. He stands for the power of creative impulse retained in impotentiality. That is why, as one critic writes, he is a metaphor so 'unspecified and unfixed' and so much 'on its own terms, to its own ends' that in the process it becomes 'not just the vehicle of a trope but a vehicle of discovery'.[82] The discovery to which Barthelme invites the reader is first of all to capture the inexhaustibility of the not-known of the literary act. Second, and more importantly, it might also be the discovery of an elusive intersection within the structure of any belief system or norm of individual life and control of power apparatuses.

In Foucault's definition, *norm* is the very biopolitical mechanism of controlling a population, which works by concealing the real subjection of individual lives under the guises of morality and social and cultural standards of (re)productive existence. A norm, in this understanding, is thus a masquerade and a drag, as a prohibition on being unproductive. In this context, *The Dead Father* registering in his readers' eyes as a drag novel, and the protagonist coming off as a drag metaphor that suggests much but means nothing in particular, impress as instances of the pre-emergent sensibility of dissent towards the exclusionary work of dominant aesthetic values and styles of the second half of the twentieth century.

'Drag' means, of course, much more than cross-dressing. As a verb, to drag is to draw with force, pull heavily or slowly along, haul, trail, but also to feel listless and apathetic, to take a puff. As a noun, drag is slow, laborious movement or procedure, retardation, but also, as a nautical term, resistance to the movement of a hull through water. It seems that all these senses are at work in Barthelme's novel. The fact that the restrained Dead Father is hauled by a cable, as a weight that retards the progress of the hearse, may represent the authoritative violence of norm enslavement and its attempt to bury the individual cast of mind. The fact that the Dead Father suffers from *dyscrasia* and *dysthymia*, which are types of physical and mental depression that make him drag around listlessly and apathetically, sets the tone of the pre-emergent sensibility, as Raymond Williams would call it, of distrust and reluctance *vis-à-vis* the norm of ever-present, privacy- and individuality-consuming productiveness. Finally, the fact that the Dead Father asserts himself with a drag manual for sons, which, however nonsensical and uninstructive, occupies nevertheless the centre of the novel and slows down the action, may be understood in the nautical sense of drag as resistance to the movement of the ship. In this particular sense, the purpose of 'Manual for Sons' is to exaggerate the superficial nature of instruction in general, that is to say, the recursive structure of prescriptions and injunctions – 'ukases' as the manual calls them – aimed at increasing produc- tiveness at all costs. The Manual urges never resting in the process of 'reproducing every one of the enormities touched upon in this manual'.[83] Interestingly, one of the most important enormities to be reproduced 'as soon as possible' is to substitute the current 'work ethic, which is a dumb one' with the ethic of fear. This brings us back to Thomas Brecker, the scholar of *acedia*, who said that the fear ethic embedded in *acedia* is the only way to be free from any form of submission. As Barthelme presents the reader with a cast of busy yet counter-productive characters, on a productive yet counter-productive burial mission, in counter-productive moods of sullenness, when their existence weighs on them like a burden, as Heidegger would say, one might treat *The Dead Father* as a unique intervention into postmodern ways of thinking in that it is a pow- erful critique of the norm of productivity. In its form and content, the theme of inert dragging around exposes the normative mask of (artistic) productivity and X-rays its subjugation mechanisms. The book, like its acediac protagonist, is anxiously yet stubbornly 'staring up into the sky . . . Decades of staring.'[84]

All in all, Barthelme's aesthetics is thus uniquely interventionist *vis-à-vis* the dominant sensibility of postmodernism, in the way that Herman Melville's Romanticism and Ernest Hemingway's modern- ism were in relation to their respective traditions. Like Melville and Hemingway, Barthelme launches a critique of his epoch's dis- tribution of the sensible by exploring its relation to the norm of productivity by means of the poetics of his time. Like Melville and Hemingway, he also recognises that this particular norm is deeply tied to and contingent upon the very production of normativity – its discourse, aesthetics and ethics. So, while Melville's mock-pastoral narration of *Typee* ridiculed Romantic didacticism and the Enlightened colonial gaze, Barthelme's work toys with postmodern aesthetics to give yet another meaning to the metaphor of laziness in order to reflect upon the aesthetic regime of postmodern exhaustion-replenishment and Rosenbergian self-fashioning. While Hemingway in *The Garden of Eden* dramatised the eclipse of artistic creativity by literary productiveness for its own sake, Barthelme enquires into the aftermath of this eclipse by refurnishing the metaphorical field of laziness in his own innovative way by exploring the counter-normative potential of the themes of inertia and *acedia*.

Notes

1. Donald Barthelme, 'January', *The New Yorker*, 6 April 1987, 41.
2. Ibid., 44.
3. Ibid., 44.
4. Helen Moore Barthelme, *Donald Barthelme: The Genesis of a Cool Sound* (College Station, TX: A&M University Press, 2001), 14.
5. '"Nothing but Darkness and Talk?"': Writers' Symposium on Traditional Values and Iconoclastic Fiction', *Critique* 31.4 (1990), 249.
6. Michel Foucault, *The Order of Things: An Archaeology of the Human Sciences* (1966) (New York: Vintage, 1994), 351–2.
7. Anton Ehrenzweig, *The Hidden Order of Art: A Study in the Psychology of Artistic Imagination* (Berkeley: University of California Press, 1967), 141.
8. Donald Barthelme, 'After Joyce', *Location* 2 (1964), 14.
9. Ibid., 14.
10. Ibid., 14.
11. Ehrenzweig, *The Hidden Order of Art*, 32–3.
12. Ibid., 42.
13. Donald Barthelme, 'Not-Knowing', *The Georgia Review* 39.3 (1985), 509–10.
14. Ehrenzweig, *The Hidden Order of Art*, 35.
15. Ibid., 37.
16. Ibid., 39.
17. Barthelme, 'Not-Knowing', 510.
18. Ibid., 513.
19. Foucault, *The Order of Things*, 351.
20. Ibid., 355. Foucault doesn't use the word 'biopolitical' in *The Order of Things*, but it seems fitting if we read his words from the 1966 book, anachronistically, through the concept of biopolitics which the idea of 'empirico-transcendental doublet' seems to anticipate.

21. Ibid., 351.
22. Barthelme, 'After Joyce', 15.
23. Ibid., 16.
24. Ibid.
25. Johnny Payne, *Conquest of the New Word: Experimental Fiction and Translation in the Americas* (Austin: University of Texas Press, 2014), 39.
26. Donald Barthelme, 'Paraguay', *The New Yorker*, 6 September 1969, 32.
27. Ibid., 32, 34.
28. Ibid., 33.
29. Ibid., 32.
30. Ibid., 32.
31. Bernard Stiegler, *States of Shock: Stupidity and Knowledge in the 21st Century* (Cambridge: Polity Press, 2015), 45.
32. Theodor Adorno and Max Horkheimer, *Dialectic of Enlightenment* (Palo Alto: Stanford University Press, 2002), xvii.
33. Ibid., xvii; Barthelme, 'Paraguay', 32.
34. Barthelme, 'Paraguay', 33.
35. Ibid., 33–4.
36. Ibid., 34.
37. John Locke, *The Philosophical Works and Selected Correspondence of John Locke. Of the Conduct of the Understanding*, 5th edn (Charlottesville, VA: InteLex Corporation, 1995), 63.
38. Barthelme, *Donald Barthelme*, 91.
39. Ehrenzweig admits in *The Hidden Order of Art* that his idea corresponds to Winnicott's transitional objects. Ehrenzweig, *The Hidden Order of Art*, 283.
40. Giorgio Agamben, 'Resistance in Art', European Graduate School Inaugural Lecture, Saas- Fee, Switzerland, 2014, https://www.youtube.com/watch?v=one7 mE-8y9c (accessed 28 January 2019).
41. Donald Barthelme, 'The Balloon', *The New Yorker*, 16 April 1966, 46.
42. Ibid., 48.
43. Barthelme, 'After Joyce', 14.
44. Donald Barthelme, 'The Falling Dog', *The New Yorker*, 3 August 1968, 28.
45. Ibid., 28, 29.
46. Ibid., 29.
47. See Zuzanna Ladyga, *Rethinking Postmodern Subjectivity: Emmanuel Levinas and the Ethics of Referentiality in the Work of Donald Barthelme* (Frankfurt am Main: Peter Lang, 2009).
48. For a detailed analysis of those works from this angle, see my *Rethinking Postmodern Subjectivity* and Zuzanna Ladyga, 'Faking the Artificial in Donald Barthelme's *Paradise*', *American Studies* 21 (March 2004), 7–15.
49. Alan Wilde, 'Middle Grounds', in *Studies in Contemporary American Fiction* (Philadelphia: University of Pennsylvania Press, 1987), 165.
50. Jeffrey T. Nealon, 'Disastrous Aesthetics: Irony, Ethics, and Gender in Barthelme's "Snow White"', *Twentieth Century Literature* 51.2 (2005), 125, 135.
51. Donald Barthelme, *Snow White* (New York: Atheneum, 1977), 59.
52. Ibid., 59.

53. Ibid., 80.
54. Ibid., 102.
55. Ibid., 59.
56. Ibid., 59.
57. John Leland, 'Re-Marked: Barthelme, What Curious Signs!', *Boundary 2* 5.3 (1977), 806.
58. Morris Dickstein, *Gates of Eden: American Culture in the Sixties* (New York: Basic Books, 1977), 62.
59. Nealon, 'Disastrous Aesthetics', 126, 130.
60. Barthelme, *Snow White*, 51.
61. Ibid., 4.
62. Ibid., 4.
63. Ibid., 62.
64. Ibid., 6.
65. Ibid., 106.
66. Ibid., 112.
67. Ibid., 139.
68. Ibid., 13.
69. Ibid., 13.
70. Ibid., 13, 94.
71. Ibid., 27.
72. Ibid., 94.
73. Donald Barthelme, *The Dead Father* (1975) (New York: Farrar, Straus and Giroux, 1986), 3.
74. Richard Todd, 'Daddy, You're Perfectly Swell!', *Atlantic Monthly*, December 1975, 112.
75. J. D. O'Hara, 'The Dead Father', *Library Journal* 100.20 (15 November 1975), 217.
76. Donald Barthelme, 'Pacifica Radio: Interview with Charles Ruas and Judith Sherman, 1975', in *Not-Knowing: The Essays and Interviews of Donald Barthelme*, ed. Kim A. Herzinger (New York: Random House, 1997), 212.
77. Ibid., 212–13.
78. Ibid., 226–7; J. D. O'Hara, 'Interview with Donald Barthelme: The Art of Fiction LXVI', *Paris Review* (summer 1981), 181; Jo Brans, 'Interview with Jo Brans: Embracing the World, 1981', in Herzinger (ed.), *Not Knowing: The Essays and Interviews of Donald Barthelme*, 294.
79. Barthelme, 'January', 42.
80. Lois Gordon, *Donald Barthelme* (New York: Twayne, 1981), 161–2.
81. Agamben, 'Resistance in Art'.
82. Richard Walsh, 'The Dead Father: Innovative Forms, Eternal Themes', in *Critical Essays on Donald Barthelme*, ed. Richard Francis Patteson (New York: G.K. Hall, 1992), 175.
83. Barthelme, *The Dead Father*, 145.
84. Ibid., 3.

CHAPTER 7

Acedia and David Foster Wallace's *The Pale King*

Premium on activity!

Luc Boltanski and Eve Chiapello

The legacy of Donald Barthelme's Dead Father in his 1975 novel, staring at the sun in the pose of a monk possessed by *daemon meridianus*, eventually made its way into the literature of the second generation of postmodernists. However, the circumstances were not favourable. For the majority of writers of the Program Era born in the 1960s and 1970s, and thus raised and trained in the spirit of hyper-productivity, the pursuit of what Lauren Berlant called in *Cruel Optimism* 'small self-interruptions' may have seemed like the betrayal of the writerly profession and identity.[1] A certain anxiety about the implications of the politics of self-interruption among the writers of this generation who were expected to make it new again – David Foster Wallace, Jeffrey Eugenides, Jonathan Franzen and Dave Eggers – manifested itself via their quiescent relinquishing of such dissensual ambitions and identification with what they called 'old-fashioned' modes of literary realism. One might ask, what else was there to do?

Among those who most openly confessed to this fear was Wallace, earmarked after the success of his *Infinite Jest* to be the voice of his generation, who, as Josh Roiland observes, desired to 'get away from it all' but could not tolerate the desire. In his essays, Wallace would often seek the 'trope of escape', whose embodiment would then 'unsettle' him greatly.[2] Writing about Fyodor Dostoyevsky's characters, Wallace would list those who exuded vitality only to remark that he sees in them parts of himself that he 'can barely look at'.[3] Writing about holidaying, he would be disgusted and 'disappointed in a way you can never admit' with the ignorant lack of consciousness that vacationers indulge in.[4] Writing about sport, he would envy professional athletes the ability to 'bypass their heads'.[5] In Roiland's words, Wallace was 'not only troubled by their lack of consciousness, but the excess of his own weigh[ed] on him'.[6]

In 'E Unibus Pluram: Television and U.S. Fiction' (1993), which is often compared to Barth's 'Literature of Exhaustion' (1967) in its status as a generational statement, Wallace ambivalently vacillates between confessions of his own addiction to the TV-induced 'cycle of indulgence, guilt, and reassurance', and the modalities of engagement without demanding, rational analyses of how television co-opts postmodern metafiction and irony, and outbursts of unrestrained contempt for the 'profound shallowness' of televisual experience.[7] All in all, neither the old-fashioned Melvillesque formats of getting away nor the more contemporary modes of disengaging the consciousness worked for Wallace. Or at least, they are not the kind of escapist tropes he was looking for. In the opinion of Wallace's critics, this profound dissatisfaction with postmodern aesthetics was the main cause of his writer's block at the time when he was working on his 'next big thing' after his 1996 epic *Infinite Jest*. Diagnosing the block, Samuel Cohen suggests that at

> the root of Wallace's difficulties in writing . . . was the problem of not knowing what fiction was supposed to be and do, the lack of 'base clause of conviction' about what he wrote for . . . He had not resolved to his own satisfaction the problem of how to write after Gaddis, Pynchon, and DeLillo.[8]

What Wallace did recognise, however, was that there was a certain 'supposed to be and do' about his own career in the literary world, and that as the voice of his generation and a McArthur genius-fellow he was expected to deliver – to put his mind into the act. Therefore, against Cohen, I would rather argue that Wallace's problem was that he *did* know what fiction at his time was supposed to be and do, that is to say, that it was forced by the rule of the market to make one participate in the biopolitical technologies of disempowering self-ownership, 'the fashions that are so easy to criticize but are so incredibly powerful and authentic-seeming when we're inside them, [which] tyrannize us'.[9] What Wallace did not seem to know (for a long time, considering his writer's block) was how to transform this knowledge into his own version of the trope of escape.

The Blank Amorphous Glare, or the Trope of *acedia*

Of some help in the direction of finding the trope and getting out of the dialogues with his conscience, his 'worrying about not writing' as he put it in the interview with Charlie Rose, might have been the advice of an older writer to whom Wallace owed so much: Thomas Pynchon. In his 1993 *New York Times* piece 'Nearer, My Couch, to Thee', Pynchon was simply saying take it easy:

> In his classical discussion of the subject in the *Summa Theologica* Aquinas termed Sloth, or acedia, one of the seven capital sins. He said he was using 'capital' to mean 'primary' . . . [yet] the word also meant 'deserving of capital punishment' . . .
>
> But come on, isn't that kind of extreme, death for something as light-weight as Sloth? Sitting there on some medieval death row, going, 'So, look, no offense, but what'd they pop you for anyway?'
>
> 'Ah, usual story, they came around at the wrong time of day, I end up taking out half of some sheriff's unit with my two-cubit crossbow, firing three-quarter-inch bolts on auto feed. Anger, I guess . . . How about you?'
>
> 'Um, well . . . it wasn't anger . . .'
>
> 'Ha! Another one of these Sloth cases, right?'
>
> '. . . fact, it wasn't even me.'
>
> 'Never is, slugger – say, look, it's almost time for lunch. You wouldn't happen to be a writer, by any chance?'

Writers of course are considered the mavens of Sloth. They are approached all the time on the subject, not only for free advice, but also to speak at Sloth Symposia, head up Sloth Task Forces, testify as expert witnesses at Sloth Hearings. The stereotype arises in part from our conspicuous presence in jobs where pay is by the word, and deadlines are tight and final – we are presumed to know from piecework and the convertibility of time and money. In addition, there is all the glamorous folklore surrounding writer's block, an affliction known sometimes to resolve itself dramatically and without warning, much like constipation, and (hence?) finding wide sympathy among readers. Writer's block, however, is a trip to the theme park of your choice alongside the mortal sin that produces it. [It can lead to] guilt and depression . . . [or] to rushing without rhyme or reason . . . It is of course precisely in such episodes of mental travelling that writers are known to do good work.[10]

I quote from Pynchon at such length not only because of how his tone counterbalances Wallace's excruciation about his inability to let go of the block, but also because it suggests a way out of identification with the productivising technologies of engagement. While acknowledging the commercial constraints of creative endeavours, the passage sends an encouragement that 'good' works of literature (by which Pynchon by default means works of literature that pocket counter-systemic resistance) come from none other than a writer's acediac disposition. *Acedia* may lead one to the crisis of self-invention in that it may feel like a version of writer's block, the term capturing the Romantic fantasy that inspiration should come from beyond the self, but this is precisely the experience that may also make the writer discover that he owns the keys to the 'theme park' of *his* 'choice'.

That Wallace might have taken this advice to heart is definitely visible in his 2004 short story collection *Oblivion*, whose title already declares a Pynchonesque/Nietzschean approach to those engaged modes of living and writing. The closing story in the collection, 'The Suffering Channel', attacks the writer's block through a juxtaposition of two artist-figures: a prolific soft-news journalist Skip Atwater, who reports controversial topics in a column of *Style* magazine, and a secretive rural artist from Illinois named Brint Moltke, who possesses the unusual gift of producing bowel movements that are replicas of the world's famous sculptures. The first is a tireless 'consummate pro' who invests himself in his job; the second is a freak, who feels tormented by his talent. Brint would like to remain anonymous but is nevertheless sought out by the entertainment industry, because suffering and self-torment sell best. In a sense, those two figures represent two conflicted sides of Wallace's artistic persona. Skip, who travels to interview Brint in his home and later supervises the television broadcast of the bowel-action sculpture in process, represents the writer who has succumbed to the drills of the publishing market without protest. Brint, on the other hand, is like Pynchon's blocked writer whose resolved affliction would make the world overjoyed with the input of the intimately private into his artistic act. The conflict between the two is, however, resolved at the end of the story, which features an event that interrupts this exploitation of privacy for the sake of the entertainment industry. During the live broadcast of Brint's action art, as artist's block – or, to use Pynchon's simile, 'constipation' – is supposed to resolve into a replica of the Hellenic sculpture of Nike, the winged victory of Samothrace, the technicians of the Suffering Channel (the entertainment TV channel designed to air real footage of painful experiences 24/7) face a last-minute problem:

> There's also some eleventh hour complication involving the ground camera and the problem of keeping the commode's special monitor out of its upward shot, since video capture of a camera's own monitor causes what is known in the industry as feedback glare – the artist in such a case would see, not his own emergent *Victory*, but a searing and amorphous light.[11]

The interruption of the camera is thus as haphazard as it is decisive: the feedback glare may be the cause of the show's failure to deliver entertainment. Figuratively, this glare, however, is of course much more than fierce light. For 'glare' the *OED* has 'to look fiercely or fixedly', 'to shine dazzlingly or disagreeably', 'to express hate and defiance by a look'. The word also refers to 'oppressive public attention'. Thus, the unexpected obstinacy of the equipment symbolically represents a sentiment of disagreement and defiance towards the oppressiveness of the attention to the private aspect of artistic production, a sentiment Wallace often identified as his own.[12] The freak artist in 'The Suffering Channel' cannot stand up to his humiliation on TV, but the technical instrumentarium relieves him from his task through a glitch in its wiring. Read allegorically, the last lines of the story thus deliver a model for an intervention into the contemporary modes of writing that could interrupt the paradigm of the postmodern writer as an 'action artist', forced to invest his entire private self in the artistic act. In the manner of a feedback glare, it is to use the instrumentarium of fiction to produce a blank, 'amorphous' reflection – a late postmodern version of what Jean-François Lyotard famously called the loss of the referent – which cannot in any way be appropriated by the affective technologies of engagement.

This is, of course, easier said than done. The strategy of using language to produce blank, amorphous reflection seems to be the right solution to the problem of what a writer can do to dissent from the demands of the contemporary publishing world, its ritual of book promotion tours, interviews and media appearances, without getting away from it all. But given Wallace's literary silence after *Oblivion*, the strategy was not easy to develop. Critics and readers awaited his 'next big thing' impatiently, yet with Wallace being a 'five-draft man'[13] the result was slow to come. The effort was eventually interrupted by his suicide in 2008. But as the 2011 posthumous publication of an edited manuscript of his unfinished novel *The Pale King* proved, it was not an effort that was ever abandoned.

And, one may add at this point, it was a particularly worthwhile effort considering how much of a celebrity Wallace was in academic circles and among his audiences by 2008 – and also how much of a popular icon he became after his suicide. Although the Wallace industry, like the Bartleby industry, continues to thrive, Wallace's untimely death made it expand to entropic proportions. In the first decade of the twenty-first century, internet reading communities were bursting at the seams with ordinary readers' comments and reactions. Literary studies were witnessing an outpouring of new interpretations, most as brilliantly illuminating as they were often frustratingly redundant. The Wallace Archive in Austin, Texas, was becoming a peregrination point. In short, the industry was experiencing the feedback glare problem without any intervention by the author himself. However, that Wallace had aimed to deliver an aesthetic performance of the feedback glare became evident in 2011 with the posthumous publication of *The Pale King*.

If read like an ordinary piece of fiction, *The Pale King* is an existential reflection upon the tragically boring mundaneness of everyday life, dramatised through the life stories of the tax officers employed by the Internal Revenue Service. It has therefore has been qualified by critics as part autobiography, part experiment in narrative plotlessness, part ideological commentary on capitalism and the commercial status of literature, provoking reflection upon such presumably settled issues as 'the death of the author', the mimetic limits of self-writing and the paradoxes of the literary market. That the novel was unfinished did not trouble the critics very much. Marshall Boswell, Wallace's most influential critic, considers *The Pale King* to have a special role in Wallace's canon, because it confirms that his was the aesthetics of non-closure.[14] According to Boswell, *The Pale King* is no more unfinished than Wallace's entire *oeuvre*, and it exemplifies his notorious preoccupation with suspension of conclusions and plots leading nowhere, to the point that notions such as climax and denouement lose all meaning.[15] In this classically metafictional interpretation, special emphasis is placed on the subversive role of authorial intrusions. Using an all-too-familiar line of deconstructive reasoning, Boswell says that chapters such as 'Author's Foreword' or 'Author here' are glaringly autobiographical in how the life narrative of an IRS officer named David F. Wallace allegorically alludes to Wallace's own career as a writer, while at the same time undercutting this allusion and at the same time legitimating it, only so as to undermine it again. From Vladimir Nabokov's 1957 novel *Pnin* to John Barth and back, American literature knows countless examples of this technique; thus Wallace's authorial intrusions are one more proof of his canonical greatness. In other words, Boswell recognises Wallace's dissensual strategy of the blank amorphous glare, yet he is inclined to count it as part of a coherent image of Wallace, the canonically postmodern aesthete.

Another critic, Henry Veggian, takes this analysis a step further, proceeding from the premises of the no-nonsense historicist branch of the Wallace industry which situates *The Pale King* first and foremost within the context of its archive.[16] By archive, Veggian does not mean biographical trivia such as Wallace's notes, references to books he read at the time of writing the novel, and so on. What he means instead is the context of the publishing market and the processes of institutionalised commodification of aesthetic labour.

A case in point for Veggian is that *The Pale King* begins with a note from Wallace's life-long editor, Michael Pietsch, who advertises the novel as a postmodern commodity with Wallace's name as its trademark. Indeed, given Pietsch's list of corrections made for the sake of narrative comprehensibility, it is difficult to disagree with Veggian's critical diagnosis. The pitch for *The Pale King* was not 'the successor of *Finnegans Wake*' but rather 'the last words of wisdom from the author of the Kenyon commencement speech'.[17] Pietsch's 'Note' declares that he has edited the manuscript 'only lightly', making 'cuts for sense and pace', correcting 'unintentional distractions and confusions so as to allow the reader to focus on the enormous issues David intended to raise and to make the story and characters as comprehensible as possible'.[18] By no means can one call such interventions 'light', for they turn an obscure piece of writing that was perhaps aimed to stay such into a digestible product.

What is even more interesting than the changes themselves is the main marketing point: Pietsch promises in his 'Note' that *The Pale King* allows readers 'to look once more inside that extraordinary mind' of David Wallace.[19] In that sense, *The Pale King* is a complete product, if not entirely a complete or finished novel to Wallace's standards.[20] The role of the 'Editor's Note' as part of *The Pale King* alters the classical meaning of metafiction, because meta-*textuality* becomes also a form of meta-*valuation*.[21] This, however, is less of a problem than an opportunity in the sense that the tension between *The Pale King* as published commodity and *The Pale King* as unfinished narrative helps to calibrate our interpretations of Wallace's text and its self-reflexive strategies to the issue of the relation between writers' self-ownership and publishing institutions. While Veggian's critique stays on the theoretical level *vis-à-vis* the outcome of those strategies, with statements such as '*The Pale King* passes through the production and valuation of its own literary commodity form in such a way that illuminates the production and valuation of literary commodity forms in general', I would like to move beyond theory to the level of stylistic analysis of how this self-commentary is dramatised in the novel.[22]

Part and parcel of Wallace's stylistic strategy, which I have referred to above as the aesthetics of the blank, amorphous glare, is his version of laziness: the theme of acediac disengagement, or as some (including Wallace himself) have called it, boredom. According to Wallace's note attached to his unfinished manuscript, quoted by Michael Pietsch in 'Notes and Asides' at the end of the Little, Brown edition of *The Pale King*, the themes of boredom and tedium are explicitly intended as the novel's 'broad arc'. The note states: 'paying attention, boredom, ADD, machines vs. people at performing mindless jobs'.[23] While Wallace's note finds frequent reference in criticism of his last novel, the themes of boredom and disengagement have not been extensively examined. This is perhaps because at first glance the novel, depicting the 'massively, spectacularly dull' lives of some officers of the IRS Regional Examination Center in Peoria, Illinois, lends itself all too easily to being read as a modernised version of Melville's 'Bartleby, the Scrivener' slashed with *Moby Dick*.[24] But despite those associations, *The Pale King* does not repeat Melville's critique without variance. In Wallace's novel, the *parrhēsiac* 'formula for non-will', if we want to use Deleuze's famous term for 'I'd prefer not to', is uniquely its own.[25]

One of the first and direct references to boredom is made in the chapter entitled 'Author's Foreword' where the 'author' says: 'It is impossible to overstate the importance of boredom' because, as the IRS has discovered, the more 'dull, arcane and mind-numbingly complex' its procedures are, the more the agency is 'insulated against public protest and political opposition'.[26] Boredom is thus depicted as a protective shield, which works in two ways. If the IRS is here an epitome for the publishing institutions, then from their standpoint, boredom is a tactic that shields their work from the attacks of the opposition. On the part of the employees (i.e. writers), however, the implication goes, the shield of boredom may also offer protection from the system's incursions into private lives and feelings, and thus be a form of self-interruptive dissent. As the narrator recalls his time spent training at the Peoria Center (Wallace himself did indeed take a course in accounting and interviewed IRS employees in Peoria in preparation for the novel),[27] he confesses to having learned in that time 'something about dullness, information, and irrelevant complexity. About negotiating boredom as one would a terrain, its levels and forests and endless wastes. Learned about it extensively, exquisitely.'[28] In other words, the lesson is that boredom is indeed the key to some deeper sensibility that

we are trying to distract ourselves from. Why do we recoil from it?
Wallace's narrator answers:

> Maybe because dullness is intrinsically painful; maybe that's where
> phrases like 'deadly dull' or 'excruciatingly dull' come from. But there
> might be more to it. Maybe dullness is associated with psychic pain
> because something that's dull or opaque fails to provide enough stimula-
> tion to distract people from some other, deeper type of pain that is always
> there, if only in an ambient low-level way, and which most of us spend
> nearly all our time and energy trying to distract ourselves from feeling, or
> at least from feeling directly or with our full attention . . . living people do
> not speak much of the dull. Of those parts of life that are and must be dull
> . . . There may, though, I opine, be more to it . . . as in vastly more, right
> here before us all, hidden by virtue of its size.[29]

In what seems to be an echo of Bartleby's famous response to the
lawyer: 'Do you not see for yourself?', Wallace's IRS officer is certain
that exploring the abysses of dullness is the key to understanding
some essential truth about humanity.

The deeper sort of pain that is always there, if only in an ambient
sort of way, is an almost exact paraphrase of Heidegger's definition
of fundamental boredom, or *Lässigkeit*, a state in which we feel that
something weighs on us and holds us in limbo. That something
is not people or things or time but something more, 'as in vastly
more': the sheer fact of being. As one of Wallace's characters will
say later in the novel, existentialist philosophy might indeed be
the only place to go to articulate this feeling, because of how 'vast'
its secret terrain turns out to be if you experience it in a boring
job. But there is a difference from Heidegger too. The author of
Fundamental Concepts of Metaphysics distinguished between *ordinary
boredom*, where the weight of time and things can be dispersed by
procrastination, and *fundamental boredom*, which is experienced in
the absence of distractions, whereas in Wallace's fictional universe,
these two experiential phenomena are merged into one. The dull,
the arcane, the mind-numbing elements of the IRS officer's work
all weigh on the narrator in their irrelevant complexity to the point
where their exoteric weight is not felt any more and what remains
is the burden of life itself.

The sentiment of *acedia* is not limited to the narrator, but is dispersed among all the characters and episodic plots, which the editor of *The Pale King* so eagerly wished to cohere, but which nevertheless disseminate in the novel and disappear without closure, 'rhyme or reason' (to recall Pynchon's quote from Aquinas). Wallace has been cited as planning this particular structure of 'series of setups for things to happen but nothing ever happens', which has usually been understood as plotlessness, but it seems that a lot more is at stake.[30]

In chapter 22, the narrator's *Bildung* narrative, the latter submits to his readers' attention: 'I'm not sure I even know what to say . . . From what I understand, I'm supposed to explain how I arrived at this career. Where I came from, so to speak, and what Service means to me.'[31] The indeterminacy transpiring from these opening words is not a matter of a formula, as in the case of Melville's Bartleby, but an abysmal indifference, a suspension of all engagement: 'I was like a piece of paper on the street in the wind . . . my essential response to everything was "Whatever".'[32] To affect theorists such as Lauren Berlant this sentence may read as exemplary of the contemporary 'structures of unfeeling', of under-performative, passive non-affect by means of which we communicate our ambivalence about social interactions.[33] But despite appearances, Wallace's character does not entirely fit Berlant's diagnosis, for although his confession recalls countless instances of indolent drifting, he browses his memories for ruptures to the autopilot mode.

In chapter 20, he begins by tracing the genealogy of the (un)feeling, which he developed as a child during 'wet, dissented Sunday afternoons', his sense of boredom growing through all the small games, 'toys and developmental projects' his mother tried to distract him with.[34] Boredom, for him, was clearly a burden, something horrible, which brought in an anxiety without a 'proper object', as if it was its object itself. 'I'd look out the window', the narrator recalls, 'and see the glass instead of anything past it', because the sensation was so autotelic.[35]

Whatever distractions came into the picture – his parents' divorce, the death of his father, terrifying attacks of profuse sweating, his discontinuous education and, finally, countless addictions – they always brought him, he claims, to this tedious 'awareness of awareness of awareness'.[36] As he recalls in a fashion bringing to mind Heidegger's description of 'ordinary boredom' at a railway station, as discussed in detail in Chapter 1, life felt 'like taking the train', spacing out and riding along with all fun and games, with the gnawing sense of weight 'at the outer periphery of your vision' which you 'can't see when you try to look directly at it' always there.[37]

There was, however, a moment when the sensation felt more urgent. The narrator recalls one particular day spent in front of a TV show, 'As the World Turns', whose interpellative 'You're watching "As the World Turns"' puts him, 'slumped there like something without any bones', face to face with limbo.[38] It was not simply a feeling of 'whatever', for that too was a distraction strategy, 'something he chose', as opposed to the striking sensation that was not of his choice.

At the time, I was aware only of the concrete impact of the announcer's statement, and the dawning realization that all of the directionless drifting and laziness and being a 'wastoid' which so many of us in that era pretended to have raised to a nihilistic art form, and believed was cool and funny (I too had thought it was cool, or at least I believed so – there had seemed to be something almost romantic about flagrant waste and drifting, which Jimmy Carter was ridiculed for calling 'malaise' and telling the nation to snap out of it) was, in reality, not funny, not one bit funny, but rather frightening, in fact, or sad, or something else – something I could not name because it has no name. I knew sitting there, that I might be a real nihilist, that it wasn't always just a hip pose. That I drifted and quit because nothing meant anything, no one choice was really better. That I was, in a way, too free, or that this kind of freedom wasn't actually real – I was free to choose 'whatever' because it didn't really matter. But that this, too, was because of something I chose – I had somehow chosen to have nothing matter. It all felt much less abstract than it sounds to try to explain it. All this was happening while I was just sitting there, spinning the ball. The point was that, through making this choice, I didn't matter, either. I didn't stand for anything. If I wanted to matter – even just to myself – I would have to be less free, by deciding to choose in some kind of definite way. Even if it was nothing more than an act of will.[39]

The directionless drifting and laziness which so fundamentally define his life and narrative style bring him to the brink of a consciousness of something which, as he says, is not simply frightening, or sad, but something he cannot name 'because it has no name'. It evades the regime of signification and floats on its horizon as a supplement to the symbolic order, but it is a non-abstract, tangible feeling of a painful realisation that whatever connection to freedom the narrator's inert existence has so far maintained, it was not real freedom.

This turning point has no status of a revelation. The narrator dispels any doubt as to whether it could be interpreted in parallel to Franklin's awakening in the project of moral perfection, for his realisation is not of the type as, for instance, '*I am going to think about life and my place in it and what's truly important to me, so that I can start forming concrete, focused goals for my adult career.*'[40] In his understanding, the conversion model may have worked for his college roommate's girlfriend in flowery cowboy boots, who once told him how she was awakened by the voice of the preacher as if spoken directly to her, but it does not explain his experience, which was not at all transcendental, unless in the generic Kantian sense, as coming from within the '*bathos*' of things in their immediacy rather than from above.[41] In short, the narrator's epiphany is born out of the tactile experience, as if within the lump weight of his disengaged body watching himself in limbo.

That the epiphanic discovery is more tactile than spiritual is confirmed on the level of plot, for his testimony in chapter 22 soon moves to a description of a life-changing class in Advanced Tax that he took by accident and a speech given there by a strange, Jesuit-looking instructor. The first thing recalled by the narrator is the unusual appearance of the teacher, whose 'expression had the same burnt, hollow concentration of photos of military veterans who'd been in some kind of real war, meaning combat'.[42] The instructor looks 'amorphous', 'slender and pale looking . . . like someone in an archaic photo or daguerreotype'.[43] The way he gazes around is such that he seems to be looking at everyone and no one at the same time, making the narrator feel 'singled out, spindled on those eyes in a way I neither liked nor didn't'.

He stood very still – noticeably stiller than most people stand when they stand still . . . he seemed to be 'indifferent' – not in a meaningless, drifting, nihilistic way, but rather in a secure, self-confident way . . . The whites of his eyes were extremely white . . . His complexion . . . was that of someone who had rarely been out in the sun . . . he cast no shadow on any side.[44]

The unmistakably Bartlebean appearance of the tax instructor, brought into the reality of the classroom straight from some daguerreotype, awes the narrator with the aura of powerful aloofness. The pallid gaze communicates nothing, but in a reflective sort of way singles the narrator out (while being reflected in the glasses of others), inducing an 'electric coolness' in his head and a sensation 'as though he and I were at opposite ends of some kind of tube or pipe'.[45] In what seems like a dramatised version of the inner mechanism of a feedback glare – as readers of this interocular exchange between characters we are also let into the textual machine caught up in recursion – we thus witness the narrator getting into the mode of tactile attunement with the authority of his pale instructor, prior to any communication. It is only after attention to the exoteric details of the situation is induced haptically that the instructor puts it into words:

I wish to inform you that the accounting profession to which you aspire is, in fact, heroic . . . Enduring tedium over real time in a confined space is what real courage is . . . The truth is that the heroism of your childhood entertainments was not true valor. It was theater . . . it was . . . all designed to appear heroic, to excite and gratify an audience . . . Gentlemen, welcome to the world of reality – there is no audience. No one to applaud, to admire. No one to see you . . . No one is interested. True heroism is minutes, hours, weeks, year upon year of the quiet, precise, judicious exercise of probity and care . . . True heroism is *a priori* incompatible with audience or applause or even the bare notice of the common run of man.[46]

The speech goes on for a long time, but its point is clear from the outset: namely, that the electrifying power of the instructor's indifferent presence comes from his recognition of the profound meaning of life as experienced under the weight of its most banal exoteric manifestations. Those exoteric things are not just piles of documents but also 'repetition, tedium, monotony, ephemeracy, inconsequence, abstraction, disorder, boredom, angst, ennui', because just like pencils or bootlaces, 'they are real'.[47] The instruction communicated in this passage is caught up in a peculiar affective recursion: boredom leads to heroic recognition of the essence of existence inasmuch as it is also the 'true hero's enemy': that is, it stands in the way of this recognition. It is the eye-opening experience to which one should attune oneself as well as stay 'immune'.[48]

If there is any moment in *The Pale King* when the trope of the blank, amorphous glare inaugurated in 'The Suffering Channel' is staged, it is certainly at this point, where *acedia* takes on at once the haptic, the affective and the philosophical sense; in other words, when it is a bodily sensation of being poised but inert, of feeling attuned but disconnected, and thinking about the essence of existence while retaining a Stoical neutrality towards that essence. The acediac disposition (of the narrator and of the characters) starts working as the motor force of Wallace's feedback glare writing technique. The blank, amorphous, interocular embrace between the narrator and the instructor is also the blank, amorphous glare of the exchange between the writer and his audience.

In the oft-quoted 'Author here' chapter of *The Pale King*, the 'author' explains that the ambition of his story is not to 'pretend that the mind works any other way than it literally does' as well as not to 'inflict' on the reader 'a regurgitation of every last sensation and passing thought I happen to recall'.[49] 'I am about art here', he insists.[50] If taken at face value, this insistence may be read as an invitation to extend the above interpretation to the metafictional level, where the feedback glare technique is read as Wallace's way out of the postmodern paradigm of the action-artist. If Wallace is about art in *The Pale King*, he is less interested in commercial success than in creating that which Berlant calls a momentary heterotopia of sovereignty. As long as the language of *The Pale King* produces the effect of the blank, amorphous glare, it also secures the heterotopic space for the writer to retain freedom of control over his writing self against the usurpatory modes of the publishing world. The blank, amorphous mode of communication between the character of the narrator and his instructor represents the glitch in the machine which turns the writer–audience exchange into a commercial feast. Moreover, even when 'I'm about art here' is taken as utterly ironic and not to be taken at face value, the feedback glare strategy still operates to shield freedom of self-ownership. In other words, by means of his recursion strategy anchored in the trope of *acedia*, Wallace in *The Pale King* manages to avoid the fate of a Rosenbergian 'Somebody' who transfers himself into the work, but remains a self-owned agency who effectively blocks this transfer at a critical point. His feedback glare strategy is, in my view, as close as one gets to what Agamben calls the conservation of one's power by not putting it into an act which one nevertheless performs. Or, to say it differently, of putting into the performance the capacity to *not* perform.

From this perspective, the logic of the feedback glare underlies the teleological structure of Wallace's novel. First, it controls the most private sphere of the characters' lives, such as sleep, for example. The narrator recalls dreaming about rows of 'blank', emotionless faces, performing 'endless small tasks' with 'placid hopelessness', and although the dream 'seemed to take hours', the clock's hands upon his awakening do not seem to have moved.[51]

Furthermore, the feedback glare mechanism controls the characters' memories. The memory of one of the clerks of his first sexual encounter is only a memory of the girl's stare of 'blank terminal sadness', which leads him to develop a habit of staring in (rather than out of) a window.[52] Another memory stored as anonymous testimony no. 943756788 is about 'the stare' that the speaker remembers as originally her father's, but now as being hers:

in a stare, you are not really looking at this thing you are seeming to stare at, you are not really noticing it – however neither are you thinking of something else. You in truth are not doing anything, mentally, but you are doing it fixedly, with what appears to be intent concentration. And now I too do this. I find myself doing it. It's not unpleasant, but it is strange. Something goes out of you – you can feel your face merely hanging loose, with no muscles or expression. It frightens my children, I know. As if your face, like your attention, belongs to someone else.[53]

Just as no. 943756788 has acquired her impenetrable gaze to the point of it becoming her second nature, so does the character named Toni Ware, whose traumatic memory of an abusing step-father features a scene where, lying in bed next to her sleeping mother, she locks eyes with the man who is about to rape her, and yet manages to appear to look 'so dead' that he would leave her alone. As a result, Toni develops a habit that paves her way into the narrative: 'This is what had started the story; David Wallace or someone else remarked that Toni Ware was creepy because, even though she wasn't shy or evasive and maintain eye contact, she seemed to be staring at your eyes rather than into them', like a fish in a tank which is aware of the gaze.[54] The blank stare is 'unsettling because it [isn't] anything like the way a human being seems aware of you when he meets your gaze'.[55]

Finally, the feedback glare logic permeates the characters' occa-sional outbursts of creativity. No. 917229047 brags about an idea for a play, which would be 'totally real, true to life' and 'unperform-able'. The setting would be 'bare and minimalistic' and on the stage there would just be a 'wiggler' (a fidgety office clerk) by a desk with a clock behind him. All he would do would be to turn pages in his pad and take notes. The play would be so long that everybody in the audience would leave, and only then could 'the real action of the play start'.[56] What is interesting about the idea of no. 917229047 is not so much its meta-textual status *vis-à-vis* the larger narrative frame of which it partakes – *The Pale King* is, of course, the long boring thing, with protagonists turning pages and scribbling notes in their pads – but its reliance on the idea of 'unperformability'. An unper-formable play which would nevertheless be performed when the audience left out of boredom represents an imaginary terrain of the author's sovereignty and privacy. But the unperformable play is not just a metaphor. In chapter 25, all the characters of the novel literally stage its scenario: 'Chris Fogle turns a page. Howard Cardwell turns a page. Ken Wax turns a page. Matt Redgate turns a page. "Groovy" Bruce Channing attaches a form to file. Ann Williams turns a page', and so on for a couple of *The Pale King*'s pages. Pages are turned and blankly stared at rather than read by the reader.[57]

One particularly intense moment of the feedback glare tech-nique that deserves to be mentioned in this discussion, as it shifts emphasis from 'staring' to the more haptic modes of experience, features in chapter 33. Here, one of the characters, Service Officer Lane A. Dean Jr, experiences what we might term an attack of *acedia*. Filing protocols in a windowless office room, Dean goes crazy with the mundane task of filing IRS forms, of which he has completed the fewest of anyone in the office, and longs for a break. Looking at the clock 'despite all best prior intentions', Dean drifts off towards all sorts of demonic fantasies followed by dejection of spirit:

> In four minutes it would be another hour, and half hour after that was the fifteen minute break. Lane Dean imagined himself running around on the break waving his arms and shouting gibberish and holding ten cigarettes at once in his mouth like a panpipe. Year after year, a face the same color as your desk. Lord Jesus. Coffee wasn't allowed because of spills on the files . . . He knew what he'd really do on the break was sit facing the wall clock in the lounge and despite prayers and effort sit counting the seconds tick off until he had to come back again and do this again. And again and again and again.[58]

As his mind wanders off to a bizarre vision of a circus strongman tearing a phonebook in half, Dean summons 'all his will and bore' down, and resumes work, only to begin thinking of suicide, 'imagining different high places to jump off of', killing himself with Jell-O, stopping his heart by holding his breath.[59] As the narrator notes at this point, Dean 'felt in a position to say he knew now that hell had nothing to do with fires or frozen troops', but rather with being held in limbo by time which does not seem to pass.[60] Dean is bored beyond recognition as well as stifled by the discomfort of his body, which is nailed to the chair.

As it turns out, Dean's suicidal fantasies and stupor are only a gentle prelude to the real bout of *daemon meridianus* – the Evagrian name being in this case more than just a metaphor. At one point, 'half asleep and dreaming', Dean registers the awkward figure of a 'big older fellow with a seamed face and picket teeth' who does not 'cast a shadow'. The man speaks to Dean about boredom:

> But now that you're getting a taste, consider it, the word. You know the one . . . Word appears suddenly in 1766. No known etymology. The Earl

of March uses it in a letter describing a French peer in the realm . . . The French of course had *malaise* and *ennui*. See Pascal's fourth *Pensée*, which Lane Dean heard as *pantsy* . . . But nothing in English prior March, Earl of. This means a good five hundred years of no word for it you see, yes?[61]

As the shadowless man's lecture continues on *accidia, daemon meridianus*, Donne's *lethargie, otiositas*, tristitia, Winchilsea's *black jaundice*, Quaker Green's *spleen-fog* and Kierkegaard, Lane Dean, who still cannot believe that this is real 'as in like who is this fellow', begins to think he is dealing with 'the phantom'.[62] In corporate terminology, as the narrator explained earlier, the name phantom is reserved for individuals whose role is to silently monitor and motivate by their sheer presence the work in an office. Phantoms are part and parcel of the phenomenon of the evil eye which, to recall Silvan Tomkins's explanation referenced in my discussion of Melville's *Typee* in Chapter 2, had been introduced in American corporate environments in the 1950s, as an efficient because culturally universal strategy of motivating work among employees. To this day, the corporate role of the phantom has been to motivate by staring and sending occasional evil looks to further exert pressure.

In Lane Dean's eyes, the phantom appears just as real as he is also ephemeral and imaginary: 'Lane Dean had heard of the phantom, but never seen it. The phantom of the hallucination of repetitive concentration held for too long a time.'[63] Dean, it seems, is not sure whether the situation is happening inside or outside his mind. Thinking he might have lost his mind, he considers praying.[64] However, the phantom's presence is absolutely real to the other workers as well: 'Now for the first time the fellow at the Tingle to the right turned briefly to give the man a look and turned just as fast back around when the man made his hands into claws and held them out at the other wiggler like a demon or someone possessed.'[65]

So even though the man is clearly an office monitor, hired to give an evil eye to anyone who appears unproductive or distracted, Lane Dean cannot distinguish him from his own projections, because whenever he looks at the clock, he discovers that 'no time had passed at all, again'.[66] Rather than as a reflection, boredom signifies in Dean's gestures, for the narrative passage that follows his last glance at the clock is followed by half-page-long paragraph of tax calculation formulas: 'IRM §781 (d) AMT Formula for Corporations: (1) Taxable income before NOL deduction, plus or minus (2) All AMT adjustments excepting ACE adjustment, plus (3) Tax preferences, yields (4)' and so on.[67] It is now the reader's turn to see the phantom.

Throughout the episode of the uncanny visitation, Dean stays notably motionless and stiff, his discomfort being both psychological and physical. Bodily tension is not only Dean's problem. Nearly all the characters in *The Pale King* suffer chronically from body issues, whose extensive list is delivered at the beginning of the novel in the form of a note of a memorandum from the Human Resources Management and Support Office of Employees Assistance. The list features forty-two somatic and psychosomatic disorders, among which are chronic or temporary 'paraplegia' (motor dysfunction of lower limbs), 'sciatica' (migrating pain), 'paralysis agitans', 'paresis' (muscular weakness), 'spasmodic dyskinesia', 'dihedral lordosis', 'spasmodic torticollis' (abnormal head positioning), 'cyclothemia', 'acial and digital ticcing', 'Krendler's syndrome' (auto-cannibalism) and many others.[68] While some characters exhibit more symptoms than others, there is no one in *The Pale King* who does not suffer from some form of work-related disorder, without necessarily recognising it as such. The unpopular Leonard Stecyk, who as a boy trains his body to be able to perform the most bizarre sorts of contortions – his ambition as a child was to be able to see his own back – continues to train his body (and mind) in 'tolerance for pain'.[69] He tries to control his profuse sweating, and develops hypomaniac, obsessive office rituals that are a psychological form of Krendler's syndrome as well as the source of his lack of esteem. Just as Stecyk does not consider his ailments as work-related but as extensions of his contortionist hobby, his colleague, the 'fact psychic' Claude Sylvanshine, does not properly recognise his problems. He treats the office inurement techniques as part of his private, isometric exercise routine, and mistakes his 'peripheral hallucinations', 'dissociative fugues' (amnesia) and 'diplopia' for a supernatural, psychic ability. Even Lane Dean, who suffers from hemeralopia (inability to see in bright light), does not relate his illness to work. All in all, therefore, given the consistency with which the bodies of the novel's characters are exposed to hypertension, both from without and from within, it is clear that the object of *The Pale King*'s ideological critique is not capitalism in general, but its intervention into our biological life. The haptic dimension serves as a poetic means in Wallace's critique of biopower, the extent of whose intrusion into the intimate sphere of his characters' lives is laid bare in the disorderly ways their bodies' muscular, digestive and neurological systems respond to external and internalised discipline.

What about the ways in which biopower intervenes in the life of a writer? In terms of artistic self-expression, Wallace's tactile poetics stands in some contrast to Melville's. For the writer of the American Renaissance, the body appeared as the frontier on which to negotiate the right to privacy and moral self-ownership. Writing *Typee*, Melville switched to the haptic to create the campy poetics of excess and to allegorically signal the desire to abandon the ocularocentric perspective together with its moralising pressure and pressure to moralise. In the absence of a technology that could prompt the recursive glitch-pattern, Melville built his self-expressive machinery out of pastoral elements: he chose a risky theme, over-stylised his setting, and made his characters overact laziness, often without rhyme or reason. Wallace, in contrast, seems to be saying that the poetics of excess are not enough in twenty-first-century capitalist reality. After all, he had tried the method before *The Pale King*. Over-excessivising procrastination in *Infinite Jest*, the *'non plus ultra'* as the novel called it, eventually turned out to his disadvantage, as far as his vision of what art was for was concerned. It did not bring him writerly freedom but a disciplining expectation that he become a Rosenbergian 'Somebody'.

In this light, the haptic aesthetics in *The Pale King* appears to be less a code for communicating dissent and the freedom of self-ownership, as if the latter were an available option and as if body-aesthetics was a way to capture the contours of individual agency, than a manner of laying bare the absence of such an option. The body cannot be re-owned but only used as a glitch-producing shield. The tactile poetics lays bare the extinction of counter-systemic resistance. In *The Pale King*, the characters' contortions, isometric exercises, refluxes and diplopias mediate the way in which the capitalist institutionalisation of the artistic profession of self-expression reappropriates the tactile, intimate dimension of an artist's life as its own. Reading Wallace's fiction, especially *The Pale King*, through the prism of *his* depression, *his* 'contest with himself', *his* suicide seems to miss this important point and read him in a Rosenbergian way.[70] Given that the body is not a marker of intimacy and authenticity but an object of regulation and cultivation, it is notable therefore that the telos of *The Pale King* is dictated by the theme of examination, which whether taken in medical, educational or conceptual terms is, as Foucault reminds us, always a form of disciplining.

The use of haptic references in Wallace's last novel does not stand in contrast with or in addition to the technique of the blank, amorphous glare with its obviously optic underpinning. It is an absolutely integral part of the strategy – the subversive glitch it produces depends as much on the vision-related element of *blankness* as it does on the body-related element of *amorphousness*. To produce the subversive glitch in the text while still performing an act of literature, Wallace combines the two phenomena in the trope of *acedia*, which harmonises and amplifies the frequency of their pitch. I have claimed above that by anchoring his strategy in the trope of *acedia*, Wallace manages to avoid in *The Pale King* the fate of a Rosenbergian 'Somebody' – an action-artist who transfers his entire self into the work and thus surrenders to the art market – because he effectively blocks this transfer at a critical point. I have also argued that the feedback glare strategy is as close as one gets to what Giorgio Agamben calls *sterēsis*, or 'the power to *not* act'. The reason why *sterēsis* is a unique exercise of power is that it stems from the conservation of one's capacity by not putting it into an act which one nevertheless performs, of putting into the performance the capacity *to not perform*.[71] What now deserves to be added to those earlier conclusions is a reflection on how such under-performative gestures as Wallace's become minimal events of heterotopic sovereignty. Where's the dissent in the blank, amorphous glare?

The most succinct answer is given by one of *The Pale King*'s characters. Debating the topic of consent to the norms and institutions, he remarks that boredom has something to do with 'personal freedom and appetite and moral license' though, as he puts it, 'I'm damned if I can figure it out.'[72] Ironically, the closer Wallace's acediac characters are to figuring it out, the more 'damned' and oppressed they become, as though the indolent mode was indeed a way – perhaps *the* way – to efficiently resist the agency-devouring apparatus of normativity and maintain a minimum of personal freedom. No wonder the indolent mode is also the prime target of this apparatus's disciplining attacks.

'Freedom is the faculty to begin an event by oneself', Kant once remarked.[73] Although in the contemporary world, 'oneself' as a self-sustained agency is arguably no longer a valid category, Wallace's *The Pale King* seems to be in tune with Kant's idea. Mobilising the tropological potential of *acedia* and its modalities, the novel stages the event of freedom from biopolitical norms over and over again, through serialised sequences of characters' bodily and mental experiences of stoppage and inactivity. All of them follow the pattern established in the fateful tax class that the narrator stumbles into during his slothful campus peregrinations. As the image of the demon-like tax instructor merges with the spectre of melancholic Bartleby, the pallid gaze of the biopolitical apparatus that the teacher represents encounters 'an eleventh hour complication' as it coalesces with the blank stare of the acediac subject represented by the narrator. The disciplining lesson is thus both learned and unlearned, both internalised and rejected. For the subject who enunciates himself in *The Pale King*, the recursive force of the interchange between power and powerlessness, engagement and disengagement, intensity and lethargy – all encapsulated in the trope of *acedia* as a postmodern version of laziness – creates a series of micro events of self-interruption which guard the heterotopic territory of his artistic sovereignty and grant immunity to the interpellative calls of the book industry.

Notes

1. Mark McGurl uses the term 'the Program Era' to denote a generation of writers whose writing styles and careers were shaped to a large degree by creative writing programmes. The programmes, he argues, have come to be the key determinant in the formation of post-1960s aesthetics and its affective modalities. See Mark McGurl, *The Program Era* (Cambridge, MA: Harvard University Press, 2009).
2. Josh Roiland, 'Getting Away from It All: The Literary Journalism of David Foster Wallace and Nietzsche's Concept of Oblivion', in *The Legacy of David Foster*

Wallace, ed. Samuel S. Cohen and Lee Konstantinou (Iowa City: University of Iowa Press, 2012), 29.

3. David Foster Wallace, 'Joseph Frank's Dostoyevsky', in *Consider the Lobster and Other Essays* (New York: Little, Brown, 2005), 265.

4. David Foster Wallace, 'A Supposedly Fun Thing I'll Never Do Again', in *A Supposedly Fun Thing I'll Never Do Again: Essays and Arguments* (New York: Little, Brown, 1997), 240.

5. Roiland, 'Getting Away from It All', 33.

6. Ibid., 32.

7. David Foster Wallace, 'E Unibus Pluram: Television and U.S. Fiction', in *A Supposedly Fun Thing I'll Never Do Again*, 41.

8. Samuel Cohen, 'To Wish to Try to Sing to the Next Generation: *Infinite Jest's* History', in Cohen and Konstantinou (eds), *The Legacy of David Foster Wallace*, 71.

9. David Foster Wallace, 'Some Kind of Terrible Burden, interview by Steve Paulson' (17 June 2004), in *To the Best of Our Knowledge: Last Interview and Other Conversations* (New York: Melville House, 2012), 87.

10. Thomas Pynchon, 'The Deadly Sins/Sloth; Nearer, My Couch, to Thee', *New York Times*, 6 June 1993, https://www.nytimes.com/books/97/05/18/reviews/pynchon-sloth.html (accessed 28 January 2019).

11. David Foster Wallace, *Oblivion* (New York: Little, Brown, 2004), 329.

12. David Lipsky, *Although of Course You End up Becoming Yourself: A Road Trip with David Foster Wallace* (New York: Broadway Books, 2010).

13. Wallace, 'Some Kind of Terrible Burden'.

14. Marshall Boswell, 'David Foster Wallace's *The Pale King*', *Studies in the Novel* 44.4, special issue 'David Foster Wallace Part 2' (2012), 367–70.

15. Marshall Boswell, 'Author Here: The Legal Fiction of David Foster Wallace's *The Pale King*', *English Studies* 95.1 (2014), 25–39.

16. Henry Veggian, 'Anachronisms of Authority: Authorship, Exchange Value, and David Foster Wallace's "The Pale King"', *Boundary 2* 39.3 (2012), 97–124.

17. In 2005 Wallace delivered a commencement address at Kenyon College entitled 'This is Water', which was widely publicised on the Internet and contributed to his celebrity status: https://www.youtube.com/watch?v=8CrOL-ydFMI (accessed 28 January 2019).

18. Michael Pietsch, 'Editor's Note', in David Foster Wallace, *The Pale King: An Unfinished Novel* (New York: Little, Brown, 2011), ix.

19. Ibid., vii.

20. Veggian, 'Anachronisms of Authority', 101.

21. Ibid., 102.

22. Ibid., 101.

23. Wallace, *The Pale King*, 545.

24. Ibid., 83.

25. Gilles Deleuze, 'Bartleby; or, the Formula', in *Essays Critical and Clinical* (London: Verso, 1998), 68–90.

26. Wallace, *The Pale King*, 83.

27. See D. T. Max, *Every Love Story Is a Ghost Story: A Life of David Foster Wallace*

(New York: Viking, 2012).

28. Wallace, *The Pale King*, 85.
29. Ibid., 85.
30. Pietsch, 'Editor's Note', viii.
31. Wallace, *The Pale King*, 154.
32. Ibid., 154.
33. Lauren Berlant, 'Structures of Unfeeling: Mysterious Skin', *International Journal of Politics, Culture, and Society* 28.3 (2015), 191–213.
34. Wallace, *The Pale King*, 253–4.
35. Ibid., 254.
36. Ibid., 188.
37. Ibid., 185.
38. Ibid., 223.
39. Ibid., 223–4.
40. Ibid., 190.
41. In an answer to the critique of his term 'transcendental' as 'higher' by Christian Garve, Kant wrote: 'On no account *higher*. High towers and the metaphysically great men that resemble them . . . are not for me. My place is the fertile *bathos* of experience, and the word: transcendental . . . does not mean something that surpasses all possible experience, but something that indeed proceeds from experience (*a priori*) but that, all the same, is destined to nothing more than to make cognition from experience possible.' Immanuel Kant, *Prolegomena to Any Future Metaphysics That will be Able to Come Forward as Science, with Kant's Letter to Marcus Herz, February 27, 1772* (1783), ed. James W. Ellington and Paul Caurus, 2nd edn (Indianapolis: Hackett, 2001), 128.
42. Wallace, *The Pale King*, 218.
43. Ibid., 217.
44. Ibid., 227.
45. Ibid., 218, 230.
46. Ibid., 229–30.
47. Ibid., 231.
48. Ibid., 438.
49. Ibid., 259.
50. Ibid., 259.
51. Ibid., 253.
52. Ibid., 50–1.
53. Ibid., 116–17.
54. Ibid., 441.
55. Ibid., 441.
56. Ibid., 106.
57. Ibid., 310.
58. Ibid. 379.
59. Ibid., 379–80.
60. Ibid., 379.
61. Ibid., 383.
62. Ibid. 383.

63. Ibid., 383.

64. Ibid., 385.

65. Ibid. 385.

66. Ibid. 385.

67. Ibid., 386.

68. Ibid., 87–8.

69. Ibid., 114.

70. Jeff Staiger, 'David Foster Wallace's Contest with Himself', *New England Review* 36.2 (2015), 90–111.

71. See Chapter 1 for my discussion of Agamben's relation between *sterēsis* and freedom.

72. Wallace, *The Pale King*, 135.

73. Kant, *Prolegomena to Any Future Metaphysics*, 98.

Epilogue

Writing *The Labour of Laziness* was my response to a cultural tendency to overvalue productivity in every area of human life at the cost of private freedom. I was troubled by the cross-dressing of this biopolitical, economy-based norm in ethical frills of self-improvement, self-management or political quasi-activism. And I saw this drag everywhere. I saw it in the Fitbit fad and Quantitative Movement's encouragement to monitor my sleep-patterns and step ratio, so that I become the healthiest and most productive version of myself. I saw it in the organised leisure activities in the lives of my children's friends, whose birthday parties would be orchestrated by skilled animators, and whose summer camps offered so many fun games that there would be no free time to do nothing. Finally, I saw it in my work place, academia. And I am not just talking about the injunction to publish more and more – the dreadful 'publish or perish' doctrine – or to translate individual, free thoughts into grant parlance. After all, it is not breaking news that the neoliberal academic system treats intellectual effort as a commodity.

What I found more troubling was the behaviour of my students, whose routine response to a class without handouts and slides was panic. I could sense their anxiety that the knowledge they had expected to be delivered might not be real, useful, degree-granting knowledge if it didn't have a reified, manageable and reproducible form. Another problem was academic conferences. Sitting in talks and presentations, I saw young scholars' notebook screens gleaming not so much with notes but with short, catchy phrases that the speaker used, phrases they would later insert into their own writing just to mark their awareness of new names and trends and identify themselves with some intellectual faction. They seemed to have internalised the logic of intellectual industry: it is so much more controllable and reproductive if throwing in the name of Bruno Latour or Jane Bennett works like a conference badge telling everyone where we've come from and what we do. Third, I saw and was greatly disturbed by a crusade to save the humanities, led by such authorities as Martha Nussbaum, Gayatri Spivak and Sidonie Smith, in the spirit of the Romantic model of education through aesthetics. What disturbed me about their fervent defence of the humanities' key role in intellectual industry was that the line of argument was structured around humanities' potential for social productiveness.

The frame of this model, restaged in Nussbaum, Spivak and Smith, is that humanities education is capable of shaping our individual and collective morality. Nussbaum, a moral philosopher, believes that literature expands our sense of virtuousness, thus training us in social responsibility. Were it not for the models of association and social sympathy provided by fiction, she claims in *Poetic Justice* (1996), there would be no social reform.[1] A similar point is made by Spivak in *An Aesthetic Education in the Era of Globalization* (2012), which reinvigorates the Schillerian model and argues that in the contemporary context of global communication, the ethical and the political concerns of literature should be treated as primary to its aesthetic mission.[2] Finally, Smith's *Manifesto for the Humanities* (2015) puts stress on the social activism that the humanities have the capacity and responsibility to promote and invigorate.[3] While these are important ideas that do a lot of good for the academic community, the ethical regime they establish does not necessarily allow much space for intellectual freedom. Such criticism re-legitimates and perpetuates the mechanism of humanities' co-optation into the power apparatus as an element of its subjectivation technology rather than exploring the juncture of the aesthetic and the ethical from outside its didactic frame.

The outside of the didactic frame is where *The Labour of Laziness* belongs. The book contests the Schillerian model, as its spirit is closer to what Marjorie Perloff expressed in her PMLA letter:

'Intellectuals, I would posit, cannot function without at least a degree of independence from the self-perpetuating power structure . . . of not having to pay lip service to the latest fashion, with writings that might not contain a single reference to Judith Butler or Homi Bhabha.'[4] Independence as opposed to social didacticism and activism is what Perloff considers the cornerstone of resistance to norms and dominant artistic and intellectual values. 'Perhaps the greatest threat to intellectual life is that of an institution,' Perloff adds – institution meaning here the normativised structure of any discipline such as art, literature or critical theory.[5]

It was therefore the undisciplined, unruly thought that I was looking for in selecting authors for *The Labour of Laziness*. All the writers, from Washington Irving to David Foster Wallace, wrote in the spirit of independence and resistance to the very aesthetic and ethical norms they inhabited, but they also went further in risking rejection and failure by trying to explore the very core of how the production of norms and the normativisation of productivity registered in their respective epochs. To use Adorno's phrase, they all departed from the well-trodden path of genres and poetic trends of their time. With fascination, I was discovering that what they all had in common was the use of the trope of doing nothing and exploring various shades and tonalities of unproductivity such as loafing, passivity, inertia, *acedia*, inaction and so on. My theoretical intervention in *The Labour of Laziness* was the delineation of this metaphorological field under the banner of the concept-metaphor of laziness, which with its stigmatic connotations and history of exclusion from all spheres of human activity seemed to be the ultimate marker of that which is exterior to Western thought. Throughout the process of building the theory of laziness as a trope of resistance to normativity *per se*, I was reassured by the thought of such radical and undisciplined thinkers as Martin Heidegger, Emmanuel Levinas, Theodor Adorno, Michel Foucault, Giorgio Agamben, Roland Barthes, Donald Winnicott and Anton Ehrenzweig, all of whom were certain that there is something fundamentally and powerfully rebellious about doing nothing that makes it one of the most crucial philosophical, ethical, intellectual and aesthetic positions. That is what Heidegger said about the fundamental boredom of *Lässigkeit*, what Levinas and Barthes said about the indolence of *paresse*, what Agamben meant by the power to not of *sterēsis*, and what Ehrenzweig and Winnicott understood as creative inattention and transitionality.

I wasn't trying to salvage laziness as a mode of living from the realm of stigma to which it has always belonged. What I was trying to do was to show how the very exploration of its metaphorological field points to the hubs and pivots in the process of norm emergence and naturalisation, in the course of which that norm co-opts into the radius of its apparatus greater and greater fragments of our private bodily and intellectual freedom. In the simplest terms possible, what laziness-as-metaphor does when it appears in a literary work is reveal the ideological underpinnings of an epoch's value system, while at the same time offering a glimpse into the possible strategies for rebelling against the status quo. In that, it is perhaps the only, or one of the very few, non-normatively ethical concept-metaphors that permit us to talk about normativity from outside the didactic frame.

It was never my deliberate idea to write an interventionist book. But looking at *The Labour of Laziness* now, situating it in the course of my intellectual life, I think it became a book about ethics that argues against the contemporary re-legitimation of the Romantic model of aesthetic education. The theoretical apparatus I have developed proposes a style of non-normative ethical criticism that makes it possible to negotiate the relation of the ethical and the aesthetic beyond the limits of moralistic didacticism. I am convinced that such negotiation is necessary if the question of literature's ethical potential is to be taken seriously.

Will *The Labour of Laziness* help my students to be more open to undisciplined, unruly thought? Will it help my children to be more critical of their organised leisure activities? This is certainly not the intention. If anything, it could perhaps make them all a little more alert to the ever-present valorisation and standardisation of activity and productiveness, and to be less judgemental towards those who prefer vagabond thoughts and untrodden paths, and trust vacancies of attention. Perhaps even less submissive to the norms they live by, at least when, say, my daughter listens to another podcast about how to rewire her mind and body software to become a hyper-version of her best, most productive self.

Leszek Kołakowski, a Polish philosopher who has been my guiding voice throughout my career, once said that in the ideal world, as far as publishing books and getting academic titles was concerned, everyone should begin their intellectual careers with full professorship and be deprived of one title with every publication. In this way, scholars would only publish books that meant a lot to them, in which they had something genuine to say and wanted to share it with others. This is how I feel about *The Labour of Laziness*.

Notes

1. Martha Craven Nussbaum, *Poetic Justice: The Literary Imagination and Public Life* (Boston: Beacon Press, 1996).
2. Gayatri Chakravorty Spivak, *An Aesthetic Education in the Era of Globalization* (Cambridge, MA: Harvard University Press, 2012).
3. Sidonie Smith, *Manifesto for the Humanities: Transforming Doctoral Education in Good Enough Times* (Ann Arbor: University of Michigan Press, 2015).
4. Marjorie Perloff, 'Intellectuals in the Twenty-First Century', in *Poetics in A New Key: Essays and Interviews*, ed. Jonathan Y. Bayou (Chicago: University of Chicago Press, 2013), 222–6, 225.
5. Ibid.

INDEX

References to notes are indicated by n.